HANDBOO
OLD CHURCH S
PART I

OLD CHURCH
SLAVONIC GRAMMAR

LONDON EAST EUROPEAN SERIES
(LANGUAGE AND LITERATURE)

Under the auspices of the Department of Language and Literature
School of Slavonic and East European Studies
University of London

GROUP I. DESCRIPTIVE GRAMMARS

Handbook of Old Church Slavonic, Parts I and II
I. *Old Church Slavonic Grammar*, by G. NANDRIŞ
II. *Texts and Glossary*, by R. AUTY

GROUP II. HISTORICAL GRAMMARS

W. K. MATTHEWS. *Russian Historical Grammar*

GROUP III. READINGS IN LITERATURE

J. PIETRKIEWICZ. *Polish Prose and Verse*
E. D. TAPPE. *Rumanian Prose and Verse*
G. F. CUSHING. *Hungarian Prose and Verse*

HANDBOOK OF
OLD CHURCH SLAVONIC
PART I

OLD CHURCH SLAVONIC GRAMMAR

BY

GRIGORE NANDRIŞ

*Professor of Comparative Philology
of the Slavonic Languages in the
University of London*

London and Atlantic Highlands, NJ
THE ATHLONE PRESS

This paperback edition
first published 1988 by The Athlone Press Ltd
44 Bedford Row, London WC1R 4LY
and 171 First Avenue, Atlantic Highlands, NJ 07716

First impression, 1959
Reprinted with corrections, 1965
Reprinted 1969

© G. Nandris   1959, 1965

British Library Cataloguing in Publication Data
Nandris, Grigore.
Handbook of Old Church Slavonic.—
(The London East European series).
Part 1: Old Church Slavonic grammar.
1. Old Church Slavonic Language
I. Title   II. Series
491.8'1701
ISBN 0-485-17520-7

Library of Congress Cataloging-in-Publication Data
Nandris, Grigore, 1895–1968.
Old Church Slavonic grammar.
Reprint. Originally published as part 1 of Handbook of Old Church
Slavonic. London : University of London, 1959.
Bibliography: p.
Includes indexes.
1. Church Slavic language—Grammar. I. Title.
PG619.N36   1988   491.8'1701   88-3481
ISBN 0-485-17520-7 (pbk.)

Printed in Great Britain by Antony Rowe Ltd, Chippenham

PREFACE

THIS Grammar is intended to help students of Slavonic philology to interpret Old Slavonic texts and to provide a starting-point for studying the history of the Slavonic languages. An attempt has therefore been made to present the facts, particularly of the phonetic system, from a descriptive and historical point of view and to draw attention to those regular correspondences between phonemes of cognate languages which seem to indicate constant principles operating in linguistic changes. It does not claim to be a historical grammar of Old Church Slavonic: its aim is to give the student in Slavonic philology a clear picture of the system of the first Slavonic literary language. As Common Slavonic is not recorded and Slavonic linguistic unity lasted until the sixth to seventh century A.D., Old Church Slavonic supplements our knowledge of Proto-Slavonic and so is an introduction to comparative Slavonic philology.

The method and plan of the Grammar conform to its purpose and aim. As it has been assumed that students will use the Grammar to read and interpret texts, the number of examples has been limited; but an attempt has been made to indicate to the student that Old Church Slavonic represents only one recorded moment of a section of a spoken language continuously changing in time and space. Fluctuations in so-called linguistic rules have been noted in order to draw the attention of students to the fluidity of linguistic phenomena and to possibilities for further research. Dialectal features and opinions based on hypotheses have also been indicated. All examples have been verified in the texts of the available editions.

Unlike phonetics and morphology, syntax has not been treated in a special chapter. As morphology and syntax are in practice interdependent, and as Old Church Slavonic syntax is based on that of the original Greek texts, its study seemed too complex to be included in this Grammar. But its characteristic features appear in the chapters devoted to conjunctions and prepositions as well as in the examples illustrating the various parts of speech.

The author is very conscious of his great debt to his predecessors, among whom he would especially name P. Diels, A. Vaillant, and N. van Wijk. As the manuscript was sent for printing in September 1954, he has not been able to make use of studies published since.

The author wishes to express his gratitude and thanks to Professor B. O. Unbegaun, Professor of Comparative Slavonic Philology in the University of Oxford, to Dr. R. Auty, Lecturer in Slavonic Studies in the University of Cambridge, and to Mr. E. D. Tappe, Lecturer in Rumanian in the School of Slavonic and East European Studies of the University of London, for reading the manuscript and suggesting improvements; to Miss S. C. Gardiner for compiling the subject-index and helping with the Cyrillic word-index; and to the Athlone Press for ensuring that the Grammar was produced under the best technical conditions.

If the Grammär succeeds in guiding the student in the field of Slavonic philology, as a branch of Indo-European linguistics, it will have achieved its purpose.

G. N.

CONTENTS

MORPHOLOGY AND WORD-FORMATION

SELECT BIBLIOGRAPHY

(For works on the Cyrillo-Methodian texts, see Part II, pp. xi–xii)

I. GRAMMARS AND CHRESTOMATHIES

DIELS, P. *Altkirchenslavische Grammatik*, I. Teil: Grammatik, Heidelberg, 1932; II. Teil: Ausgewählte Texte und Wörterbuch, Heidelberg, 1934; 2. Auflage 1963.

HAMM, J. *Gramatika starocrkvenoslavenskog jezika*. Pregled gramatike starocrkvenoslavenskog jezika s hrestomatijom i rječnikom, i, Zagreb, 1947.

—— *Čitanka starocrkvenoslavenskog jezika s hrestomatijom i rječnikom*, ii, Zagreb, 1947.

KUL'BAKIN, ST. *Le Vieux Slave*, Paris, 1929 (with a chapter on the dialectal forms in OCS).

LESKIEN, A. *Handbuch der altbulgarischen (altkirchenslavischen) Sprache* (contains a selection of texts and a glossary), Heidelberg, 1922[6].

—— *Grammatik der altbulgarischen (altkirchenslavischen) Sprache*, Heidelberg, 1919[2, 3].

ŁOŚ, J. *Gramatyka staroslowiańska*, Lwów-Warszawa-Kraków, 1922.

LUNT, H. G. *Old Church Slavonic Grammar*, 'S-Gravenhage, 1955. See the appreciation by W. K. Matthews of this American handbook in *The Slavonic and East European Review*, vol. xxxv, No. 84, 1956, pp. 286–288.

MEILLET, ANTOINE (a general introduction to the history of the Slavonic languages), *Le Slave commun*[2], Paris, 1934.

MILETIČ, L. *Starobălgarska Gramatika*, Sofia, 1925[9].

ROMANSKI, ST. *Starobălgarski ezik v obrazci*, Sofia, 1945.

SELIŠČEV, A. M. *Staroslavjanskij jazyk*, i, Vvedenie, Fonetika; Moskva, 1951; ii, Teksty, Slovar', Očerki Morfologii; Moskva, 1952.

SŁOŃSKI, S. *Gramatyka języka staroslowiańskiego (starobulgarskiego)*, Warszawa, 1950.

—— *Wybór tekstów staroslowiańskich*, Lwów, 1926.

VAILLANT, A. *Manuel du vieux slave*, i, Grammaire; ii, Textes et Glossaire, Paris, 1948; 2e éd. rev. et augm., 1963–4.

WIJK, N. VAN. *Geschichte der altkirchenslavischen Sprache*, I, Laut- und Formenlehre, Berlin–Leipzig, 1931.

VONDRÁK, W. *Altkirchenslavische Grammatik*, Berlin, 1912[2].

—— *Kirchenslavische Chrestomathie*, Göttingen, 1910.

—— *Církevněslovanská Chrestomatie*, Brno, 1925.

WEINGART, M. *Rukovět' jazyka staroslověnského* (2 vols.), Praha, 1937–8.

WEINGART, M. and KURZ, J. *Texty ke studiu jazyka a písemnictví staroslověnského*, Praha, 1949².

II. DICTIONARIES

MIKLOSICH, F. *Lexicon palaeoslovenico-graeco-latinum*, Vienna, 1862–5 (contains Middle Bulgarian, Old Serbian, Old Russian vocabulary).

SADNIK, L. and AITZENMÜLLER, R. *Handwörterbuch zu den altkirchenslavischen Texten*, 'S-Gravenhage–Heidelberg–Leiden, 1955.

Slovar' cerkovno-slavjanskago i russkago jazyka (sostavlennyj vtorymŭ otděleniemŭ Imperatorskoj Akademiji Naukŭ), Sanktpeterburg, 1867².

ABBREVIATIONS

A./acc.	accusative	L./loc.	locative
act.	active	masc.	masculine
adj.	adjective	M	Middle
adv.	adverb	Mar.	Marianus
aor.	aorist	MHG	Middle High German
AS	Anglo-Saxon	Mn	Modern
Ass.	Codex Assemanianus	n.	noun
Av.	Avestan	neut.	neuter
B	Bulgarian	N./nom.	nominative
C	Croatian	num.	numeral
caus.	causative	OCS	Old Church Slavonic
cf.	conferatur (compare),	OHG	Old High German
	refer to	OPr	Old Prussian
Cloz.	Glagolita Clozianus	ord.	ordinal
coll.	collective	OS	Old Saxon
comp.	comparative	Ostr.	Ostromir's Gospel-
conj.	conjunction		Book
CS	Common Slavonic	p.	past
Cz	Czech	P	Polish
D./dat.	dative	part.	participle
dial.	dialectal	pass.	passive
dim.	diminutive	pf.	perfect
Dor.	Doric	pft.	perfective
du.	dual	pers.	person
E	English	plur./pl.	plural
Euch. Sin.	Euchologium Sinaiticum	poss.	possessive
Finn.	Finnish	pr.	present
fem.	feminine	Prague Fr.	Prague Fragments
Fr.	French	prep.	preposition
Freis.	Freising Texts	pron.	pronoun
fut.	future	prop. n.	proper name
G	German	PrS	Proto-Slavonic
G./gen.	genitive	Ps. Sin.	Psalterium Sinaiticum
Goth.	Gothic	R	Russian
Gr	Greek	refl.	reflexive
IE	Indo-European	Savv. Kn.	Savvina Kniga
imp.	imperative	SCr	Serbo-Croatian
impf.	imperfect	sing./sg.	singular
impft.	imperfective	Skt	Sanskrit
inf.	infinitive	Slk	Slovak
I./instr.	instrumental	Sln	Slovene
int.	interjection	sup.	supine
intrans.	intransitive	Supr.	Suprasliensis
it.	iterative	T	Teutonic
Kiev Miss.	Kiev Missal	trans.	transitive
Lat.	Latin	v.	verb
Latv.	Latvian	V./voc.	vocative
Lith.	Lithuanian	Zogr.	Zographensis

SYMBOLS

> becomes
< from
* hypothetically reconstructed form
~ links words derived from the same root or different apophonic grades of a root
^ marks palatalization; over a vowel (in SCr) marks the intonation (§ 4)
' marks place of reduced vowel
: cognates or loan-words, derivative relation
[ ] phonetic transcription
( ) explanatory or alternative words or morphological definition of a form
' after or above a consonant marks the softness of the consonant (§ 3 *a*); the same symbol over a vowel marks the stress or the intonation (§ 4)
‿ over a vowel indicates its short quantity
‐ over a vowel indicates its long quantity
ˌ under a vowel (*u̯, i̯*) marks the consonantic function of the phoneme
₀ under a consonant (*n̥, m̥, l̥, r̥*) marks the vocalic function of the phoneme

For the understanding of some philological terms the useof a dictionary of linguistic terminology is valuable, like that by J. Marouzeau, *Lexique de la terminologie linguistique*.

THE OLD CHURCH SLAVONIC
LANGUAGE

OLD CHURCH SLAVONIC is a South Slavonic dialect from the region of Macedonia used, in the ninth century, by two Greek scholars, Constantine (Cyril) and Methodius of Thessalonica, for their missionary purposes in the Slav countries of Moravia and Pannonia. The Introduction to Part II summarizes our present knowledge of the historical events surrounding the formation of the two alphabets, *Glagolitic* and *Cyrillic*; but it may be briefly stated here that Glagolitic was largely based on the Greek minuscules (cursives), and Cyrillic on the Greek majuscules (uncials) of the period. There. are preserved tenth- and eleventh-century Moravo-Pannonian texts, in South-Slavonic recensions, written in both alphabets.

The South Slavonic character of the first Slavonic literary language is apparent in its phonetic structure. An original Indo-European and Proto-Slavonic dental followed by *j* is represented in OCS by *št*, *žd*, which occur elsewhere only in Bulgarian, as this language belongs to the same group of dialects as OCS. So, to OCS *svešta* < PrS **svetja* 'light', OCS *mežda* < PrS **medja* (cf. Lat. *media*) correspond: B *svešta*, *mežda*, SCr *svijéća*, *mèd'a*, C *svíce*, *meze*, P *świeca*, *miedza*, R *sv'ečá*, *m'ežá* (§ 21·2). However, even the earliest Slavonic texts show dialectal influences of the region where they were written.. So one finds in these texts isolated forms with Western Slavonic correspondents for original *tj*, *dj*, e.g. *rozĭstvo* 'birth' for *roždĭstvo* (§ 31 *c*); two texts, the *Kiev Missal* and the *Prague Folia*, are characterized by such correspondences called *bohemisms* (*moravisms*).

The reduced vowels illustrate the dialectal and chronological aspects of OCS. These phonemes were already in the oldest texts on the way to losing their independent value and to being used only to define the character of the preceding consonants. One observes therefore in the oldest texts a certain fluctuation in the use of the letters corresponding to these sounds. They are sometimes interchanged, vocalized, or dropped altogether (§ 33).

Various dialectal influences penetrated into OCS texts through

the spoken language of the copyists. So, for example, the epenthetic *l* after labials was inconsistently written in words like *zemjia/ zemlja* (§ 17 *b*, *c*). Further, the nasal ǫ is changed into *u* under the influence of the Serbo-Croat dialect spoken by the scribes of certain MSS (§ 32.4, § 35). These and other phonetic, morphological, and lexical features group the OCS texts into several regional and chronological categories. The Gospels of Ostromir (1056–7) contains many East Slavonic characteristics and is considered as the oldest Russian text. After the eleventh century the local influences penetrated more and more into the written language and the Slavonic texts of this period are classified according to their local dialectal features as *Middle Bulgarian* (called so because Old Bulgarian was improperly used for OCS), *Old Serbian*, *Czecho-Moravian*, *Slavo-Russian* (Old Russian). It is difficult to trace a hard line between OCS and later Slavonic texts; the year 1100 has been conventionally accepted as the borderline between OCS and the various branches of Old Slavonic.

The Slavonic linguistic unity lasted till relatively late in the Middle Ages, so that OCS serves, for philological purposes, as surrogate for Common Slavonic (Proto-Slavonic), and forms a basis for the history of the Slavonic languages. Cyril's and Methodius' works have a literary and also a fundamental cultural and religious importance. Through their activities Byzantium won the Slav world for the Eastern Church. Before Cyril and Methodius's mission some Slavs had been converted to Christianity by the Western Church. For that reason the Church terminology, common to all Slavs, is either of Western Latin or of German origin, e.g. OCS *olŭtarĭ* 'altar' < OHG *altâri* < Lat. *altare*; *postŭ* 'lent' < OHG *fasto*; *crĭky* 'church': OHG *chirihha* < Gr. κυριακόν, or translation loan-words like *nepriĕznĭ* 'devil': OHG *unholdo* m. 'devil'.

Through the Middle Ages Old Slavonic was called, in Slavonic literary usage, словѣньскъіи ѩзъікъ (*slovĕnĭskyj językŭ*); it became the language of culture for the Orthodox peoples of eastern Europe, for Slavs and for non-Slavs as well, and this language played in eastern Europe a role similar to that of Latin in the West.

WRITING SYSTEMS AND SOUNDS

§ 1. TABLE OF ALPHABETS

Cyrillic	Numerical value	Glagolitic	Numerical value	Transcription	Slavonic names of the letters	Pronunciation
А	1		1	a	azŭ	
Б	—		2	b	buky	
В	2		3	v	vědě	
Г	3		4	g	glagoli	
Д	4		5	d	dobro	
е	5		6	e	estĭ	e in *end*
Ж	—		7	ž	živěte	s in *pleasure*
Ѕ, ʒ	6		8	dz	dzělo	see § 25
З, z	7		9	z	zemlja	
I (ï)	10		10	i	iže	
И	8		20	i	ižei	
(ħ)	—		30	ǵ	ǵa, djerv	g in *coagulate*
К	20		40	k	kako	
Л	30		50	l	ljudije	
М	40		60	m	myslite	
Н	50		70	n	našĭ	
о	70		80	o	onŭ	
П	80		90	p	pokoj	
ρ	100		100	r	rĭci	
с	200		200	s	slovo	
Т, ш	300		300	t	tvrĭdo	
оу, 8	400		400	u	ukŭ	
ф. ф	500		500	f	frĭtŭ	
Ѳ	9		—	th, θ	fita	t or θ, th
Х	600		600	x, (ch)	xěrŭ	ch in *loch*
ω	800		700	o	otŭ	
ш	—		800	št	šta	sht
ц	900		900	c	ci	ts in *hats*
ч	90		1,000	č	črĭvĭ, ča	ch in *church*
ш	—		—	š	ša	sh in *sharp*
'ъ	—		—	ŭ, ('ъ)	jerŭ	reduced, obscure like -*er* in *father*
ь	—		—	ĭ, (ь)	jerĭ	reduced *i*

B 2

Cyrillic	Numerical value	Glagolitic	Numerical value	Transcription	Slavonic names of the letters	Pronunciation
ЪІ	—	ɞⱚ	—	y	jery	similar to P y, R ы in syn
ѣ	—	Ⰰ	—	ě	jatĭ	}ya in yam, }yak
ꙗ	—	Ⰰ	—	ja	—	
ІЄ	—	—	—	je	—	ye in yet
ю	—	Ⱆ	—	ju	—	you, jü
ѧ, Ⰰ	900	Ⰵ	—	ę	jusŭ, ęsŭ	nasal like Fr. fin
ѫ	—	Ⰶ	—	ǫ	jusŭ, ǫsŭ	nasal like Fr. bon
ѩ	—	Ⰶ	—	ję	jusŭ, jęsŭ	nasal like Fr. bien
ѭ	—	Ⱚ	—	jǫ	jusŭ, jǫsŭ	nasal like Fr. lion
ѯ	60	—	—	ks	—	ks
ѱ	700	—	—	ps	—	ps
ѵ, ѷ	400	Ⰱ	—	i, v	ižica	i in ship, u, ü
—	—	—	—	j (yod, jot, iota)	—	y in E yes, you

The Phonetic System

§ 2. I. The vocalic phonemes may be divided into : (1) a *front* (soft) series, and (2) a *back* (hard) series of vowels. In each of these series there are : (a) *oral* vowels, (b) *nasal* vowels, and (c) *reduced* (semi) vowels :

1. *Front vowels*

(a) oral:
    ѣ, є, и
    [ě, e, i]

(b) nasal:
    ѧ [ę]

(c) reduced:
    ь [ĭ]

2. *Back vowels*

(a) oral:
    а, о, оу, ъі
    [a, o, u, y]

(b) nasal:
    ѫ [ǫ]

(c) reduced:
    ъ [ŭ]

The *jery* (ъі, ъи) is a central (mixed) vowel.

II. The consonantal phonemes could be grouped according to their place and way of articulation in:

1. *Liquids (lateral):*
    ρ, ʌ [*r, l*]
2. *Nasals:*
    ʍ, ʜ [*m, n*]
3. *Spirants:*
    (*a*) labio-dental:
        в, (ф) [*v, f*]
    (*b*) dental hiss-type:
        з, с [*z, s*]
    (*c*) dental hush-type:
        ж, ш [*ž, š*]
    (*d*) velar:
        χ [*x*]

4. *Affricates (semi-occlusives):*
    (*a*) dental:
        ѕ, ц [*dz, c*]
    (*b*) palatal:
        ч [*č*]
5. *Stops (occlusives):*
    (*a*) labial:
        в, п [*b, p*]
    (*b*) dental:
        д, т [*d, t*]
    (*c*) velar:
        г, к [*g, k*]

1. The Glagolitic alphabet has a special letter for soft *g'* (affricate) (ѥ) which is transcribed in Cyrillic by ѓ or by ħ (the latter is a graphic development from the Glagolitic ѥ, and was used in late Serbian (Bosnian) manuscripts): анħелъ, анѓелъ 'angel', ħеона, ѓеона = Gr. γέεννα 'Gehenna', ħетъсиманн = Gr. Γεθσημανεί 'Gethsemane', ѥħүпьтъ, еѓюптъ = Gr. Αἴγυπτος 'Egypt'.

2. The Cyrillic alphabet has four letters which are used in words of foreign origin or as numbers: ѳ [Gr. θ] = 9, ѯ [*ks*] = 60, ѱ [*ps*] = 700, ѵ [Gr. *v*] = 400. The letter щ [*št*] is a ligature of ш and т.

3. The OCS phonetic system contained a sonant [*j*] = consonant [*i̯*]. For this *yod*-sound neither of the two Slavonic alphabets has a special letter. The Cyrillic alphabet marks this sound (by a ligature) when it is followed by a vowel, with which it forms a phoneme: ꙗ [*ja*], ѥ [*je*], ю [*ju*], ѩ [*je̜*], ѭ [*jǫ*]. It is not marked before [*i*], and is inconsistently marked before [*e*]. It may be assumed that ю had a phonetic value of [*ü, jü*], as ѣ, which is often interchanged with ꙗ, might have sounded like a preiotized [*jä*] (§ 32.5).

4. The Glagolitic alphabet writes: Ⰵ for [*e*] and [*je*], Ⱑ for [*ě*]

and [*ja*]; ⰳ for [*ju*] and ⰵ for [*u*], ⱔⰵ for [*ję*] and ⰵ for [*ę*], ⱖⰵ for [*jǫ*], and ⰸⰵ for [*ǫ*]. The Glagolitic letters for preiotized *ę* and *ǫ* are ligatures, but it is not clear what sounds their component parts represent.

5. In the Cyrillic transcription of the Glagolitic texts new letters have been devised by the editors in order to distinguish between the three Glagolitic letters for [*i*]: ⰺ, ⰻ, ⰻ, though these letters are not used consistently in the texts. The Cyrillic letter ⰻ (н later form) usually transcribes the Glagolitic ⰺ, the Cyrillic letter ⰻ (ī) corresponds to Glagolitic ⰻ and ⰻ. Later ʊ was devised (by Jagić) for the transcription of the Glagolitic ⰻ, and Leskien uses й for marking [*jĭ*] as in nom. sg. ꙁⰿⰻⰻ [*zmiji̯*] : nom. pl. ꙁⰿⰻⰻⰻ [*zmiji*] 'dragon(s)'.

6. The OCS spellings of liquids followed by reduced vowels (ръ, рь, лъ, ль) represent either a CS vocalic liquid, soft or hard, [*r̥, r̥', l̥, l̥'*] or a combination of a CS liquid followed by a reduced vowel [*r+ŭ, r+ĭ, l+ŭ, l+ĭ*]. This distinction is practically non-existent in OCS, though it may be detected in the orthography of some texts (Zogr.), which confuse the reduced vowels representing original vocalic liquids and write, for example, прьвъ instead of прьвъ 'first', съмрътъ instead of съмрьтъ 'death'. The original phonetic values are apparent in the development of some Slavonic languages, e.g. Russian shows consistently the original vocalic liquid by a vowel developed before the liquid, whereas the group liquid followed by a reduced vowel developed into a liquid followed by a vowel: OCS прьвъ 'first', влькъ 'wolf', тръгъ 'market', длъгъ 'long': R первый, волк, торг, долг, whereas to OCS трьхъ 'in three', слъза 'tear', крьвь 'blood', плътъ 'flesh' correspond in R трёх, слеза, кровь, плоть (§ 17).

7. The semicircle (apostrophe) ˘ over certain consonants indicates their softness: *l̓, r̓, n̓, g̓, k̓, x̓, p̓, b̓*: любити 'to love', морⱖ 'sea', нива 'field', ангелъ 'angel', кесарь 'Caesar', хероувимъ 'cherub', пристѫпльь 'having come', корабⰵь 'boat'. The apostrophe ' marks the omission of a vowel: ч'то for чьто 'what'. These signs appear, however, only in some texts and are used inconsistently. A line ¯ or ⌐ (tittle) over the letters indicates their use

as numbers or abbreviations; the words abbreviated frequently have a sacred character: а̄ = 1, бг҃ъ = богъ 'God'. A ⸝ before a letter indicates 'thousand'. The sign is an original χ, the first letter of Gr. χίλιοι = 1,000: ⸝г = 3,000.

HARD, SOFT, AND PALATAL CONSONANTS

§ 3. A consonant could be pronounced soft or hard according to whether it was followed by a front or back vowel. Thus the consonant system is made up of pairs of consonants distinguished by the presence or absence of softness (palatalization). This distinction was, however, not phonemic and it is not graphically marked. A narrow transcription should distinguish between soft and hard consonants, e.g. пьсати 'to write' would be transcribed [p'ĭsat'i] with soft p and t and with hard s. If the soft consonants had been felt by the speakers of OCS to be different phonemes, opposed to the hard consonants, the creators of the Slavonic alphabets would have devised special letters for them.

The sonant [j] (jot) changes the preceding consonant (whether labial, dental, or velar) into a palatal one; in the case of the labials into a consonant group ending in a palatal sound (§ 17). Therefore we have to distinguish between palatal consonants produced by jot, which changed the preceding consonant into a different phoneme, and soft consonants, which appear before any front vowel, being softened (slightly palatalized) but not changed into new phonemes. The jot is a fundamental feature of the OCS phonetic system (§ 17.c, § 21, § 30) and changes the preceding consonant:

Hard consonant	Soft consonant	Palatal consonant
[r] рабъ [rabŭ] 'servant'	рѣка [rěka] 'river'	море [morje] 'sea'
[l] коло [kolo] 'wheel'	мыслити [mysliti] 'to think'	мышлѭ [myšljǫ] 'I think'
[m] имати [imati] 'to have'	имѣти [iměti] 'to have'	иемлѭ [jemljǫ] 'I shall take'

Hard consonant	Soft consonant	Palatal consonant
[n] на [na] 'on'	небо [nebo] 'heaven'	напльнꙗти [naplŭnjati] 'to fill up'
[v] слава [slava] 'glory'	славити [slaviti] 'to glorify'	славлѭ [slavljǫ] 'I glorify'
[z] казати [kazati] 'to explain'	казити [kaziti] 'to destroy'	кажѭ [kažǫ] 'I destroy' < *kaz-jǫ
[s] пьсати [pĭsati] 'to write'	письць [pisĭcĭ] 'scribe'	пишѭ [pišǫ] 'I write' < *pis-jǫ
[ž] жаба [žaba] 'frog'	живъ [živŭ] 'alive'	драже [draže] 'dearer' < *drag-je
[š] шоумъ [šumŭ] 'noise'	шесть [šesti] 'six'	
[dz] двизати [dvidzati] 'to move'	бози [bodzi] 'gods'	движѭ [dvižǫ] 'I move' < *dvig-jǫ
[c] црькꙑ [crŭky] 'church'	отьць [otĭcĭ] 'father'	
[č] чаꙗти [čajati] 'to wait'	число [čislo] 'number'	оучѭ [učǫ] 'I teach' < *uk-jǫ
[b] братръ [bratrŭ] 'brother'	любити [ljubiti] 'to love'	люблѭ [ljubljǫ] 'I love' < *ljub-jǫ
[p] коуповати [kupovati] 'to buy'	коупити [kupiti] 'to buy'	коуплѭ [kupljǫ] 'I shall buy' < *kup-jǫ
[d] родъ [rodŭ] 'birth'	родити [roditi] 'to give birth'	рождѭ [roždjǫ] 'I shall give birth' < *rod-jǫ

Hard consonant	*Soft consonant*	*Palatal consonant*
[t] врата [*vrata*]	вратити [*vratiti*]	врашти [*vraštǫ*]
'door'	'to turn'	'I shall turn'
		< *vrat-jǫ*

(*a*) Soft velars occur only in loan-words: хитонъ [*x'itonŭ*] 'under-garment', Gr. χιτών; кедръ [*k'edrŭ*] 'cedar', Gr. κέδρος; геона [*g'eona*] 'hell', Gr. γέεννα. The voiceless spirant [*f*] occurs only in loan-words: фараосъ [*faraosŭ*], филипъ [*filipŭ*]. For changes of velars when followed by *j* or by a front vowel see: § 21, § 23, § 30, § 31.

(*b*) The softness of the consonants is not marked in the transcription because, in the historical period, a hardening process affected them (§ 31). In a narrow transcription initial *i* of a word or syllable should be preiotized: имати [*jimati*] 'to have', прѣити [*prějiti*] 'to pass over', as *e* and *ę* are usually preiotized in initial positions: ѥстъ [*jestŭ*] 'he is', ѩти [*jęti*] 'to take', but сънѩти [*sŭnęti*] 'to come together'.

QUANTITY, STRESS, AND INTONATION

§ 4. By a comparative study of the Slavonic languages one can infer that OCS had continued long and short vowels from CS. We may infer that OCS had long *a*, *ě*, *i*, *y*, *u*, *ǫ*, *ę*, *r̥*, *l̥*, which in certain positions became short. The vowels *e*, *o* were in general short; the vowels *ŭ*, *ĭ* were reduced vocalic elements, with a tendency to disappear in weak positions and to become full vowels in strong positions (§ 33).

The OCS texts, with the exception of the Kiev Miss., do not mark the quantity or the stress. The Kiev Miss. frequently uses diacritic signs over vowels (´ ` ˇ ˆ); these signs were probably intended to indicate the quantity or the stress, though they are used inconsistently. The double vowels in contractions, as добрааго (gen. sg. masc. neutr.), may also have marked the length. There is, however, no direct evidence concerning quantity, stress, and intonation in the historical period of OCS.

It is, moreover, only by a comparative study of stress and

intonation (or quantity) in the modern Slavonic languages, especially in Russian and Serbo-Croat, that one can conclude that CS had a free (movable) expiratory stress and a musical intonation (pitch). This could be either acute (rising ´) or circumflex (rising-falling ˜). ʻThe expiratory stress results from the concentration of a stronger physical emphasis on a particular syllable. The intonation consists in pronouncing the syllables on different musical tones. When the musical tone was lower at the beginning of the syllable and was raised towards the end, the intonation was rising (acute); when the tone rose, fell and rose again the intonation was falling (circumflex).

In CS, these three phonemic elements (quantity, stress, intonation) were independent of each other, i.e. an unstressed vowel could be long, and a stressed vowel could be short; and the intonation operated on stressed and on unstressed vowels. A somewhat similar situation exists in SCr dialects, which have long and short vowels, which may be stressed or unstressed, while the stress is movable, without exercising any influence on the timbre of the vowel. Russian also has preserved mobility of stress, which, being strongly expiratory, changed the timbre of the vowels, but lost all traces of intonation.

The relationship between the stress and the intonation is established by very complicated rules, which are far from explaining all cases. The intricacy of these relations is complicated by the changes in the intonation systems of the Slavonic languages, which took place after CS split into various distinct dialects.

For instance, in the course of the Balto-Slavonic period, the stress is thrown forward from a syllable carrying a falling tone or, being short, onto the following syllable, when this carried a rising tone. This rule has been formulated by Ferdinand de Saussure in a study ʻAccentuation lituanienne' (*Indogermanische Forschungen*, *VI*, *Anzeiger*, 1896, p. 157); it was first communicated at the Congress of Orientalists in Geneva, in 1894. A. Meillet established its validity for the Slavonic accent in an article ʻNote sur un déplacement d'accent en slave' (*Mémoires de la Société de linguistique*, xi, 1900, 345–51).

By the terms of this rule is explained the relationship between,

for example, R *zimá* (nom. sg.) where the final syllable had originally rising intonation and R *zímu* (acc. sg.) because here the intonation of the last syllable was falling.

From the modern Slavonic forms one can infer the quantity and intonation in CS. The R forms *byl* (*dóbyl, príbyl, úbyl*) compared with *bylá* 'she was' (*dobylá, pribylá, ubylá*) presuppose a rising tone of the fem. ending and a falling tone of the thematic vowel. However, some isolated forms contradict the general trend, e.g. *zabýla* 'she forgot', *péla* 'she sang', *vólja* 'will' : *zemljá* 'earth'. For details see N. van Wijk, 'Die baltischen und slavischen Akzent- und Intonations-Systeme' (*Verhandelingen d. k. Ak. d. W., Letterkunde* xxiii, nr 2, Amsterdam, 1923); A. Meillet, *Le slave commun*, 2nd ed., Paris, 1934, 137 sq.; especially Linda Sadnik, *Slawische Akzentuation. I. Vorhistorische Zeit*, Wien, 1959. For Indo-European: J. Kurylowicz, *Accentuation des langues indo-européennes*, 1958[2].

SYLLABIC DIVISION

§ 5. In the OCS phonetic system no syllable ended in a consonant. The tendency to open originally closed syllables is due to the increasing wave of sonority in the rhythm of syllables and this caused many phonetic changes which created the specific OCS phonological pattern. Owing to this tendency the prehistoric diphthongs *ě̄i, āi, ōi, ěu, āu, ōu* were monophthongized (§ 10, § 12); *or, ol, er, el* were changed by metathesis and lengthening of the vowel (§ 6.3, § 10.4); *on, un, en, in* were nasalized (§ 13, § 14); *ŗ, ļ, ŗ', ļ'* developed vocalic elements (§ 16.2, § 17, § 18); groups of consonants were simplified and the syllabic division changed its original place: **ob-viti* > **o-bviti* > *o-bi-ti*, овити 'to wind round': вити 'to wind'; погребѫ 'I will bury': погрети 'to bury' < **po-greb-ti* (§ 29.9, 11). (A. Leskien, *Grammatik der altbulgarischen (aksl.) Sprache*, 1919, 53, 59, 62; N. van Wijk, *Geschichte der altkirchenslavischen Sprache*, 1931, 46; P. Diels, *Altkirchenslavische Grammatik*, 1932, 120 sq.)

Loan-words from languages with a different syllabic structure often insert a vowel in order to open the syllable: Gr. Σαλμανά > салъмана; Gr. πορφύρα > поръфира, Porphyrius: поръфоури; σπόνδυλος 'spindle' > спонъдило.

The Vowels

§ 6. The vowel *a* continues an IE long *ā* or long *ō*:

1. To Lat. *frāter*, Gr. φράτηρ = member of a φρᾱτρία 'brotherhood', Skt *bhrå̆tar-*; to Lat. *māter*, Gr. (Dor.) μᾱ́τηρ, Skt *mātá̆* which represent IE *bhrā-ter, *mā-tēr correspond OCS братръ, братъ, мати (gen. матере); in loan-words Lat. *pǎgānus*, OCS поганъ 'pagan'.

2. To Lat. *dōnum*, Gr. δῶρον; Lat *co-gnōsco*, Gr. γι-γνώσκω correspond OCS даръ 'present', знати 'to know'.

3. The vowel *a* may represent an IE *o* of the liquid diphthongs *or*, *ol* at the beginning or in the middle of a word. These groups *ort-*, *olt-*, *tort*, *tolt*, following the tendency towards open syllables, were changed by metathesis of the consonant and by lengthening the vowel (*t* in these groups symbolizes any consonant): CS *ordlo (cf. Lat. *arātrum*) > OCS рало 'plough'; CS *olkomŭ > OCS лакомъ 'hungry'; CS *gordŭ (cf. Lat. *hortus*, E 'yard') > OCS градъ 'town'; CS *golva (cf. Lith. *galvà*) > OCS глава 'head' (§ 36).

4. CS *ě* which continues an IE *ē* (§ 10) developed, when preceded by *j, č, ž, š, št, žd*, into OCS *a*: стоӕти 'to stand' < *stojěti : трьпѣти 'to suffer'; ѣсти (cf. Lat. *ēdĕre*), ӕсти, асти 'to eat' < *jěsti; кричати 'to shout' < *kričěti : видѣти 'to see'; лежати 'to lie down' < *ležěti: оумѣти 'to understand'; слышати 'to hear' < *slyšěti; поуштати 'to set free' < *pustjěti; троуждати 'to weary' < *trudjěti.

§ 7. The vowel *o* continues an IE short *a* or short *o*:

1. To Lat. *axis*, *arare*, Skt *ákṣaḥ*, Gr. ἄξων, ἀρόω correspond OCS ось 'axle', орати 'to plough'; in loan-words Lat. *altare* ⸰ OCS ол(ъ)тарь.

2. To Lat. *domus*, *oculus*, *ovis*, Gr. δόμος, ὄχος 'cart', ἐ-φύγ-ο-μεν (1st pl. aor.) correspond OCS домъ 'house', око 'eye', овьца 'sheep', возъ 'cart', нес-о-мъ (1st pl. aor.).

3. The IE *ə* (*shva*) is represented in certain positions by *o*: OCS *sto-jati* 'to be standing' corresponds to Gr. στατός 'placed',

Lat. *stătus* 'still', Skt *sthitáḥ* < IE **sthə-t-os*; sometimes IE *ə* disappears: OCS *dŭšti* 'daughter': Gr. θυγάτηρ, Skt *duhitá*, in which *ə* is represented by *a* or *i*, as IE **dhugh(ə)tér-* shows.

4. The IE diphthong *eu̯* developed into *ev* > *ov*, and the syllabic frontier was changed (§ 25): **neu̯-os* > *no-vŭ*, OCS новъ 'new', Lat. *novus*, Gr. νέος; **k'leu̯os* > Gr. κλέϝος > κλέος : OCS слово; **pleu̯-om-* > пловѫ 'I sail' (cf. Gr. πλέ(ϝ)ω): **pleu̯-ti* > **pljuti* > плоути 'to sail'. The last change, into *pluti*, is on the analogy of the present stem *plovǫ* (§ 19.3). The change *e* > *o* is due to the following back vowel.

§ 8. The vowel *u* developed from the IE diphthongs *au̯*, *ou̯*, *eu̯*:

1. As IE short *a* became Slavonic *o* (§ 7), the diphthong *au̯* > *ou̯* and developed further into *u*: Lat. *taurus*, Gr. ταῦρος, OPr *tauris*: OCS тоуръ 'aurochs'; Lat. *auris*, Lith. *ausis*: OCS оухо; Lith. *báudinti* 'to urge', Skt *bodháyati*: OCS боудити, боудитъ 'to wake up, he awakens'.

2. The diphthong *eu̯* developed into a preiotized *'u* [*ju*]: Gr. πεύθομαι 'I search', Lith. *baũsti* 'to punish', Goth. *biuda* 'I order', AS *bēodan* 'to order': CS **bjudti* > OCS блюсти 'I observe, watch'; Goth. *liufs*, AS *lēof*, OHG *liup*: OCS любъ 'beloved'. The IE formulae are **bheu̯dh-*, **leu̯bh-*.

§ 9. The vowel *y* has been preserved (as a separate sound from *i*) in Polish and in Russian. It is assumed to have been a hard back sound pronounced without rounding of the lips and with the top of the tongue raised towards the hard palate.

1. *y* continues a long IE *ū* as appears from the following examples: Lat. *fūmus*, Lith. *dúmai*, Skt *dhūmáḥ*: OCS дыимъ 'smoke'; Lat. *mūs*, Gr. μῦς, OHG *mūs*, Skt *mūṣ*: OCS мышь 'mouse'; in loan-words: Lat. *būbalus* > OCS быволъ 'buffalo'; OHG *hūs* (T **hūza*) > OCS хызъ 'house'.

2. In final position *y* corresponds to IE *ā*, *ō*, *ū* followed by *s* (*-ās*, *-ōs*, *-ūs*) or *a*, *o*, *u* followed by *ns* (> *-āns*, *-ōns*, *-ūns*): сыины (acc. pl.) represents IE **sūn-uns*, влъкы (acc. pl.): IE *u̯l̥qons*; свекры: Skt *śvaśrúḥ*; ны (nom. pl.), вы (nom. pl.): Lat. *nos*, *vos*; рѫкы (gen. sg.) < **ronkās* (§ 46.1.2.6.7).

3. The sound combination *ŭ+j* changed into *yj*: CS *dobrŭjĭ* > OCS добръıи 'good'; CS *mŭjọ* > OCS мъ̈ıѭ 'I wash'. The vowel *y* also alternates with other grades in some verbal stems (§ 37.5): OCS д'ъм҃ѫ : -д'ъıмаѭ (it.) 'I blow up'; гоүьнти: гъıбнѫти 'to perish'.

§ 10. The *ě* (*jat'*) is generally considered to have been a very open preiotized *e* [ịä, ịa]. It is the soft counterpart of *a*. The Glagolitic alphabet had one single letter for *ě* and for *ja*: ⱑ, though the two sounds were not identical (§ 2.3.4).

1. Historically *ě* continues an IE *ē*: видѣти 'to see':Lat. *vidēre*; сѣмѧ 'seed':Lat. *sēmen*; дѣти 'to do':Gr. τί-θη-μι.

2. Under unknown conditions, dominated probably by rules of intonation, the final diphthongs IE *ai̯*, *oi̯* changed into *ě* or into *i*: вльци (nom. pl.), вльцѣ (loc. sg.) represent the same IE formula *u̯l̥qoi̯*; женѣ (dat. sg.):Lat. *feminae*; рабѣхъ (loc. pl.):Gr. λόγοις; бери (2nd imp. sg.):Gr. φέροις (§ 46.2.10.15.16).

3. In medial position the diphthongs IE *ai̯*, *oi̯* are represented by *ě*: снѣгъ 'snow':Goth. *snaiws*, OPr *snaygs*, Lith. *sniēgas*, Lat. *nix*; лѣвъ 'left':Lat. *laevus*, Gr. λαιός < λαιϝος; берѣте (2nd pl. imp.):Gr. φέροιτε (optative), Goth. *bairáiþ*; in loan-words цѣсарь: Lat. *Caesar*, Goth. *kaisar*.

4. The vowel *ě* represents an IE *e* of the liquid diphthongs *er*, *el* in initial position of the groups *ert-*, *elt-*, for which there are no certain examples, or in medial position of the groups *tert-*, *telt-* in which *t* symbolizes any consonant:брѣза 'birch tree' < CS *berz-a*:Lith. *béržas*, Skt *bhūrjaḥ*, AS *beorc*, *bierce*; брѣгъ 'hill' < CS *bergŭ*:AS *beorg*, Goth. *bairgahein* 'mountain region'; млѣко 'milk' < CS *melko*:AS *milc*, *meolc*. It is controversial whether this Slavonic word is a Teutonic loan-word, or cognate with the Teutonic.

§ 11. The vowel *e* has two origins:

1. *e* continues the IE *e*: везѫ 'I drive':Lat. *veho*; ѥстъ 'he is': Lat. *est*; десѧть 'ten':Lat. *decem*, Gr. δέκα.

2. Original *o* preceded by *j*, or by a palatal consonant: *č*, *š*, *ž*, *št*, *žd*—in a later period also after *c'*, *dz'*, *n'*, *r'*, *l'*—changed into *e*, and

this change divided the OCS declension into two types: a hard-stem declension and a soft-stem declension (§ 37.6, § 38.2, § 55.2):

того (gen. sg.) 'of that': іего (gen. sg.) 'of him, his'

томоу (dat. sg.) 'to that': іемоу (dat. sg.) 'to him'

село (nom. sg. neut.) 'village': полге (nom. sg. neut.) 'field'

жено (voc. sg. fem.) 'woman!': доуше (voc. sg. fem.) 'soul!'

женоѭ (instr. sg. fem.) 'with the woman': доушеѭ (instr. sg. fem.) 'with the soul'

градомь (instr. sg. masc.) 'with the town': мѫжемь (instr. sg. masc.) 'with the man'

градомъ (dat. pl. masc.) 'to the towns': мѫжемъ (dat. pl. masc.) 'to the men'

градома (dat. instr. du. masc.) 'with (to) two towns': мѫжема (dat. instr. du. masc.) 'with (to) two men'

тоѭ (instr. sg. fem.) 'with her': іеѭ (instr. sg. fem.) 'with her'

тои (dat. loc. sg. fem.) 'to her': іеи (dat. loc. sg. fem.) 'to her'

томь (loc. sg. masc. neut.) 'in that': іемь (loc. sg. masc. neut.) 'in him'

тою (gen. loc. du. masc. neut. fem.) 'of (in) them two': іею (gen. loc. du. masc. neut. fem.) 'of them two'

то (nom. acc. sg. neut.) 'that': іе (nom. acc. sg. neut.) 'it'

§ 12. The vowel *i* continues an IE *ī*, or an IE diphthong *ei̯*.

1. OCS живъ 'alive' corresponds to Lat. *vīvus*; пити 'to drink': Gr. πίνω; грива 'mane', гривьна 'necklace': Skt *grīvá* 'neck', Latv. *grīva* 'mouth of a river'.

2. OCS видѣти: Gr. εἶδος < ϝειδος, Lith. *véid-as* 'face, visage'.

Of diphthongal origin is *i* in flexional endings of the masc. nom. pl. -o- stems and of the imperative forms (§ 10.2, § 40, § 71). In these and in other flexional endings *i* alternates with *ě* of diphthongal origin:

градѣ (loc. sg. masc.): мѫжи (loc. sg. masc.)

градѣхъ (loc. pl. masc.): мѫжихъ (loc. pl. masc.)

лѣтѣ (loc. sg. neut.): поли (loc. sg. neut.)

лѣтѣхъ (loc. pl. neut.): полихъ (loc. pl. neut.)

женѣ (dat. loc. sg. fem.): доуши (dat. loc. sg. fem.)

лѣтѣ (nom. acc. voc. du.): доуши (nom. acc. voc. du.)

бєр҄клъ (1st pl. imp.): бнимъ (1st pl. imp.)
бєр҄кте (2nd pl. imp.): бните (2nd pl. imp.)
бєр҄кв҄к (1st du. imp.): бнив҄к (1st du. imp.)
бєр҄кта (2nd du. imp.): бнита (2nd 3rd du. imp.)
т҄клъ (instr. sg. masc. neut.): нлъ (instr. sg. masc. neut.)
т҄клъ (dat. pl. masc. neut. fem.): нлгъ (dat. pl. masc. neut. fem.)
т҄кли (instr. pl. masc. neut. fem.): нли (instr. pl. masc. neut. fem.)
т҄кхъ (gen. pl. masc. neut. fem.): нхъ (gen. pl. masc. neut. fem.)
т҄кма (dat. instr. du. masc. neut. fem.): нма (dat. instr. du. masc. neut. fem.)

3. In Slavonic *i* may represent the development of *ĭ+j* > *ij*: гостые (nom. pl.) > гостиіе 'guests' (§ 16.4); знаменье (nom. sg. neut.) > знаменние 'sign' (§ 33.3).

4. Initially *i* represents a development of *j+ĭ*: нго 'yoke' < *jĭgo* < *jŭgo*: Lat. *iugum*, нмѧ 'name' < *jĭmę* (§ 33.4).

5. Of early Proto-Slavonic origin is *i* < *y* after *j* or consonants which result from the influence of *j* (*š, ž, č, št, žd; c, dz*) as shown by the endings of the instr. pl. masc. neut. of the hard and soft stems: градъı : крaи = *kraji* < *krajy* (§ 45.14); cf. also шити 'to sew' < IE *sjū-* as shown by Lith. *siúti*.

6. The vowel *i* alternates with *ĭ* in verbal stems and characterizes the imperfective forms: пр҄клъстити 'to cheat': пр҄клиштати (impft. -it.) (§ 37.5).

§ 13. The back nasal vowel *ǫ* represents an original oral back vowel followed by a nasal consonant belonging to the same syllable.

1. OCS зѫбъ 'tooth' corresponds to Gr. γόμφος 'bolt', Skt *jámbha* 'tooth', Lith. *žaṁbas* 'sharp edge'; here the OCS nasal represents an original *om*. In пѫть 'road': Lat. *pons, pont-is* the nasal represents *on*. In ѫзъкъ 'narrow' the nasal represents an original *an* as is shown by Lat. *angustus*, Lith. *aňkštas* 'tight, narrow'; Gr. ἄγχω 'I press, close', Goth. *aggwu* (nom. sg. neut.) 'narrow',

Skt *anhīyas* (comp.). There are no clear examples for ǫ representing an IE *am*. As the original short *a* fell together with *o*, in an early period, the development of *am* was identical in OCS with the development of *om*. In Germanic loan-words *an* is represented by ǫ: χѫдогъ 'skilful' : Goth. *handugs* 'wise'.

2. The nasal ǫ may correspond to *un*, *um* for which, however, there are only scarce examples: гѫБа 'sponge' corresponds to Lith. *gumbas* 'swelling'. IE *snubh-* (Lat. *nuba*, Gr. νύμφη) with a *n*-infix is represented in Slavonic by P *dziewosłąb* 'match-maker' < *-snǫb*, Sln *snóbok* 'match-maker', Cz *snoubiti* 'to wed', which go back to CS *snǫbŭ*.

3. The acc. sg. fem. ending of the *a*- stems corresponds to an original *-ām*: жен-ѫ: Lat. *femin-ām*; рѫк-ѫ: OPr *rank-am*, Lith. *rañk-ą* 'hand'.

§ 14. The front nasal ę has the following origins:

1. It corresponds to original long or short *en*, *em*, e.g. пѧть 'five':Gr. πέντε, Lith. *penki*, Lat. *quinque*; свѧтъ 'holy':Lith. *šveñtas*; тѧтива 'gut-string': Lith.*temptúvas* 'stretcher, bowstring'; сѣмѧ 'seed':Lat. *sēmen*; мѧ < *mem*.

2. It represents original *n̥*, *m̥*: дєсѧть:Lat. *decem*, Gr. δέκα, Lith. *dešimtis* < IE *dek'm̥(-tis)*; памѧть 'memory':Lat. *mentis* (gen.), Lith. *atmintìs*, Goth. *ga-munds* < *mn̥ti*; пѧти (inf.) < *pn̥-ti/ *pen-ti*:Lith. *pinti* 'to twist, to plait'.

3. In final position, in the endings of the acc. pl. of the fem. *-ja-* stems, and of the masc. *-jo-* stems, the ę goes back to *-jons*; opposed to the hard stems acc. pl. жен-ъı, рав-ъı, in which the ending *-y* represents *-ons* (§ 9.2), are the soft stems доушѧ, крагѧ in which the ending *-ę* represents *-jens* < *-jons* (§ 45.6, 7). The gen. sg. fem. доушѧ is by analogy with the acc. pl. The same origin *-jon+t* > *-jen-t* > *-ję* accounts for the ending of the pr. part. of the soft verbal stems: знагѧ < *gno-jonts* (cf. Lat. *fug-ient-is*) (§ 45.6, § 67.1, § 73).

4. In loan-words the nasal ę represents original *in*: цѧтa 'coin': Goth. *kintus*, *kinta*; къназь:OHG *kuning*, AS *cyning*, cf. Finnish *kuningas* (Germanic loan-word); чѧдо 'child':OHG *kind* (§ 30.2).

§ 15. The OCS vocalic system contained two reduced vowels which already in the earliest texts show the tendency to disappear or to develop into full vowels according to their position (§ 33, § 34).

1. The hard reduced vowel *ŭ* continues an IE *u*: мъхъ 'moisture': Lat. *muscus* 'moss'; дъшти 'daughter': Gr. θυγάτηρ, Skt *duhitá*, Lith. *duktė̃*.

2. OCS *ŭ* developed from original syllabic (sonant) *m̥, n̥, l̥, r̥*: дъмѭ 'I blow' goes back to IE **dhm̥-*: Lith. *dumiù*; гънати 'to drive' represents the root **ghn̥-*: Lith. *giñti, giniaũ*. (The Lithuanian reflexes are not entirely clear.) In isolated cases OCS *ŭ* corresponds to initial *m̥, n̥*: въторъ 'the other, the second' (§ 59.2), together with Lith. *añtras*, Goth. *anþar* 'other', Gr. dial. ἄτερος, goes back to **n̥tor-*; съто 'hundred' may go back to **k'm̥tóm* as shown by Gr. ἑ-κατόν, Lat. *centum*, Skt *śatám*, Goth. *hunda* (nom. pl. neut.), Lith. *šim̃tas*. The Slavonic *sŭto* has been explained also as an Iranian loan-word. влъна 'wool' represents **vl̥na*: Lat. *lāna*, Goth. *wulla*, Lith. *vilna*, Skt *ūrṇā*; кръма 'rudder' < CS **kr̥ma*: Gr. πρύμνη; слъньце 'sun': Lat. *sol* (§ 2.6).

3. In the ending of the acc. sg. of the masc. -o- stems the -*ŭ* represents an IE -*om*: влькъ 'wolf' < **u̯l̥qom*: Lat. *lupum*.

§ 16. The soft reduced vowel *ĭ* continues:

1. An IE *i*: OCS вьсь 'village' is cognate with Lat. *vīcus*, Skt *víś* (fem). 'house, tribe, settlement'. Lat. *vīcus*, Gr. dial. ϝοῖκος 'house', Skt *vēśáḥ* 'neighbour', Lith. *vēšéti* 'to stay, to be a guest', *vēš-pat(i)s* 'master', require a root with a diphthongal grade, whereas OCS вьсь postulates **u̯ik'is* (§ 37.3). OCS дьнь 'day' is cognate with Lat. *nun-dīn-ae* (pl.) 'things pertaining to the ninth day'. Also in loan-words *ĭ* appears for *i*: OCS льсть 'deceit' < Goth. *lists*.

2. OCS *ĭ* corresponds to a vocalic element developed from IE syllabic (sonant) *m̥, n̥, l̥, r̥* (§ 15.2), when in CS these sonants were soft. IE had only one series of sonants; CS developed a soft, as well as a hard series: тьма 'darkness' (the form тъма is secondary as shown by the further development in Slavonic тьмьница > темьница 'prison') represents an original **tm̥-*; пьнѭ 'I stretch' continues an IE **pn̥-*, Lith. *pinti* 'to twist'; влькъ 'wolf': Gr. λύκος; прьвъ 'first': Lat. *pri-mus*; мрьтвъ 'dead',

мьр-ѣти (before vowels) 'to die' < *mṛ́-, Lith. *miriaũ* (1st pret.), *miȓti* 'to die'.

The opposition of hard and soft liquid sonants appears clearly in OCS examples containing an original velar palatalized before soft liquid sonants, and preserved before hard ones: чльнъ 'boat', жльтъ 'yellow', чрьнъ 'black', жрьны 'mill' had in CS ṛ́; глъкъ 'noise', кръкъ 'neck', грънъ 'kettle' had in CS ṛ.

3. OCS *i* corresponds to an IE *m̥* in final position: OCS матерь (acc. sg.): Lat. *matr-em* < *māter-m̥* (§ 44.5) with different vowel-gradation (§ 37.3).

4. OCS *i* corresponds to the IE diphthong *ei̯* followed by a vowel: гостые (nom. pl.) 'guests' < IE *ghostei̯-es*; трье : Lat. *tres* < *trei̯es* (§ 12.3).

5. In CS the semivowel *ĭ* developed from an *ŭ* preceded by *j, č, ž, š, št, žd, (c, z)*: иго 'yoke' < *jĭgo < *jŭgo*: Lat. *iugum*, Lith. *jùngas*, Goth. *juk*, Skt *yugam*; краи 'limit' [*kraji*] (nom. acc. sg.): рабъ 'slave'; мѫжь (nom. acc. sg.): градъ 'city'; доушь 'soul' (gen. pl.): женъ; овьць (gen. pl.): змии 'dragon' [*zmiji*]; ѩзь 'disease' (gen. pl.): женъ. Nom. sg. forms of the past part. act. 1 such as хождь : двигъ illustrate the same vowel gradation *ŭ/ĭ* (§ 12.4, 5, § 37.6).

THE CONSONANTS

§ 17. The OCS liquids continue either original liquids or original sonants *ṛ, ḷ* (§ 2.6). The orthography does not distinguish between the two historically different liquids. We find съмрътъ 'death', плънъ 'full', сръдьце 'heart', влъкъ 'wolf' where the liquid represents an original *ṛ, ḷ*, as appears in the further development of the language: SCr *smrt*, P *śmierć*, Cz *plný*, R *сердце*, *волк*, P *wilk*. The same spelling is used for кръвь 'blood', плъть 'flesh', крьстъ 'cross', црькы 'church' which historically represent a liquid followed by a vowel (cf. Lat. *crŭ-or* 'blood', Lat. *Cristus*, Gr. κυριακή > *κυρική* > OHG *chirihha*: *cĭriky*) and had a different development: R *кровь*, *плоть*, *крест*, *церковь*, that shows that the pronunciation of the liquids in the two categories was not the same (§ 1.6).

(a) The liquids can be followed by any vowel: лѣто 'summer, year', кладѫ 'I put', молѭ 'I pray', морье 'sea', рѧдъ 'row, line';

рабъ 'servant'. The spelling does not show the soft character of the consonants followed by front vowels, because it was not a phonemic distinction. Softness of consonants will therefore also not be indicated in the transcriptions in this book: *lěto, kladǫ, moljǫ, morje, rědǔ, rabǔ*, which in a narrow transcription should be reproduced *l'ěto, kladǫ, mol'jǫ, mor'je, r'ědǔ, rabǔ*.

When the scribes wished to indicate the softness of certain palatal consonants, especially of *l*, *n*, *r*, they placed a semicircle above them: земл҄и (dat.), цѣсар҄ь, мор҄ю (dat.), н҄ива (§ 2.7).

(*b*) The labial consonants followed by *j* developed a palatal *l*, called epenthetic *l*: съпати (inf.) 'to sleep': съпл҄ѭ (1st sg. pr.); любити (inf.) 'to love': любл҄ѭ (1st sg. pr.); ꙗвити (inf.) 'to show': ꙗвл҄ѭ (1st sg. pr.); земи (dat., loc. sg.) 'earth': земл҄ꙗ (§ 3).

(*c*) This epenthetic *l* disappears in the further history of OCS, though it is preserved, with greater tenacity, when followed by certain vowels. It shows the tendency to disappear when followed by *i* or *ĭ*, e.g. оставь (p. part. act. 1) alongside оставл҄ь 'having left behind', земьскъ 'earthen': земл҄ьскъ, корабь 'ship': корабл҄ь, земи (dat., loc. sg.): земл҄и, whereas before other front vowels it tended to remain; forms like благословенъ 'blessed', възлюбенъ 'beloved', прославенъ 'glorified' lost the epenthetic *l* by the dissimilatory influence of the *l* in the stem.

The OCS texts are not uniform as regards the incidence of epenthetic *l*: the Kiev Miss. consistently shows forms with *l*; the Zogr. writes *l* pretty regularly before е, ѣ, ꙗ, ѭ, ю, less regularly before и, ь; in Cloz., Mar., Euch. Sin. *l* is usually left out before и, ь; in Supr. the omission of *l* is normal, Ps. Sin. and Savv. Kn. also have forms without *l*.

(*d*) In the later period Russo-Slavonic, Old Serbian, and Old Croatian texts show a regular epenthetic *l*, but it is dropped as a rule in Macedo-Bulgarian and in the medieval Western Slavonic languages (Czech, Polish). It would therefore appear that the distribution of forms with or without epenthetic *l* points to a prehistoric dialectal division of Slavonic linguistic area in an East-South and a West region.

(*e*) In OCS texts the distinction between original hard and soft liquids, representing original liquids or vocalic liquids, is in pro-

cess of disappearing. In the Kiev Miss. original ŗ is represented by ρъ, and original ŗ' by ρь, ļ by лъ, ļ' by ль: скръбьни (nom. pl.) 'sorrowful', тврьдь 'fortress, firmness', напльнени (nom. pl.) 'filled', въплътити са 'to become incarnate'. In later copies of OCS texts the difference between soft and hard vocalic ŗ is not marked. Zogr. shows spellings like прьвъ and пръвъ, срьдьце and сръдьце. There is a tendency to continue to indicate the difference between ļ and ļ'. Original liquids followed by a reduced vowel (r+ŭ, r+ĭ, l+ŭ, l+ĭ) are generally kept separated in spellings: кръвь 'blood', трьхъ 'three', плъть 'flesh', пльвати 'to spit', кръстити 'to baptize', бльштати 'to shine'. Other OCS texts do not distinguish between original soft and hard liquids. The reduced vowels, in the original combinations r+ŭ &c., are sometimes vocalized in strong position, according to the laws governing the development of the reduced vowels: въскресъ (Mar., Ass., Ps. Sin.) for въскрьсъ, крестъ 'cross' (Cloz.) for крьстъ, слезъ (gen. pl.) 'tear' (Ps. Sin., Euch. Sin.) for сльзъ. There is no vocalization of reduced vowels when they represent ŗ, ļ (= ρъ, лъ), because there was no reduced vowel in the pronunciation of these sonants (§ 2.6, § 33.1).

§ 18. The nasal consonants continue IE *n*, *m*: зима 'winter':Lat. *hiems*, огнь 'fire':Lat. *ignis*, матерь:Lat. *mater*, сынъ : Goth. *sunus*, or IE ṇ, ṃ > CS ĭn, ĭm (Balto-Slavonic *in, im*) (§ 16.2).

The tendency towards open syllables (§ 5), caused these original nasals that closed a syllable to be absorbed in the preceding vowels: *an, am, on, om* > ǫ; *en, em* > ę; *un, um* > ǫ; *in, im* > ę (§ 13, § 14).

§ 19. OCS had only one labio-dental spirant *v*; *f* appears only in foreign words: Фарисѣи = Gr. Φαρισαῖος. The *v* continues an IE *u̯*, and was probably bilabial in an early period of OCS.

1. The *v* in вьдова 'widow', видѣти 'to see', вѣдѣ 'I know', corresponds to the *u̯* in Lat. *vidua, vidēre*, Gr. οἶδα < ϝοιδα, IE *k'leu̯os* > CS *slovo*.

2. A prosthetic *v* was developed in CS before initial ŭ-, у-: въпити 'to call' < *u-pi-ti; выдра 'otter' < *-ūdra:Gr. ὕδρα; въторыи 'the other':Lat. *uter* 'which of the two'; вазати 'to tie': ѫза 'tie' (§ 32.1).

3. The OCS *v* developed from the second element of IE *oụ*, *eụ* when followed by a vowel: плоүти 'to flow' (inf.), пловѫ (1st sg. pr.): Gr. πλέω < πλεϝω; *ov* goes back to *eụ* as in IE *neụ-os > новъ 'new': Gr. νέος < νεϝος, Lat. *novus* (§ 7.4). The development was the same when the original diphthong was long: сѣверъ 'north': Lith. *šiáurė* 'north'.

The *v* in the verbal ending *-ovati* (of the type *kup-ova-ti*) goes back to a diphthong *oụ*: *kup-oụa-ti/*kup-i-ti*. In the 2nd pers. *kupuješi* represents *kup-oụ-ješi (§ 8): T *kaupjan, Goth. *kaupōn* < Lat. *caupo* 'publican'.

§ 20. The spirants *s*, *z* continue CS and IE spirants, or represent IE soft velars (*k'*, *k'h*; *g'*, *g'h*), or developed within Slavonic from velars or dentals:

1. The IE voiceless spirant *s* is continued in OCS сꙑнъ 'son': Lith. *sūnùs*, Skt *sūnus*; сънъ 'sleep': Gr. ὕπνος, Lat. *somnus*. The IE *z* appears in OCS only combined with *d*, *g* (*zd*, *zg*): мьзда 'reward, pay': Goth. *mizdō*, Gr. μισθός; мозгъ 'marrow of bones': Av. *mazga-* 'brain'.

2. OCS *s*, *z* represent an IE soft velar: съто 'hundred: Lat. *centum*, Gr. ἑκατόν < IE **k'ṃtóm*; осмь 'eight' < **ok'tōu-* (cf. Lat. *octo*); срьдьце 'heart': Lat. *cord-is*, Gr. καρδία, Lith. *širdis* < IE **kṛd-*; знати 'to know': Lat. *co-gnō-sco*, Gr. γνῶσις < IE **g'nō-*.

3. The spirants represent original velars that were palatalized in Slavonic (§ 30.2): богъ 'God' (nom.): бозѣ, бозѣ (loc. sg.), бози, бози (nom. pl.); доухъ 'spirit' (nom.): доусѣ (loc. sg.), доуси (nom. pl.); влъхвъ 'seer' (nom.): влъсви (nom. pl.).

4. Original *tt* and *dt* are represented in OCS by *st*: чисти 'to read' (inf.) < *čit-ti : чьтѫ (1st sg.); власти 'to rule' (inf.) < *vold-ti: владѫ (1st sg.); вести 'to lead' (inf.) < *vedti: ведѫ (1st sg.) (§ 29.10). This change occurs in many IE dialects: Indo-Iranian, Greek, Italic, Celtic, Teutonic.

§ 21. The palatal spirants *š*, *ž* resulted from the first palatalization of the velars (§ 30.1):

1. Original *x*, *g* followed by a vowel of the front series (*e*, *ě* < *ē*, *ę*, *i* < *i* or *eị*, *ī*, *ṛ'*, *ḷ'*) or by *j* changed into *š*, *ž*: доухъ 'spirit' (nom.): доуше (voc.); слꙑшати (inf.) 'to hear' < *slyxēti: слоухъ (n.)

'listening'; соүшити (inf.) 'to dry': соүхъ (adj.), съхнѫти (inf.) 'to dry up'; мъшьца 'midge, gnat': моүха 'fly'; доүша 'soul' < *dux-ja: доүхъ 'spirit' (§ 30.1). богъ 'God' (nom.): боже (voc.); жаръ 'heat' < CS *žěrŭ < IE *gēr- (cf. Lith. garas 'steam', OCS gorěti 'to burn' < IE gṵher-); жѧти 'to harvest': Lith. geněti (inf.) 'to trim'; живъ 'alive': Lith. gývas, Skt jīváḥ, Lat. vīvus; жьдати < *gĭd-: Lith. geidžù 'I desire'; жьрѫ 'to swallow' < *gr̥'-: Lith. girkšnoti 'to drink', Skt giráti 'he swallows'; жльтъ 'yellow' < *gl̥'t-: Lith. geltas 'brown'; стражь < *storg+jĭ 'guard' (cf. ратаи = rata+jĭ 'ploughman'); лъжь < *lŭg+jĭ 'lie, liar' (cf. льгати, лъжѫ).

2. Palatal spirants developed from dentals followed by j (tj, dj), and from certain groups of consonants followed by j (stj, skj, zdj, zgj): свькштѫ (1st sg.) < *svět-jǫ: свѣтити (inf.) 'to shine'; межДоү (adv.) 'between', межДа (n.) 'limit' < *med-ja: Lat. medius, Skt mádhyaḥ. When considering the origin of OCS št, žd we have to distinguish between:

(a) st+j > št, zd+j > žd: поүстити (inf.) 'to send out': поүштѫ (1st sg.) < *pust-jǫ; зьдати (inf.) 'to build': зиждѫ (1st sg.) < *zĭd-jǫ.

(b) sk+j, zg+j > št, žd: искати 'to search': иштѫ 'I search' < *isk-jǫ; мозгъ (n.) 'marrow in bones': мождднъ (adj.) < *mozg-janŭ (§ 30.1).

(c) The palatalizing effect of j on preceding consonantal groups was not consistent when the first member of the group was a dental. So one finds forms like съмотрѭ (1st sg. pr.) alongside съмоштрѭ from съмотрити (inf.) 'to consider, to contemplate'.

The sounds št, žd are characteristic features of the OCS phonetic system shared only by Bulgarian among the Slavonic languages.

§ 22. The velar spirant x developed from an IE s:

1. An original s preceded by i, u, r, k and followed by a vowel developed in CS into x. (Whether this x developed from a š followed by back vowels is controversial. The fact that Lithuanian and Indo-Iranian present a š where OCS shows x (cf. OCS врьхъ 'peak': Lith. viršùs) induced some scholars to assume that š was the intermediary stage also for Slavonic x.) The following

examples will illustrate the development *i*, *u*, *r*, *k*+*s*+*vowel* > *i*, *u*, *r*, *k*+*x*+*vowel*: тихъ 'mild': Lith. *teisùs* (adj.) 'just'; ветъхъ 'ancient': Lat. *vetus*; снъха 'daughter-in-law': Lat. *nŭrus*, Skt *snuṣá*; ръкъ (aor.) 'to say' < *rĕk-xŭ* < *rēk-sŭ*: Gr. *ἔλυσα* (aor.), whereas before consonants the *s* remained: искати 'to seek for', мьзда 'reward'.

2. The aorist ending *-xŭ* has been generalized also to cases where the original *s* could not develop into *x*: дахъ < *dad-sŭ* 'I gave'. Similar analogical developments occurred in the flexion of the nouns; the ending *-xŭ* developed from *-su* in the declension of the *-o-*, *-u-*, and *-i-* stems (рабѣхъ < *rabojsu*, съинъхъ < *sūnusu*, гостьхъ < *gostĭsu*), and analogically this ending spread also to the *-a-* stems: женахъ (loc. pl.) (§ 45.16).

3. In a restricted number of examples the OCS *x* represents an IE *kh*: соха 'tree-branch, piece of wood used for ploughing': Lith. *šakà* 'branch', Skt *śākhā* 'branch'; храбъръ 'daring': Skt *kharaḥ* 'hard, rough', Gr. *κάρχαρος* 'sharp', Latv. *skarbs* 'sharp, stiff'.

4. The change of IE *s* into CS *x* is a very old process. It took place earlier than the change of IE *k'* into *s* (§ 20.2) because this *s* did not change into *x*: прасѧ 'pig' < *pors-* < *pork'-*: Lat. *porcus*. When the *s* was of IE origin it changed into *x*: прахъ 'dust' < *porso-*. This development shows also that the change *s* > *x* took place earlier than the metathesis of the liquid diphthongs (§ 6.3). In пръсть (fem.) 'dust' the *s* is preserved probably because it was immediately followed by a consonant: *pṛsti-* (cf. A. Meillet, *Le slave commun*, 1934, 34).

5. The change *s* > *x* is an earlier development than the monophthongization of *oj*, because after *ě* representing this diphthong the change takes place: мѣхъ 'bag': Lith. *maišas* 'a net, a bag', OPr *moasis* 'bellows', Skt *mēṣá* 'wether'; this means that *s* > *x* in a stage *moix-* < *mais-*.

§ 23. The dental affricates are results of CS developments:

1. The voiced affricate *dz* (ѕ) which changed into *z* (з) (§ 25) represents an original *g* palatalized according to the second and third palatalizations (§ 30.2, 3):

(a) $g+\check{e}$ ($< o\underset{\cdot}{i}$), i ($< o\underset{\cdot}{i}$) $> dz > z$: восѣ (loc. sg.), восн (nom. pl.): вогъ (nom. sg.).

(b) $\check{i}$, i, ϱ, $\underline{\jmath}'+g > \check{i}$, i, ϱ, $\underline{\jmath}'+dz > z$: говьзь 'abundant' $<$ Goth. gabigs (gabeigs) 'rich'; двизати: двигнѫти 'to move'; кънѧзь 'chief' $<$ *kuning-; трьгнѫти 'to pull': трьзати (impft.)$<$ *-$\underline{\jmath}'g$- (§ 30.3).

(c) In the South Slavonic languages, and so also in OCS, and in the East Slavonic languages g is palatalized also when separated by v from the front vowel $\check{e}$, i: OCS звѣзда 'star', звиздати 'to whistle':P gwiazda, Cz hvízdati $<$ CS *gvězda, *gvizdati (§ 30.2).

2. The voiceless affricate c developed on the same lines from an original k:

(a) $k+\check{e}$ ($< o\underset{\cdot}{i}$), i ($< o\underset{\cdot}{i}$) $> c$: чловѣцѣ (loc. sg.), чловѣци (nom. pl.), чловѣцѣхъ (loc. pl.): чловѣкъ (nom. sg.) 'man'; рѫцѣ (dat. loc. sg., nom. acc. du.): рѫка (nom. sg.) 'hand' (§ 30.2).

(b) $\check{i}$, i, ϱ, $\underline{\jmath}'+k > \check{i}$, i, ϱ, $\underline{\jmath}'+c$: отьць 'father' $<$ *otĭkŭ (cf. Gr. ἄττα); овьца 'sheep' $<$ *ov-ika (cf. Lat. ovis); мѣсѧць 'month' $<$ *mēs+en+ko (cf. Skt mās 'the moon', Lat. mensis); мрьцати 'to darken': мрькнѫти $<$ *-$\underline{\jmath}'k$-.

(c) The group $kv+\check{e}$, $i > cv$ in OCS, and in the other South Slavonic languages, as well as in the East Slavonic languages: OCS цвѣтъ 'to flower', цвисти 'to blossom':P kwiat, kwitnąć $<$ CS *květŭ (§ 30.2).

§ 24. The palatal affricate $\check{c}$ developed in CS from an IE k under similar conditions to those which gave rise to the palatal spirants $\check{s}$, $\check{z}$ (§ 21):

Front vowels palatalized the preceding velar k into $\check{c}$: $k+e$, $\check{e}$ ($< \bar{e}$), ϱ, $\check{i}$, i ($< \check{i}$, $e\underset{\cdot}{i}$), $\underline{\jmath}'$, $\underline{l}'$, $j > \check{c}e$: чело 'forehead' $<$ *kel-: Lith. kélti 'to lift', Lat. collis; чесати 'to comb' $<$ *kes-: коса 'hair'; чадъ 'smoke' $<$ *kĕd- $<$ *kēd; чѧстъ 'thick' $<$ *kęd-: Lith. kimštas part. from kimšti 'to stuff'; рѣчь $<$ *rēk-i; почити 'to rest': покои 'rest' (n.); чрьта 'line' $<$ *k$\underline{\jmath}'t$-:Lith. kiřsti 'to cut'; чльнъ 'boat' $<$ *k$\underline{l}'n$-: OHG scalm; начѧти 'to begin' $<$ *k$\underline{n}$-: искони, коньць 'end' (n.) (cf. Lat. re-cens); плакати (inf.) 'to cry':плачѫ (1st sg.) $<$ *plakjǫ (§ 3, § 21, § 30.1).

§ 25. The affricate s [dz] developed in an early period into a

spirant з [z]. In the historical period s appears in Ass. and Ps. Sin., less consistently in Zogr. and Mar. in words like гоѕьꙁовати 'to abound', ѕвѣꙁда 'star', ѕѣло 'very', кънѧꙁь 'chief', польꙁа 'utility', помиꙁати 'to nod', пѣнѧꙁь 'money', стьꙁа 'foot-path', as well as before flexional endings: воꙁи (nom. pl.), ноѕѣ (dat. loc. sg.). Savv. Kn., Supr., Euch. Sin., and Cloz. know only з.

It is clear that the original Cyrillo-Methodian texts knew the affricate ѕ [dz], for the Glagolitic alphabet has a special letter for it, which also has the numeric value of 8. The affricate developed into a fricative sound, but there are still Southern Slavonic dialects, mainly in Macedonia, as well as Western Slavonic (Polish and Slovak), which have the affricate dz.

§ 26. The labials represent either IE labials or IE aspirated labials: теплъ 'warm' : Lat. *tepidus*, Skt *tápati* 'he warms'; пѣна 'foam' : Skt *phénaḥ*; волии (comp.) 'bigger' : Skt *bá-līyān* 'stronger', Lat. *dē-bilis*, Gr. βέλτερος 'better'; небо 'sky' : Skt *nábhaḥ* 'mist', Gr. νέφος.

§ 27. 1. The dentals continue either IE dentals or IE aspirated dentals: противъ 'against' : Skt *práti* 'towards', Gr. (Hom) προτι; домъ 'house' : Lat. *domus*, Gr. δόμος; дѣти 'to put, to do' : Skt *ádhām*, Gr. ἔθηκα, Lat. *facio*.

2. A dental developed in CS (and in Teutonic) in the groups *zr*, *sr* when these groups were primary ones: строуꙗ 'river' : Lith. *srovė* 'stream', Skt *srávati* 'he runs'; сестра 'sister' : Skt *svasar-* 'sister', Goth. *swistar*; иꙁдрешти 'to pronounce' < *iz+rešti; Иꙁдраиль < 'Ισραήλ; ноꙁдри 'nostrils' : Lith. *nasraī* 'mouth (of beasts)'; OCS иꙁ-д-ребръ = иꙁъ ребръ 'from the sides'. When, however, the groups *sr*, *zr* were secondary, i.e. resulted from a metathesis of the original liquid diphthongs, a dental was not inserted between the spirant and the liquid: срамъ 'shame' < *sorm- : Persian *šarm*; зракъ 'sight' < *zork- : P *w-zrok* (§ 6.3). Also when *sr*, *zr* stand for original *sr̥*, *zr̥* a dental is not inserted: сръдьце 'heart' : Lith. *širdìs*; зрьно 'grain' : Goth. *kaúrn* (§ 17).

3. A dental may develop in CS by a process of dissimilation in

the groups *zdz, sc = sts*. Now, by dissimilation the groups lost the last element: *zdz > zd, sts > st*: дрѧзга 'forest' has in dat. loc. sg. and nom. acc. du. **dręzgě > дрѧзѕѣ* (§ 30.2). Alongside this exists the form дрѧздѣ. In the same way alongside дъсцѣ (dat. loc. sg. and nom. acc. du. from дъска 'plank') exists the dissimilated form дъстѣ.

A form истѣлити alongside исцѣлити 'to heal' is to be explained by dissimilation: **iz+cěliti = *is-tsěliti >* истѣлити, исцѣлити.

§ 28. The velars continue IE gutturals (aspirated or non aspirated): ковати 'to strike': Lith. *káuti*, OHG *houwan*, Lat. *cūdō*; -стигъ 'I climbed': Lith. *staigýti* 'to hurry', Goth. *steiga* 'to climb', Skt *stighnoti* 'he climbs', Gr. στείχω 'I go'; остегъ 'garment': Lith. *stógas* 'roof', G *Dach*, Lat. *tego*, Gr. στέγω 'I cover', Skt *sthagayati* 'he covers'.

GROUPS OF CONSONANTS

§ 29. Common Slavonic shows a clear tendency towards the simplification of certain consonant groups and the opening of closed syllables (§ 5):

1. Original double consonants have been simplified: отьць 'father': Gr. ἄττα, Lat. *atta*, Goth. *atta*; юси 'thou art' < **es-si*.

2. Original *tl, dl* have been reduced in OCS, and in other regions of the Slavonic linguistic area (South and East Slavonic), to *l*: рало 'plough' < **ordlo*:P *radło*, Cz *rádlo*; плелъ 'plaited' < **pletlŭ*:Cz *pletl*, P *plótł*. This dialectal division of CS coincides with the division produced by the treatment of the groups *kv, gv* (§ 23.1*c*, 2*c*; § 30.2*c*) and it indicates a difference in the syllabic structure in the two regions.

3. The groups *tn, dn* are reduced to *n*: свьнѫти 'to begin to shine' < **svitnǫti*:свѣтъ (n.) 'light', свьтѣти (inf.) 'to shine'; бънѫти 'to awake' < **budnǫti*:боудити 'to wake up'.

4. The groups *tm, dm* are reduced to *m*: дамь 'I will give' < **dadmĭ*:дадѧтъ (3rd pl.); врѣмѧ 'time' < **uert-men-*:врьтѣти 'to turn round'. In седмъ (ord.) the group *dm* has been preserved

because, according to Meillet, it goes back to *bdm* as shown by Gr. ἕβδομος, and the *d* was maintained owing to the preceding *b*.

5. The groups *pn*, *bn*, *kn* are reduced to *n*: съпъ < *sйpnŭ, оусънѫти 'to fall asleep' < *usŭpnǫti : Lith. *săpnas* 'dream', Gr. ὕπνος, Skt *svápnaḥ*; -гънѫти 'to bend' < *gŭbnǫti : -гъібати (impft.) 'to bend', соугоувъ 'double', Latv. *gubt* 'to bend'; блъснѫти 'to glitter' < *blĭskn- : блѣскъ 'brightness', блисцати 'to lighten'. However, the groups *bn*, *pn*, *kn* were not absent in the OCS phonetic structure, and they were restored analogically at an early period. We find in OCS texts: погъібнѫти 'to perish' on the analogy of погъібъ (aor.), погъібати (impft.), топнѫти 'to plunge oneself into' : -топъ (aor.), -тапати (impft.), топити 'to make warm' (caus.); млькнѫти 'to become still', млькъ (aor.), млъчати (inf.) 'to be silent'. The last verb has preserved the *k*, as *g* has been preserved in a similar position: огнь 'fire' : Lat. *ignis*, Skt *agniḥ*, Lith. *ugnís*. When the *k* was part of the group -*kxn*- representing an IE -*ksn*- it disappeared, the group being simplified to *n*: лоуна 'moon' < *loŭksnā : OPr *lauxnos*, Lat. *luna*, (dial.) *losna*.

6. The groups *ks*, *gs*, when changed into Slavonic *kx* (§ 22.1) were simplified to *x*: ръхъ 'I said' (aor.) < *rĕk-sŭ : ръсте (aor. 2nd pl.), ръшѧ (aor. 3rd pl.); жахъ (aor.) 'I burnt up' < *žĕg-sŭ : жасте (aor. 2nd pl.), жашѧ (aor. 3rd pl.). Also a dental was dropped in the group -*tx*-: оходити 'to go away' < *ot-xoditi, or in the group -*ts*-: чисъ (aor.) 'I counted' < *čit-sŭ : чьтѫ (pr.), чьтохъ (aor.); даси (2nd sg.) 'thou wilt give' < *dadsi.

7. The groups *ps*, *bs* have been reduced to *s*: чрѣсъ (aor.) < *čĕrps- : -чръпѫ 'I shall ladle (out)'; оса 'wasp': Lith. *vapsà*, OHG *wafsa*, E wasp; гръсъ (aor.) 'I scratched' < *grĕbs- : гревѫ.

8. When the spirant preceded the occlusive the groups were maintained in Slavonic: юстъ 'he is': Lat. *est*, Gr. ἔστι, Skt *ásti*; мозгъ 'brain': Av. *mazga*, OHG *mar(a)g*, E marrow < IE *mazgh-. The voiced spirant became, by assimilation, voiceless when followed by a voiceless consonant: въставити 'to put' < *vŭz-staviti, въспросити 'to demand' < *vŭz-prositi. The groups spirant + occlusive (*sk*, *zg*, *st*, *zd*) followed by front vowel were palatalized according to the rules of palatalization (§ 30.1a, 2b).

9. The group *bv* is reduced to *b*: овити 'to wind round' < *ob-viti*; овласть 'power' < *ob-vlasti*, овлѣкѫ 'I shall cover with' < *ob-velkǫ*.

10. In the groups *dt*, *tt* the first dental was dissimilated and developed into a spirant: мєсти 'to throw' < *met-ti*: мєтѫ; класти 'to put' < *klad-ti*: кладѫ.

11. When two occlusives form a group in which the second element is a dental, the tendency is to reduce that group to the dental element: *pt* > *t*:-чрѣти 'to empty' < *čerp-ti*: чрьпѫ; *bt* > *t*: грєти 'to scratch' < *greb-ti*: грєбѫ; *bd* > *d*: сєдмъ (ord.): Gr. ἕβδομος; илєтѫ 'I plait' < *plek-tǫ*: Lat. *plecto*. If the group was followed by a front vowel it was palatalized: ноштъ 'night' < *nokti-* (cf. Lat. *nox*, *noc-tis*); мошти 'to have power' < *mog-ti*: могѫ (1st sg. pr.) (§ 30).

12. The group *tx* was reduced to *x*, and the group *zš* > *š*: оходити 'to go away' < *otŭ-xoditi*: *otiti*; рашнрити 'to extend' < *raz-širiti*.

13. The group *šč* changed into *št* which is a simplification by regressive dissimilation of *štš* = *šč*: заштитити 'to defend' < *zaš-čititi*; дъштица (dim.) < *dŭščica* < *dŭska* 'plank, board'. Similarly, the group *ždž* > *žd*: разга, розга (fem.) 'branch of vine': раждине, рождние (neut., coll.) < *rozg-ĭje* (§ 30.1*a*).

Palatalization of the Velars

§ 30. It has already been noted (§ 3, § 21) that the sonant *j* caused changes in the preceding consonants. Front vowels had a similar effect on certain preceding consonants, in certain periods of the language, causing them to change in accordance with certain principles of palatalization. The consonants affected were the velars *k*, *g*, *x*, and three processes of palatalization are usually distinguished according to the chronology and nature of the changes concerned.

1. The first, i.e. the earliest, palatalization, consists of the change of the velars *k*, *g*, *x* into *č′*, *ž′*, *š′* when followed by a front vowel or by a soft liquid sonant. The vowel *ě* produces this change only when it derives historically from *ē*, and the vowel *i* when it

derives from i or ei. We can express this change in the following formula:

$$\left.\begin{matrix} k \\ g \\ x \end{matrix}\right\} + \check{e} \ (< \bar{e}),\ e,\ i\ (<\bar{\imath},\ ei),\ \bar{\imath},\ \rho,\ \gamma',\ l' > \left\{\begin{matrix} \check{c}' \\ \check{z}' \\ \check{s}' \end{matrix}\right.$$

Examples: обычаи 'custom' < *ob-ūkēj-: въікнѫти 'to learn', оукъ 'doctrine', Lith. jùnkti 'to be accustomed' (§ 19.2, § 32.3); рожанъ 'of horn' < *rog-ēno-: рогъ 'horn' (§ 21.1); чловѣче 'man' (voc.) < *člověk-e; можеши (2nd sg. pr.) < *mog-eši: могѫ 'I am able'; -връшеши (2nd sg. pr.) < *vr̥'x-eši: връхъ (n.) 'top'; почити 'to rest' (inf.) < *po-ki-ti (cf. Lat. quiēs): покои 'rest'; ложити 'to put': -логъ; тишаи 'silent' (comp.) < *tix-ēj-: тишити (inf.) 'to appease': тихъ (adj.) 'quiet' (§ 21.1); чьто 'what' < *ki- (cf. Lat. quid); шьдъ (p. part. act. 1) 'gone' < šedŭ < *xedŭ/*xodŭ: ходити (§ 37.4); члънъ 'boat' < čĭlnŭ < *kl̥'no; чрънъ 'black' < *kr̥'n-: Skt kr̥ṣnáh, OPr kirsnan; жрънъі 'mill' < *zr̥'n-: Lith. girnos; жлътъ 'yellow' < *gl̥'t-: G gelb (§ 21.1).

(a) Under the same conditions, the groups sk, zg were palatalized into sč, zdž which changed further into šč, ždž and, by dissimilation (šč = štš), developed in OCS into št, žd (§ 21.2c): искати (inf.) 'to demand', искѫ (1st sg.): иштеши (2nd sg. pr.) < *isk-eši; разга (розга) 'branch': раждие (рождие) (coll.) < *rozg-ije. The Teutonic word skillings changed according to this tendency of the OCS phonetic system: штьлагъ 'money' > штьлазь (OR цлазь, цлагъ, цлагъ). The same word appears also with the group sk not palatalized because it entered the language in different periods, by a different way: скьлазь, склазь, стьлазь (see also § 30.3f).

(b) The groups kt, gt were palatalized into št: *noktĭ > ношть 'night', *mogti > мошти 'to be able'.

(c) Other loan-words affected by the first palatalization are: мечь < мьчь 'sword': Goth. meki (acc. sg.); жлѣдѫ, жладѫ 'I pay' < Goth. -gildan.

2. The second palatalization of the velars is a later process. The velars which had not been affected by the first palatalization, because the diphthongs oi, ai had not yet been monopthongized

into front vowels, changed into affricates or into spirant *s*. This could be expressed in the following formula:

$$\left.\begin{array}{l} k \\ g \\ x \end{array}\right\} + \check{e} \text{ or } i \ (< o\underset{.}{i}, a\underset{.}{i}) > \left\{\begin{array}{l} c' \\ dz' \\ s' \end{array}\right. > z'$$

Examples: отрокъ (nom. sg.) 'boy': отроци (nom. pl.) < *otrok-oi̯, отроцѣ (loc. sg.), отроцѣхъ (loc. pl.); богъ (nom. sg.) 'God': бози, бози (nom. pl.) < *bog-oi̯, бозѣ, бозѣ (loc. sg.), бозѣхъ, бозѣхъ (loc. pl.) *bog-oi̯; доухъ (nom. sg.) 'spirit': доуси (nom. pl.) < *dux-oi̯, доусѣ (loc. sg.), доусѣхъ (loc. pl.); рѫка (nom. sg.) 'hand': рѫцѣ (dat. loc. sg., nom. acc. du.); слоуга (nom. sg.) 'servant': слоусѣ, слоузѣ (dat. loc. sg., nom. acc. du.); моуха (nom. sg.) 'fly': моусѣ (dat. loc. sg., nom. acc. du.) (§ 46.2, 10, 15, 16).

(*a*) This process of palatalization also defines the relationship between verbal forms of the type: рекѫ (1st pers. sg.), решти (inf.) 'to say': рьци (imp.) < *rĭk-oi̯-, рьцѣте (2nd imp. pl.), рьцѣмъ (1st imp. pl.), нарицати (it.); лагѫ (1st pers. sg.): лешти (inf.) 'to lie down': лѧзи, лѧзи (2nd sg. imp.) < *leng-oi̯-, лѧзѣте, лѧзѣте (2nd pl. imp.), лѧзѣмъ, лѧзѣмъ (1st pl. imp.).

The pronoun вьсь 'each, every' is formed on the analogy of other cases in which a stem *vix- has been palatalized by the following *ě* < *oi̯* (§ 30.3*d, e*): instr. sg. вьсѣмь, gen. pl. вьсѣхъ, dat. pl. вьсѣмъ, instr. pl. вьсѣми, loc. pl. вьсѣхъ (§ 55.5) which have a palatalized stem *vix-.

(*b*) The groups -*sk*-, -*zg*- changed into -*sc*-, -*zdz*- which sometimes developed further into -*st*-, -*zd*- (§ 27.3): паска 'Easter': пасцѣ (dat. loc. пастѣ; дрѧзга 'forest': дрѧззѣ (loc.), дрѧздѣ; морьскъ 'marine': морьсцѣи > морьстѣи (Zogr., Mar.); людьскъ 'human': людьсции > людьстии (Zogr., Mar.).

(*c*) The groups *kv*, *gv*, *xv* were palatalized in OCS, and in the East and South Slavonic languages (§ 23.1. *c*, 2. *c*, § 29.2).

(*d*) Loan-words also underwent this palatalization: цѣсарь 'emperor': Goth. *kaisar* < lat. *Caesar*; цѧта 'coin': Goth. *kintus*; цръкы 'church': Goth. *kyrikō*, OHG *chirihha* < Gr. *κυρική*, κυριακή (§ 17, § 23.2).

3. The third palatalization is a separate development on the

lines of the second palatalization. Its chronological relationship to the second palatalization is not clear. Some investigators assume that it took place earlier than the second (cf. R. Ekblom, *Die Palatalisierung von k, g, ch im Slavischen*, Uppsala, 1935). The velar was palatalized when it was preceded by a front vowel and followed by a back vowel (but not by *y* or *ŭ* in two consecutive syllables). This change could be expressed in the following formula:

ĭ, i (when not of diphthongal origin), *ę, ĭ'+k, g, x > ć, dž > ź, ś*.

Examples: отьць < *otĭ-kŭ : Gr. ἄττα, Lat. *atta*; овьца < *ov-ika*:Skt *avikā*; стьsа 'path':R dial. *cmeza*; польза 'profit':R dial. *польза*; the Russian literary form *польза* is a loan-word; двиsати 'to move' (impft.):двигнѫти (pft.); сиць 'such' < *sikŭ: такъ 'such', iакъ 'such as', какъ 'of what sort'; блисцати 'to shine':блѣскъ (n.) 'shine', блискати 'to glitter'.

(*a*) Howevèr, this change (of the velars when preceded by front vowels) is not consistent, and the conditions under which it took place have not been sufficiently clarified; in двьрьникъ 'porter', and in similar derived forms, the velar has not been palatalized; льгъкъ 'light in weight', мากъкъ 'soft' preserve the velar; кънагꙑни 'princess' has preserved the velar, whereas кънаsь 'prince' < T *kuning-* (Finn. *kuningas*) changed it into *dz > z*. Moreover when the *i* preceding the velar represented an original *ęi* the velar seems to have resisted the change: тихъ 'silent' < *teis-*; лихъ 'exceeding' < *leiks-*.

(*b*) This palatalization applies also to loan-words, e.g. кънаsь, пѣнаsь (masc.) 'coin' < T *penning*, гобьsь 'rich' < Goth. *gabeigs* (*gabigs*) 'rich' (§ 23.1. *b*).

(*c*) As to the chronology of this change we can state that it was a CS development and had not been concluded by the time the Slavs came into contact with the Teutons. The chronological relationship of this development to the second palatalization is not clear. It is obvious that the first palatalization is the earliest, and that it took place earlier than the monophthongization of *oi* into *ě*. The back element *o* of this diphthong hindered the change of the guttural, which was palatalized only before front vowels so

non-diphthongal origin, e.g. the ending -*e* of the voc. sg. of the masc. -*o*- stems. In a later period, when the diphthongs were monophthongized into front vowels, the velars were changed into palatalized dentals: *c, z, s*.

(*d*) As already indicated, the so-called third palatalization may have either preceded or succeeded the second palatalization. The pronominal forms *visi* 'each', *sici* 'such' go back etymologically to the stems *vix-, *sik- ending in velars (cf. такъ, такъ). The instr. sg., gen. and dat. pl. and instr. pl. endings of these pronouns are: -*ěmi*, -*ěxŭ*, -*ěmŭ*, -*ěmi*. In opposition to these endings *otici* (showing the same palatalization of the stem consonant: *otikŭ) has in the instr. pl. *otici*, loc. pl. *oticixŭ*. The question arises which of the two patterns represents the historical development and which is an analogical formation following the soft stems: *mojixŭ*, &c.

If we assume that the change of the velars before *ě* < *oi̯* is earlier than the change of the velar after *ĭ, i, ę, r̥'* then *sicěmi* could be explained, according to the second palatalization, from *sik-ěmi < **sik-oi̯mi*. That means that at that period the nom. had **sik-*:*tak-*, &c. In a later period the velar preceded by a front vowel (*ĭ, i, ę, r̥'*) was palatalized, and *sici*, *visi* are forms due to this third palatalization. A form like *otici*, *ovica* is explained through the same palatalization. The endings of the nom. and loc. pl. *otici*, *oticixŭ* are formed from the stem *otic-* on the analogy of the soft stems: nom. pl. *kraji*, *moji*, loc. pl. *krajixŭ*, *mojixŭ*. If the change of the velar had taken place according to the second palatalization one should have *oticě, *oticěxŭ.

(*e*) However, this change seems not to have been uniform in its results, because the Western Slavonic languages show *š* instead of *s* in *visi*: OCz *vši*, *všěx*, *všěčiskaě* (*Prague Folia*), which forms are local dialectal features (cf. N. van Wijk, *Geschichte der altkirchen-slavischen Sprache*, 1931, 68 sq.).

(*f*) The change of the velars according to the third palatalization took place in a limited number of cases: (1) in the endings -ьць (masc.), -ьца (fem.), -ьце (neut.): отьць, мышьца 'arm', сръдьце 'heart'; -ица: дѣвица:дѣва 'girl'; (2) in the iterative ending -ицати/-ѣкати: -рицати 'to tell': -рѣкати, рекѫ; -тицати 'to run, to flow': -тѣкати, текѫ; двизати 'to move', двизати:

дви́гнѫти; (3) in some nominal formations: мѣсѧць 'month', заѩць 'hare', лице 'visage', ѩsа 'disease', польsа 'utility', стьза 'path'; (4) in the Teutonic loan-words: кънѧзь 'chief' < T *kuning; пѣнѧзь 'money': OHG pfenning; штьлагъ 'money', штьлѧзь < OHG skilling, гоѣьзь 'abundant' < Goth. gabeigs (gabigs) (adj.) 'rich'.

(g) The causes of the changes generally referred to as the third palatalization are partly phonetic and partly analogical. They cannot be explained by any single cause. In the case of the diminutive suffixes the change into *-ĭcĭ may postulate an original *-ĭki̯o alongside *-ĭko; the verbal forms in -icati, -idzati may have their origin in the phonetically regular imperative forms of the type рьци; the ending of кънѧзь: T *kuning could be explained through the nom. pl. кънѧзи where the change is regular (cf. R. Ekblom, Die frühe dorsale Palatalisierung im Slavischen, Uppsala, 1951). As a result of the palatalizations there are no velar consonants followed by front vowels in the structure of the OCS language.

HARDENING OF THE PALATAL CONSONANTS

§ 31. The consonants resulting from the processes of palatalization, or from combination with j (ч, ж, ш, шт, жд, ц, s > з, р̑, л̑, н̑) were originally soft: č′, ž′, š′, š′t′, ž′d′, ć, d′z′ > z′, r′, l′, n′. This is shown by some modern Slavonic languages, whose history makes it clear that the original palatalization of these consonants was lost in later periods. In OCS texts the palatalization, i.e. the soft character, of the consonants, is not consistently indicated, and it appears that these consonants were already hard. The soft character is indicated by a semicircle over the letters р̑, л̑, н̑, but only Zogr. and Supr. are consistent in the use of ˘ especially on л and н: клевета 'calumny', н̑ива 'field', кън̑игъı (pl.) 'book', сѫпьр̑ѣ, сѫпьрѩ (gen.) 'of the adversary'.

(a) The scribes did not mark the character of the other palatal consonants, no doubt because they were either hard or on the way to becoming depalatalized. The original soft character is shown by spellings with ѩ (ѣ), ю, ѭ alongside the normal spellings with а, оу, ѫ: шюлѩъ (Ps. Sin.) 'sound', доушѫ (acc.) (Euch. Sin.) 'soul' мѫжю (dat.) (Zogr.) 'man' чюдо (Savv. Kn.) 'miracle', сѫждѭ

(Mar.) 'I judge', сѫштю (dat.) (Savv. Kn.) 'being', отьцю (dat.) (Cloz.) 'father', льзѣ (nom.) (Supr.) 'profit' for льза, gen. льзѧ.

(b) The hardening of the consonants is borne out by the regular spellings with а, оу, ѫ, as well as by spellings with the hard reduced vowel after the originally palatal consonants: доушоу (gen., loc. du.) for доушю, нашъ for нашь 'our', ноштъ for ноштъ 'night', конецъ for коньць 'end', цѣсара for цѣсарѩ (gen.) 'emperor', врамѩ for врѣмѩ 'time', мороу for морю (dat.) 'sea', рождъство for рождьство 'birth'.

(c) The consonantal group шт, жд from tj, dj (§ 21.2) is represented in the Kiev Miss. by ц, з which are a dialectal feature of Moravian Slavonic: насъицені for насъиштени 'satiated', подазь for подаждь (imp.) 'give'. Traces of this treatment appear also in other texts: розьство (Cloz., Mar.) for рождьство 'birth', невѣзества (Ps. Sin.) for невѣждьства 'of ignorance'. Instead of the шт representing stj, skj the Kiev Miss. has шч: очишчение for очиштение 'purification' from очистити.

CHANGES IN THE OCS VOWEL SYSTEM

§ 32. OCS continued the tendency, inherited from Common Slavonic, to pronounce certain initial vowels with a prothetic i or u and to insert i between vowels. The reasons for this phonetic process are not clear, and in the further development of the individual Slavonic languages we also find the reverse tendency to drop i and $v < u$:

1. The verbs оучити 'to teach' and въикнѫти 'to learn' represent the same root *ūk-; въ, вън- < *ŭn (cf. Lat. en, in) въньмѫ: имѫ 'I seize'; имѫ < *ịịmǫ (cf. из-ьмѫ); иго < *ịịgo < *ịugo (cf. Lat. iugum); ѥстъ, естъ 'is' (cf. Lat. est). The OCS spelling did not regularly indicate this prothetic i [j] (§ 2. 3. 4) and it is not possible to give a clear definition of the use of this prothetic sound, or to be sure when it was pronounced without being written.

2. In the OCS texts we find forms with prothetic i alongside forms without i, varying from text to text: его 'of that, his', еже 'which', езеро 'lake', еще 'yet': ѥго, ѥже, ѥзеро; оутро 'morning': ютро; оуже: юже 'now'; авити 'to show': ѣвити, ѩвити; агньць 'lamb': ѩгньць, ѥгньць; агода 'berry': ѩгода; азъ 'I':

ѣзъ, ꙗзъ [jazŭ] (cf. B аз, ꙗз, OP *jaz*, P *ja*, Sln *jaz*); аштє 'if': ꙗштє; аблъко 'apple': ꙗблъко (cf. Lith. *óbuolas*).

3. A prothetic *u* > *v* appears in вѧзати 'to tie': ѫза, вѫза 'tie'; воꙗ 'odour': ѫхати 'to smell'.

4. In a later development of OCS appear more frequently forms with prothetic elements: осмь 'eight': восмь; ѫдоль 'valley': ꙗꙞдоль, OR юдоль; ѫза, ꙗꙞза, оуза, воуза, вѫза 'tie'.

5. The tendency to drop intervocalic *i* [*j*] appears in OCS: in the declension of the definite adjective: доврагего (masc. gen.) 'good', доброугемоу (dat.), благаꙗ (nom. fem.) 'good': доврагего, доврааго, доврагго, доброугемоу, доброугоулюу, доброулюу, благаа; in the verbal forms: даꙗти, даꙀти 'to give', покаꙗти 'to regret', вѣроугѫтъ 'they believe', обрѣтаѭ 'I discover': даати, покаати, вѣроугѫтъ, обрѣтаѭ; in nouns and pronouns: зълодѣꙀ (gen.) 'evil-doer', июдеꙗ 'Judea', моꙗ 'mine', твоꙗ 'thine', зълодѣꙗ, июдеа, моа, твоа.

These orthographies have caused some scholars to reach the conclusion that *ju* = ю was pronounced like *jü*, *ü* with more rounded lips, and *ja* = ꙗ, ѣ like *jä*, *ä* (§ 2. 3. 4).

6. There are slight divergencies between the OCS texts as to the use of the initial *a-*/*ja-* alternation; the generally accepted rule was that:

(*a*) some words appear only with *a-*: а 'but, and', агода 'berry', али 'but, if', ашоутъ 'in vain';

(*b*) others have only initial *ja-*: ꙗдро 'bosom', ꙗможе 'where to' (later texts have also амо, аможе), ꙗрость 'anger', ꙗръ 'spring of the year', ꙗрьмъ 'yoke', ꙗсли pl. 'manger', ꙗсти 'to eat', ꙗзва 'wound', ꙗхати 'to drive in a vehicle';

(*c*) in other words again *a-*/*ja-* appear indiscriminately: абие, ꙗбие 'soon', авити, ꙗвити 'to reveal', азъ, ꙗзъ 'I', ако, ꙗко 'as, in order that, because', аште, ꙗште 'if', агньць, ꙗгньць 'lamb', &c.

CHANGES OF THE REDUCED VOWELS

§ 33. The Macedonian Slavonic dialect, raised by Constantine-Cyril and his brother Methodius to the status of the first Slavonic literary language in the second half of the ninth century, contained the two reduced phonemes, called hard and soft *jers*, where they

might be etymologically expected. The first OCS texts, which are copies of the Cyrillo-Methodian originals, already show changes in these weak phonemes. These changes are due to the influence of the copyist on the language that he transcribed, i.e. to the local dialect spoken by the scribe.

The following changes and omissions of the *jers* become apparent in the OCS texts:

1. The *jers* disappear in a weak position, whereas in a strong position they are changed into a front or back vowel respectively. A *jer* is in strong position when the immediately following syllable contains another *jer*. When several consecutive syllables contain *jers*, the strong or weak position is defined by counting the syllables starting with that one which contains the last *jer*: the last *jer* is in weak position, the preceding one is strong, the next is weak. If we mark the weak position with the diacritic ˎ, and the strong position with ˏ, then the instr. sg. from съньмлъ 'meeting (place)' presents two *jers* in weak and two in strong position: съньмлъмь = sŭnĭmŭmĭ > sĭnĭmĭmĭ > senĭmemĭ written сеньлѥмь, сеньлѥм, съне́мь (cf. W. Vondrák, *Altkirchenslavische Grammatik*, 1912, 184). So we may find in the texts the form дьнесь 'today' alongside дьньсь, пра́веденъ 'just': пра́вьдьнъ, ше́дъ 'gone': шьдъ, конецъ 'end': коньцъ, денетъ 'that day': дьнь тъ, кож(ь)до 'each': къжьдо, работъ 'that servant': рабъ тъ, крѣпокъ 'strong': крѣпъкъ, четвръто́къ 'Thursday': четвръ́тъкъ, крꙑвь 'blood': кровꙑѫ (instr.), плоть 'flesh': плъть. In these examples the *jers* are vocalized in strong position, whether in a word or in a connected group of words in a sentence: dĭnĭ sĭ > dnes. Analogy intervenes to create phonetically irregular forms: pravĭdĭnŭ develops regularly into pravden, but pravĭdĭna (gen. masc., nom. fem.), pravĭdĭnu (dat. masc.) develop regularly into pravedna, pravednu. On the analogy of these forms a form praveden was constructed.

In the weak position, i.e. at the end of words, or when not followed by another reduced vowel, the reduced vowels show a tendency to disappear: къто 'who': кто, вьсь: вьсь 'all', мно́га 'much': мъно́га, вамъ 'to you': вам, коньчина 'end': кончина, дьньми 'with the days': д'ньми, отьць 'father': от'ць, сътворити 'to do': створити, пьсати 'to write': псати, къ тому 'to that':

к'томоу. The apostrophe marks the place of a dropped semi-vowel.

In the light of the vocalization of the reduced vowels we can explain also spellings with *jers* instead of the vowels that are etymologically to be expected: дъвъльно 'sufficient' for довъльно, доволино, вѣтъхъ for ветъхъ 'ancient'. Such cases show that in the mind of the scribe the letter ъ was associated with *o*, and ь with *e*, because these often stood for those sounds in his spoken dialect.

2. The reduced vowels are sometimes interchanged; already in OCS texts we find ъ [*ŭ*] for ь [*ĭ*] and the other way round: тьма 'darkness': тъма, бьдѣти 'to keep awake': бъдѣти, вьсь 'every': въсъ, въсь, хлъмъ 'hillock': хльмъ, прьвъ 'first': пръвъ.

A reason for this interchange is the assimilation of the reduced vowel to the following vowel, and the fact that in the historical period the reduced vowels show the tendency to be vocalized or to disappear. The fluctuation is due also to the fact that the traditional orthography of the scribes was confused by the pronunciation of their native dialects in which reduced vowels did not exist. In words like бьдѣти, зьлѣ, бърати 'to take' the change of the *jers* is due to regressive assimilation.

3. When followed by *j* the reduced vowels acquired the timbre of the appropriate full vowels: *ĭj* > *ij*, *ŭj* > *yj*. The orthography does not clearly show this change, but we find such spellings as абье, абие, іабие 'suddenly'; дьные 'days', дьние (nom. pl.), дьньи, дьнии (gen. pl.); пыѭ, пиѭ 'I drink'. The change of *ŭj* > *yj* is supported by the forms of the definite adjectives: добрыи 'the good' < *dobrŭ+jĭ*; въ истинѫ 'in truth' considered as a single word is found spelt въі истинѫ 'in truth'. The position of the semivowels when followed by *j* has been called 'intense' (§ 9. 3, § 12. 3).

The OCS texts differ as to the spelling with ь or и: the Kiev Miss. has both spellings: милостьѭ, -ниѭ (acc. sg.) 'pity', съпасение 'salvation', зълъ (nom.) 'evil', зълии (gen. pl.). Mar., Savv. Kn., and Supr. spell as a rule with и, and the examples with ь are

exceptions. Ass. has only и spellings. Zogr. avoids, but for a few exceptions, the spelling ьи, replacing it by ии; in a part of the codex, however (Ev. Mk. and Ev. L.), the spelling with ь prevails, in certain positions. Ps. Sin. has both ьи and ии. Euch. Sin. regularly has -ьи, -ью, but -иıе, -и҃к, -иıа, -ииѧ, -ииѫ.

4. When the reduced vowel *ĭ* is preceded by *j* it develops into a full vowel *i*: *jĭže* > *jiže* = иже 'who'; *jĭgŭla* > *jigŭla* = игъла 'needle'; *dostojĭnŭ* > достоинъ 'worthy'. The hard semivowel in this position was changed into a soft one (progressive assimilation), and treated in the same way (§ 12.4): *jŭgo* (cf. Lat. *iugum*) > *jĭgo* > *jigo* = иго 'yoke'.

The Reduced Vowels in the OCS Texts

§ 34. The OCS texts reflect these changes in various degrees:

1. The most conservative text as regards the reduced vowels is the Kiev Miss. Only twice does this text confuse the reduced vowels and both examples concern the same word: въсѣхъ instead of вьсѣхъ 'in all' (§ 33. 2).

2. Zogr. uses the hard ъ instead of the soft ь followed by a back vowel in the next syllable: зъдати for зьдати 'to build', -стълати for -стьлати 'to spread out', тъма for тьма 'darkness'; but also soft ь instead of hard ъ: бьдѣти for бъдѣти 'to keep awake', зьлѣ for зълѣ 'bad', вь for въ 'in', правъда 'truth' alternates with правьдѣ, вѣрънъи 'faithful' alternates with вѣрьни.

The reduced vowels are dropped in many instances: всемь 'with all', что 'what', рци 'say!', слѣпца 'of the blind', кде 'where', кто 'who', створихомъ 'we did', for вьсемь, чьто, рьци, слѣпьца, къде, къто, сътворихомъ, &c.

In some instances the reduced vowels are vocalized in strong position: бѣсенъ, бисеръ, вьзнезъше, днесь, подобенъ, шедъ, темьницеѭ instead of бѣсьнъ 'demonic', бисьръ 'pearl', възньзъше 'those who have thrust', дьньсь 'today', подобьнъ similar', шьдъ 'gone', тьмьницеѭ 'with the prison'.

3. Another stage of the history of the reduced vowels is shown in Mar. The hard ъ shows the tendency to replace the soft ь,

especially after ш, ж, ч, шт, жд, ц: шьдъ for шьдъ 'went', жрѫдь for жрьдь 'pole', жрѫти for жрьти 'to sacrifice', къжждо for къжьдо 'every'. The hardening of the consonants (§ 31) is apparent also in: дърати, пърати, тъма for дьрати 'to tear to pieces', пьрати 'to fly up', тьма 'darkness'. Cases of the opposite type are less frequent: вь нихъ, прѣдь ними for въ нихъ 'in them', прѣдъ ними 'in front of them'. In this stage, the vocalized reduced vowels appear more frequently: шелъ 'gone', людемъ 'to the people', вонъ 'out', любовь 'love', плодо-сь 'this seed', можето-сь 'this is able', домо-тъ 'that house', for шьлъ, людьмъ, вънъ, любъвь, плодъ-сь, можетъ-сь, домъ-тъ. In Mar. the reduced vowels are more often dropped than in Zogr.

In the spelling of original ĭ followed by j, the Mar. prefers и to ь: виienъ 'beaten', виѭ 'I beat', млънии 'lightning', сѫдии 'judge' for вьienъ, вьѭ, млъньи, сѫдьи (§ 33. 3).

4. In Ass. the use of the jer letters for the reduced vowels is so inconsistent that it appears clearly that the copyist had not those sounds in his own language. He writes the letters by tradition but he puts them in wrong places. The vocalization of ь appears more frequently than that of ъ: начѧтокъ, ложь for начѧтъкъ 'beginning', лъжь (adj.) 'liar'.

5. Cloz., too, presents more cases of the vocalization of ь into e, than of ъ into o: день, честь, пришедъ for дьнь 'day', чьсть 'honour', пришьдъ 'arrived'; четврътокъ, кровьѭ, любовь for 'четврьтъкъ 'Thursday', кръвьѭ 'with blood', любъвь 'love'. In this text the interchangeability of ъ and ь is clearly dependent on the following vowel: зьлѣ, вь ньже, сьмрьть for зълѣ 'badly', въ ньже 'in that', съмрьть 'death'; тъма, мъзда for тьма 'darkness', мьзда 'payment'.

After ш, ж, шт, жд, ц the letter ь is consistently replaced by ъ: нашъ, чъто, мѫжъ, сѫштъ, рождъ for нашь 'our', чьто 'what', мѫжь 'man', сѫшть 'being', рождь 'birth'. The letters ъ and ь are often dropped.

6. Ps. Sin. shows a clear tendency to vocalize the reduced vowels in strong position: левъ for львъ 'lion', во мнѣ 'in me' for въ мьнѣ. In во кръви 'in blood' (Ps. xxix. 10) the ъ in кръви is

treated as weak. The letters ъ and ь are seldom dropped, but they
are often interchanged owing to the character of the following
vowel: въ селѣ 'in the estate' for въ селѣ, вьниде 'he entered'
for въниде. Also cases of changes independent of the following
vowel occur: зьвати for зъвати 'to call', зьлоба for зълоба
'wickedness', оупьвати for оупъвати 'to hope'.

7. Euch. Sin. regularly writes ъ after ш, ж: нашъ for нашь 'our',
слоужъба for слоужьба 'service'. After ч, шт, жд, ц, however,
ь remains: чьто 'what', даждь 'give', ношть 'night', отьць 'father'.
A following hard syllable changes ь into ъ: вѣрънъ for вѣрьнъ
'faithful', бърати for бьрати 'to take', and inversely вь вѣкъ for
въ вѣкъ 'in eternity', вьпити for въпити. Vocalization in strong
position is frequent: агнець for агньць 'lamb', сонъ for сънъ
'sleep'. The dropping of the letters ъ and ь is restricted mainly
to мwногъ for мъногъ 'many', всего for вьсего 'of all', к'то
'who', ч'то 'what' for къто, чьто.

8. Savv. Kn. replaces ь by ъ after ш, ж, ч, шт, жд: шъдъ for
шьдъ 'gone', мѫжъ for мѫжь 'man', плачъ for плачь 'weeping',
ноштъ for ношть 'night', даждъ for даждь 'give'. The interchange of the two letters appears also in other positions: дамъ for
дамь 'I shall give', възатъ for възатъ 'they lift up', бърати for
бьрати 'to take'. Also the dropping of the letters ъ, ь is frequent:
брати, кто 'who', псати 'to write'. Vocalization is less frequent
than in other OCS texts; e for ь appears in flexional endings:
людемъ for людьмъ 'to the men', именемь for именьмь 'with the
name'; o for ъ does not appear.

9. Supr. changes ь into ъ after ш: шъдъ for шьдъ 'gone', нашъ
for нашь 'our'; very often drops them in weak position; frequently
interchanges them: възати for възати 'to lift up', сь небесе
for съ небесе 'from heaven', въста for въста 'he got up', сь
нами for съ нами 'with us'. The vocalization of ь into e appears
only in the first part of the text; in the second part this is
restricted to the final syllable: дьнехъ for дьньхъ 'in the days'.
The vocalization of ъ into o is limited to three doubtful examples
(cf. N. van Wijk, *Geschichte der altkirchenslavischen Sprache*,
1931, 96).

CHANGES OF THE NASAL VOWELS IN OCS TEXTS

§ 35. The correct use of the original nasal vowels is the most important criterion which distinguishes the OCS texts written before 1100 from the later Slavonic texts of the various recensions: Middle Bulgarian, Old Serbian, Old Croatian, Old Russian. However, even with regard to this criterion some OCS texts show deviations from the rule, i.e. from the original state. Already in OCS texts the tendency appears to denasalize $\varrho > u$ and $\varrho > e$.

1. The Kiev Miss. regularly uses the nasals ѫ and ѧ where they are etymologically to be expected. The single exception (and that not certain) seems to be represented by the form of the instr. sg. fem. небесьскоѭ for небесьскꙑѭ 'with the heavenly'. If, however, we accept a form небесьскоѭ for the instr. sg. fem. then the u may represent a faulty transcription of the original glagolitic letter o. Confusion between ѫ and оу is nevertheless betrayed in this text by the word въсѫдъ 'communion', which should be spelt *въсоудъ because it is an Old High German loan-word (wizzôd).

2. Zogr. has very few irregularities in the use of ѫ, ѧ; they are mistakes or accidental and do not reveal any dialectal peculiarities in the language of the copyist. Alongside мѫдити 'to delay', мѫдьнъ 'slow' appear моудити, моудьнъ; отътоудоу, отъ-ноудоуже, иноудоу for отътѫдоу 'from there', отъиѭдоуже 'from where', инѫдоу 'from elsewhere', which could be explained on the analogy of adverbs like низоу 'down'. The e for ѧ in a few cases could be explained as faulty spellings due to the neighbouring letters or to the corruption of the original: не етъ for не ѩтъ 'he did not seize', приꙗше for приѧшѧ 'they received'. A confusion between ѧ and ѣ occurs in помѣнѫти for помѧнѫти 'to remember'.

3. Mar. has more examples of nasal ϱ developed into u, occasionally into o, and of nasal ϱ replaced by ě: соумьнѣти for сѫмьнѣти 'to doubt', коупѣли for кѫпѣль 'bath', люблю for люблѭ 'I love', собота for сѫбота 'Saturday'. Conversely it also writes вѫрѣ for воурꙗ 'tempest'. The ѧ is replaced by ѣ in: сѣдѣте for сѧдѣте (imp.) 'sit down', грѣди for грѧди (imp.) 'come', съвѣзавъше for съвѧзавъше 'having tied'. It never has

e for ę. If we admit that the language of the copyist already contained u for original ǫ then we may ascribe to him a Serbian origin.

4. Ass. has моудити 'to delay', моудьнъ 'slow' for мѫдити, мѫдьнъ. Confusion between ѫ and ѧ is shown in: помажѧтъ for помажѫтъ 'they will anoint', приемлатъ for приемлиѫтъ 'they will receive'. As in some Bulgarian dialects the two nasals have been reduced to a single one, this confusion may indicate the origin of the copyist.

5. In Cloz. there are examples of ѫ being replaced by оу: моука for мѫка 'torment', ѫтробоу (acc.) for ѫтробѫ 'intestines'. Also inversely we meet отъсѫдѫ for отъсѫдоу 'from here'. This changes reveal a Serbo-Croatian or Moravian influence. The spelling констатинѣ 'Constantine' indicates an open pronunciation of the ę. The confusion of ѧ with ѣ is testified by the regular appearance of -мѣ- in помѣнѫти for помѧнѫти 'to remember'. The inverse spelling appears in сѧдаштаго (gen. sg.) 'of the (one) seated' for сѣдаштаго. These are, however, isolated cases.

6. Ps. Sin. has many examples of ѫ replaced by о; twice it replaces о by ѫ: сѫбоѭ for собоѭ, ѫтрѫба for ѫтроба 'intestines'; this could be explained by the vicinity of the ѫ in the other syllable. The о for ѫ appears more frequently and has been explained as a dialectal influence on the language of the text, in view of the fact that in some modern Macedonian dialects (Debra) the ǫ has developed into o. This explanation is, however, not certain, for we should expect as many faulty spellings of the opposite kind (ѫ for о); but ѫ for о only appears in few isolated forms. More obvious would be to explain these spellings by a misinterpretation of the Glagolitic letter for ǫ. The form собота, in Ps. Sin. and in Mar., may go back to a Lat. Sabbata (pl.) (§ 7.1), whereas the form with nasal сѫбтоа reflects the Byzantine-Greek σάμβατον. The nasal ǫ is changed into u: моудити for мѫдити 'to delay', паоучина for пѫчина 'cobweb', which, however, could be interpreted also as a faulty spelling under the influence of the following word пооучаахѫ сѧ (Ps. lxxxix. 9). We find also cases of the opposite type: рѫкѫ for рѫкоу (gen. loc. du.). The vowel e sometimes

replaces ę: єзъщи for ιазъщи 'the Gentiles', възложєтъ for възложѫтъ (3rd pl.) 'they lay (burdens) upon' (trans.). Instances of ѧ for є are also recorded: имѧни for имєни (dat. sg.) 'name', искоушѧнъ for искоушєнъ (p. pf. pass.) 'tempted', ѣ for ѧ appears in полѣнѫти for помѧнѫти 'to remember'; however, the last spelling is as frequent as the first.

These spellings seem to indicate that the original of the text was a Moravian or Serbian dialect. The present recension is written by a Bulgarian scribe who introduced characteristics of his own language.

7. Similar spellings are to be found in Euch. Sin.: моудити моудьнъ for мѫдити 'to delay', мѫдьнъ 'late', озоιѫ for ѫзоιѫ 'with a fetter, tie', отробѫ (acc. sg.) for ѫтробѫ 'intestines', and inversely нѫжѫ for ножѫ (acc. pl.) 'knife'; e for ę appears in few examples: начельниче for начѧльниче (voc.) 'leader'. A doubtful case of confusion between ѧ and ѣ is мѧстѣ for мѣстѣ 'in the place'.

8. Savv. Kn. has only three cases of confusion of the nasals: моудити, моудьнъ for мѫдити 'to delay', мѫдьнъ 'late', плюноувъше for плюнѫвъше (nom. pl.) 'having spit'.

9. Supr. has cases of u for ǫ: соумьнѣти for сѫмьнѣти 'to doubt', гноусити сѧ, гноусьнъ alongside гнѫсити сѧ 'to be disgusted', гнѫсьнъ 'disgusting', моудьнъ for мѫдьнъ 'slow', ноудити, ноужда for нѫдити 'to compel', нѫжда 'necessity', гонезноути for гонезнѫти 'to escape', &c. The confusion ѣ for ѧ is recorded once in полѣнѫти for помѧнѫти 'to remember'. The confusion between ѫ and ѧ appears in стелѧштѧ 'spreading' for стелѭштѧ. One example presents є for ѧ: обѧдише for обѧдиша 'they accused'. Cases of ѧ for є are mistakes of the copyist: надѧжда for надєжда 'hope', помѧташѧ for помєташѧ 'they threw away'.

10. Ostr. belongs chronologically to the OCS texts, i.e. to the texts written or copied between the ninth and the eleventh centuries. This text was copied in 1056/7 by Russian scribes, for the burgomaster of Novgorod, from an East Bulgarian original of the time of the Tsar Simeon. Through the scribes vernacular

forms have been introduced into the language of the original, e.g.
ѫ is replaced by оу, ѭ by ю, or inversely in some 300 cases; ѧ is
replaced by ꙗ and ѩ by ꙗ in some 200 cases: ꙗзꙑкъ for ѩзꙑкъ
'tongue', изꙗслдвъ for изꙗслдвъ (pr. n.); ѣ appears for ѧ in
недѣлѣ (gen. sg. fem.) for недѣлꙗ 'Sunday'. The reduced vowels
are in a number of cases vocalized in strong position: темьнъ for
тьмьнъ 'dark' (§ 33).

The OCS group жд is replaced thirty-four times by the Eastern
Slavonic corresponding ж: рожьство for рождьство 'birth'. (§ 21. 2).
Apart from these and some other local influences, however, the
language of the Ostr. is nearer to the language of the first trans-
lators than are some of the older OCS texts.

DEVELOPMENT OF LIQUID DIPHTHONGS
IN OCS TEXTS

§ 36. The original initial groups *ort-*, *olt-* (*t* representing any
consonant) developed in OCS into *rat-*, *lat-* (§ 6. 3). The OCS
texts present some dialectal deviations from this development.
Supr. has several times, alongside рабъ 'slave' < *orbh-*, the
form робъ, роботд 'labour', робии (adj.) '(of the) slave', робичиштъ
'(God's) servant' and, alongside рдз-, forms with роз- (рос-):
розличьнии 'various' (pl.), розбити 'to loosen', розвѣ 'except',
ростворивъ (p. part. act.) 'disjoin', роширити 'to extend',
розбоиникъ 'brigand'. The form робъ 'slave' appears once in
Zogr. (J. xv. 15). The form розгд 'young branch' appears in
Mar., Zogr., Savv. Kn., Ass. (J. xv. 4, 6), Ps. Sin. (cviii. 7), whereas
рдзгд appears in Mar., Zogr. (J. xv. 2).   The forms with *rot-* are
peculiar to the Slavonic languages of the Western (Polish, Czech,
Lusatian) group and of the Eastern group (Russian, White
Russian, Ukrainian). One may assume that also south of the
Danube, e.g. in East Bulgarian, there existed a dialect containing
the development *ort-* > *rot-*. Another explanation of the forms
with initial *rot-* is that which considers them (especially робъ) as
Moravianisms, i.e. originating in Moravia where the first translations were written down. Alongside the usual verbal form (не)
родити '(not) to care' the OCS texts show also (не) рддити (Mar.,
Zogr., Ostr., Supr.).

Concerning the development *olt-* > *lat-*, in OCS texts appear forms showing ал-, алъ-, ла- for original ·*olt*: ладни, ладна alongside алъдьн, ал'дни 'boat'; лакати, лакомъ alongside алъкати, алкати 'to be hungry'. The form ал'дьн, алъдьн appears in Zogr., Supr. The form алъкати occurs in Mar., Ass., Euch. Sin., Savv. Kn., Supr. Also лань, лани 'hind, chamois', appears without metathesis: алнии, алъннн (cf. Gr. ἔλαφος 'stag, doe', ἄλκη 'elk', OHG ëlho, Lat. *alces* 'elk').

VOWEL-GRADATION (APOPHONY)

§ 37. In words derived from the same root occur vowel-changes which cannot be explained as phonetic developments. No phonetic rule peculiar to OCS could explain the change of the vowels in the stems of verbs or nouns of the following kind: вести 'to lead', водити 'to lead'; текж 'I am running', токъ 'course, river', притѣкати 'to rush together', такание 'the running'; бити 'to beat', быж (биж) 'I beat', разбоиникъ 'brigand', &c. These changes of vowels represent older phonetic patterns which go back to IE and are referred to as vowel-gradation (apophony, ablaut).

1. In the IE system the regular alternation of certain vowels was a means of forming word-categories from elements belonging etymologically to the same phonetic unit. The alternation was based (*a*) on the quality or (*b*) on the quantity of the vowels. The most usual alternation was that of *e/o*. The various aspects of vowel-alternation are called grades. So the alternating basis with *e* ∼ *o* is called *full grade*, *ē* ∼ *ō* is the *lengthened grade*; when the vowel is reduced and disappears the basis is called *zero-grade*. Both kinds of gradation could occur in the same group of words.

(*a*) Qualitative gradations

	Full grade:	Lengthened grade:	Zero (reduced) grade:
IE *bher-	Gr. φέρω, φορέω	Gr. φώρ 'thief'	Gr. δί-φρος
	OCS berǫ	Lat. fūr	OCS bĭrati
	Goth. baíra, bar	Goth. bērum	Lat. fors 'accident'
	Skt bhárati		Goth. -baúrans

IE *ped- Lat. ped-is   Lat. pēs   Skt upa-bda-
          Gr. ποδ-ός   Gr. πώς   'foot-step'
                          OCS pěšĭ

(b) Quantitative gradations

	Long:		Short:
Lat.	dōnum	Lat.	dătus
Gr.	δῶρον, δίδωμι	Gr.	δόσις 'gift'
OCS	darŭ, dati		
OPr	dātwei 'to give'		
Lat.	stāre	Lat.	stătus
OCS	stati	OCS	stojǫ
Gr. (Dor.)	ἵστᾱμι	Gr.	στατός
Goth.	stōls 'chair'	Goth.	staps 'place'
Skt	á-sthāt 'he stood up'	Skt	sthi-táḥ 'standing'

2. Vowel quantity had ceased to be phonemically significant in OCS, the trends of IE gradation-system continued to be operative, new alternations have been developed, and analogy has interfered and changed the original patterns of gradations.

Owing to the phonetic developments proper to Slavonic, in OCS the vowel-gradations appear in the following series:

(a) ě ~ e ~ ĭ ~ zero ~ a ~ o.
(b) ě ~ a ~ o.
(c) o ~ ŭ.

3. OCS alternations could represent also IE diphthongal apophonies. The result in OCS differed according to the element which followed after the diphthong. Schematically these apophonic series could be represented in the following way:

IE diphthongal apophonies: CS apophonies:

ēi̯ : ei̯ : i : ōi̯ : oi̯	+ cons.	=	i : ĭ (= ь) : ě
	+ vowel	=	ĭj : ĭj : oj
ēu̯ : eu̯ : u : ōu̯ : ou̯	+ cons.	=	ju : ŭ (= ъ) : u
	+ vowel	=	ov : ŭv : ov
ēr : er : r̥ : ōr : or	+ cons.	=	rě : r̥ (rŭ) : ra
	+ vowel	=	er : ĭr : or
ēl : el : l̥ : ōl : ol	+ cons.	=	lě : l̥ (lŭ) : la
	+ vowel	=	el : ĭl : ol

$$\bar{e}m:em:\eta:\bar{o}m:om \quad + \quad \text{cons.} \quad = \quad e:e:\varrho$$
$$\qquad\qquad\qquad\qquad + \quad \text{vowel} \quad = \quad em:\bar{\imath}m:om$$
$$\bar{e}n:en:\eta:\bar{o}n:on \quad + \quad \text{cons.} \quad = \quad e:e:\varrho$$
$$\qquad\qquad\qquad\qquad + \quad \text{vowel} \quad = \quad en:\bar{\imath}n:on$$

4. The various aspects of vowel-gradation appear in instances of the following kind:

An IE alternating basis *ghrebh ~ *grēbh is represented in OCS by: full grade grebǫ 'I dig, I scoop', grobŭ 'grave' ~ long grade -grěsŭ (1st aor. sg.), -grěbajǫ (1st sg. pr. impft.) ~ reduced grade -*grĭb-ěti 'to be buried' (cf. OCz hřbiti); perhaps also original long grade grabiti 'to snatch' as indicated by Lith. grόbti 'id.'; Skt grāháyati 'he seizes' (causative). The OHG grubilôn 'to bore, to drill' represents the reduced grade.

Full grade jestŭ (cf. Lat. est, Gr. ἔστι, Lith. ēsti) ~ reduced grade jistŭ (= istŭ 'true, real') ~ zero grade s-ǫtŭ 'they are', s-y (pr. part.) 'being' (Lat. s-unt).

Full grade rekǫ 'I say', rokŭ 'fixed time' ~ long grade rěxŭ (1st sg. aor.), rěčĭ 'speech, word' ~ reduced grade rĭci (2nd, 3rd imp. sg.), OR rьku, rьklъ, Cz řka, vyřkl.

Full grade tekǫ 'I run', Lith. tekù, OIrish techim 'I fly', tokŭ 'the flowing', Lith. tākas 'foot-path' ~ long grade těxŭ (1st sg. aor.), těkati (it.), takati 'to let run' ~ reduced grade tĭci (2nd, 3rd sg. imp.), -ticati (it.).

5. Vowel gradation plays a role in the morphology of the OCS verb. The sigmatic aorist of the verbs whose stems ended in a consonant was formed by lengthening the thematic vowel: нести, несж 'I carry' ~ нѣсъ (1st sg. aor.); бости, бодж 'I sting' ~ басъ (1st sg. aor.); чисти, чьтж 'to count, to read' ~ чисъ (1st sg. aor.). Also in other morphological forms: творити 'to make' ~ тварь 'creation'; сѣкж 'I cut' ~ секыра 'axe'; сѣсти 'to sit down' ~ седло 'the seat'.

(a) The gradation of vowels also serves in OCS to create imperfective verbal forms from perfective ones: po-greti (pft.) 'to bury' ~ po-grěbati (impft.); roditi 'to bear, to generate' ~ raždati (impft.). This means of creating new forms has also been extended in Slavonic to other vowels: pri-zŭvati (pft.) 'to call' ~ pri-zyvati

(impft.); *umrěti* (pft.) < **-merti, moriti* 'to perish' ~ *umǐretǔ* 'he will die', *mrǔtvǔ* (adj.) 'dead' ~ *umirati* (impft.), *umirajetǔ* 'he is dying'.

Thus, in OCS, the following regular oppositions were established:

The perfective forms have the thematic vowels: *e, o*; *ǐ, ǔ*.

The imperfective forms have the thematic vowels: *ě, a*; *i, y*.

(*b*) Gradations in bases containing original diphthongs before vowels: *pǐjǫ* 'I drink' ~ *pivo* 'drink' (n.), *pitǔ* (p. pr. pass.) ~ *pojǫ* 'I make drink', *-pajati* 'to make drink' representing an IE **pōi̯* (cf. Lat. *pōtus*, Gr. (Aeol.) πώνω, Lith. *pù'ta* 'orgy' representing IE **pōu̯*); before consonants: *cvitǫ* 'I bloom' ~ *cvisti* (inf.) ~ *cvětǔ* 'flower' with an alternating diphthong *oi̯*; *čitǫ* (1st sg. pr.) 'I read, I count' ~ *čitati* (it.), *čisti* (inf.), *čisǔ* (1st sg. aor.) representing IE **(s)kei̯d-* (cf. Lith. *skaityti* 'to read', Skt *cétati* 'he perceives').

(*c*) As the diphthong *eu̯* developed in OCS into *ju*, and the diphthong *ou̯* developed into *u* (§ 8), this gradation was not employed in OCS for morphological purposes, because the opposition *ju : u* was not phonemically significant. However, an original formation based on this gradation has survived in OCS: the IE **bheu̯dh-* is represented in Slavonic by *bljudǫ, bljusti* 'to observe, to watch', *buditi* 'to awake' ~ *bǔděti* 'to watch, to stay awake', *-bǔnǫti* 'to get up' (cf. Gr. πεύθομαι 'to ask, to inquire', Goth. *ana-biudan* 'to order', AS *béodan*, E *bid*, G *bieten*).

The same diphthong (*eu̯, ou̯*) alternated differently in open syllables, i.e. when followed by a vowel: *pluti* (inf.) 'to float' < **plou̯-ti* ~ *plovǫ* (1st sg. pr.) 'I swim, float, run', *plavati*, R *плáватъ* 'to swim' (cf. Gr. πλέ(ϝ)ω, πλό(ϝ)ος, πλω(ϝ)ω); *-pl'ujǫ* 'I spit' ~ *pl'ǐvati* (inf.) ~ *pl'inǫti* (inf.) (§ 7.4).

(*d*) Gradations of *er* diphthong:

Followed by vowel (= in open syllable): *moriti* 'to kill', *morǔ* 'plague' ~ *mirǫ* (1st sg. pr.) ~ *mirati* (it.): *u-marjati* 'to kill' (cf. Lat. *mors*, Lith. *mǐrti*, Skt *mr̥tá*, Goth. *maúrþr*); *derǫ* 'I flay', *raz-dorǔ* 'quarrel' ~ *dǐrati* (inf.), *dǐrtǔ* (p. part. pass.) ~ *u-darǔ* 'blow' ~ *-dirati* (inf.), *dira* 'split'.

Followed by consonant (= in closed syllable): *otŭ-vrěsti* 'to open' < **verz-*, *povrazŭ* 'bundle' < **vorz-* ~ *otŭ-vrŭzǫ* (1st sg. pr.); *vrěteno* 'spindle' < **vert-*, *vratiti* 'to turn round' < **vort-* ~ *vĭrtěti*, *vrŭtěti* 'to turn, to drill' ~ *vratŭ* 'turning'.

(e) Gradations of *el* diphthong:
Followed by vowel (= in open syllable): *velěti* 'to order', *volja* 'the will' ~ later form *do-vilěti* 'to be sufficient'.

Followed by consonant (= in closed syllable): *vlěkǫ* 'I pull' < **velk-*, *vlačiti* (inf.) < **volk-* ~ *vĭlkŭ* (p. part. act. I).

(f) Gradations of *em* diphthong:
Followed by vowel (= in open syllable): *gromŭ* 'thunder' ~ *grĭměti* 'to thunder' ~ *grimati* (it).

Followed by consonant (= in closed syllable): *dǫti* 'to blow up' ~ *dŭmǫ* (1st sg. pr.) ~ *na-dymati sę* 'to boast'.

(g) Gradations of *en* diphthong:
Followed by vowel (= in open syllable): *opona* 'curtain' ~ *pro-pĭnǫ* 'I shall crucify'.

Followed by consonant (= in closed syllable): *blęsti* 'to err' ~ *blǫdŭ* (n.) 'fornication', *blǫditi*; *męsti* 'to mix, stir up' ~ *mǫtŭ* (n.) 'turmoil'.

6. In view of the fact that CS only partially continued the IE system of apophony, the examples are not always clear and numerous for each series. Like the secondary gradation established in the OCS verb stems (§ 96.B.1.*b*), a vowel gradation based on the alternation of front and back vowels plays an important role in the morphology of the OCS noun. This secondary alternation divided some paradigms of the declension into a soft and hard one (§ 11.2, § 38.I.II). The vowels alternate in the suffixes of the nouns in the following way:

Hard declension (back vowel: *o, ŭ, y, a, ě < oi*):

N. sg.	*rabŭ*	*vlĭkŭ*	*lěto*	*žena*
L. sg.	*rabě*	*vlĭcě*	*lětě*	*ženě*
I. sg.	*rabomĭ*	*vlĭkomĭ*	*lětomĭ*	*ženojǫ*
A. pl.	*raby*	*vlĭky*	*lěta*	*ženy*
I. pl.	*raby*	*vlĭky*	*lěty*	*ženami*

Soft declension (front vowel: *e*, *ĭ*, *i* (*ę* in finals), *ja* (*ě*), *i*):

N. sg.	*krajĭ*	*otĭcĭ*	*lice*	*duša*
L. sg.	*kraji*	*otĭci*	*lici*	*duši*
I. sg.	*krajemĭ*	*otĭcemĭ*	*licemĭ*	*dušejǫ*
A. pl.	*kraję*	*otĭcę*	*lica*	*dušę*
I. pl.	*kraji*	*otĭci*	*lici*	*dušami*

MORPHOLOGY

The Noun

§ 38. The OCS nominal system is conservative in its relation to IE. It inherited several stem classes, seven cases, three genders, and three numbers. Each nominal form has therefore to be defined from the point of view of these four morphological categories:

1. Stems.

The declension of the noun is based on the stem, to which the case endings are added. In the ninth century, when the OCS texts were first composed, these stems were already indistinguishable as such except in a few of the nominal inflexions. The following survey of the declensions gives the nominative forms and another case in which the original stem is recognizable:

I. *-a-/-ja-* stems.—This declension comprises feminine nouns, with the exception of those nouns whose natural gender is masculine (§ 37.6, § 39):

(*a*) Hard:

жена [*žena*] 'woman', dat. pl. женамъ [*žena-mŭ*]

владъіка [*vladyka*] masc. 'ruler', instr. pl. владъіками [*vladyka-mi*]

(*b*) Soft:

доуша [*duša*] 'soul', dat. pl. доушамъ [*duša-mŭ*]

юноша [*junoša*] masc. 'young man', dat. pl. юношамъ [*junoša-mŭ*]

сждии (сжди) [*sǫdiji*] masc. 'judge', dat. pl. сждиıамъ [*sǫdija-mŭ*]

млъ́нии [mlŭniji] masc. 'lightning', dat. pl. млъ́нишамъ
[mlŭnija-mŭ]
богъ́ıни [bogyńi] 'goddess', dat. pl. богъ́ıшамъ [bogyńa-mŭ]

II. -o-/-jo- stems.—The nouns of this declension are masculine
or neuter (§ 37.6, § 40):

1. Masculine:

(a) Hard:

градъ [gradŭ] 'city', instr. sg. градолиь [grado-mĭ]
богъ [bogŭ] 'God', instr. sg. богомь [bogo-mĭ]

(b) Soft:

краи [krajĭ] 'end, extremity', instr. sg. краюмь [kraje-mĭ]
мжжь [mǫžĭ] 'man', dat. pl. мжжель́ъ [mǫže-mŭ]
отьць [otĭcĭ] 'father', dat. du. отьцема [otĭce-ma]

2. Neuter:

(a) Hard:

лѣто [lěto] 'summer, year', instr. sg. лѣтомь [lěto-mĭ]
вѣко [věko] 'eyelid', dat. pl. вѣкомъ [věko-mŭ]

(b) Soft:

полю [polje] 'field', instr. sg. полюмь [polje-mĭ]
знамению [znamenije] 'sign', dat. pl. знаменюмъ
[znamenije-mŭ]
лице [lice] 'face', dat. du. лицема [lice-ma]

III. -u- stems.—There are no soft stems in this declension, and
all nouns of this category are masculine (§ 42):

сынъ [synŭ] 'son', instr. pl. сынъ́ми [synŭ-mi]

IV. -i- stems.—The greater part of the nouns belonging to this
declension are feminine, a few are masculine. There is no distinction of 'soft' and 'hard' stems in this category (§ 43):

(a) Feminine:

кость [kostĭ] 'bone', instr. pl. костьми [kostĭ-mi]

(b) Masculine:

пжть [pǫtĭ] 'way', dat. pl. пжтьмъ [pǫtĭ-mŭ]

V. Consonant stems.—This category of stems includes masc., fem., and neut. nouns. The stem ends in one of the following consonants: -*v*-, -*n*-, -*s*-, -*nt*-, -*r*- (§ 44):

1. The -*v*- stems are usually called -*ū*- stems, because historically the -*ŭv*- stem-ending goes back by way of -*ŭu*- to -*ū*-, and the nom. ending -*y* of this group represents IE -*ūs* (§ 45.1). The nouns of this declension are feminine:

свекры [*svekry*] 'mother-in-law', gen. sg. свекръве [*svekrŭv-e*]
любы [*ljuby*] 'love', dat. sg. любъви [*ljubŭv-i*]

2. The -*n*- stems are masculine or neuter:
Masc. камы [*kamy*] 'stone', gen. sg. камене [*kamen-e*]
Neut. имѧ [*imę*] 'name', gen. pl. именъ [*imen-ŭ*]

3. The -*s*- stems are only neuter:
слово [*slovo*] 'word', gen. sg. словесе [*sloves-e*]

4. The -*nt*- are only neuter and designate young creatures:
отрочѧ [*otročę*] 'child', gen. sg. отрочѧте [*otročęt-e*]

5. The -*r*- stems are represented only by two feminine nouns:
мати [*mati*] 'mother', gen. sg. матере [*mater-e*]
дъшти [*dŭšti*] 'daughter', gen. sg. дъштере [*dŭšter-e*]

2. Genders.

The grammatical gender of a noun can be recognized from its attributive determination (adjective, pronoun), but generally also from the form of the noun, because certain endings correspond to certain grammatical genders:

Nouns of the -*o*- declension ending in -ъ [-*ŭ*], -ь [-*ĭ*] are masculine (§ 40.1, § 41, § 42).

Nouns ending in -а [-*a*], -ia, ѣ [-*ja*], -и [-*i*] are feminine with the exception of those whose natural gender is masculine (§ 39).

Nouns ending in -о [-*o*], -е [-*e*], -ѧ [-*ę*] are neuter (§ 40.2, § 44.2.3.4).

Nouns ending in -ы [-*y*] are feminine, with the exception of камы 'stone' and пламы 'flame' which are masculine (§ 44.1).

Nouns ending in -ь [-ĭ] of the -i- declension are either
masculine or feminine (§ 43). Feminine are the abstract
-i- stems in -stĭ, -ĭ: мѫдрость 'wisdom', радость 'joy',
зависть 'envy', доблесть 'fortitude', горюсть 'heat', боѣзнь
'fear', зълъ 'evil', печаль 'sorrow', &c.

3. Numbers.

The nouns are declined in three numbers (singular, dual, plural)
and seven cases. It should, however, be remembered that not every
noun has all three numbers, that some nouns have only plural
forms, e.g. врата 'gate', and that others have only singular forms,
e.g. collective nouns: дѫбие neut. coll. to дѫбъ 'oak-tree'; neuter
abstract nouns оученне 'teaching'; братрнѣ fem. coll. to братръ
'brother', which declines as in § 39c.

4. Cases.

The seven cases are: nominative, genitive, dative, accusative,
vocative, instrumental, locative. It should be remembered that: (a)
the neuter nouns have three identical forms each for nom., acc., and
voc., in sing., in du., and in plur.; (b) the fem. nouns have an identical
form for nom., acc., and voc. in plur.; (c) the masc. nouns have an
identical form for nom. and voc. in plur.; (d) the dual has three
forms only: one for nom., acc., voc., another for gen. and loc.,
and a third for dat. and instr.; (e) the masc. nouns have as a rule
one single form for nom. and acc. in sing.; (f) the masc. -o- stems
(persons) may use the genitive in the function of accusative in sing.
(§ 40.1p).

DECLENSION OF THE NOUNS

§ 39. I. The -a-/-ja- stems.
Feminine: глава 'head', нога 'foot', рѫка 'hand', доуша 'soul',
стьза (стьзѣ, стьза) 'path', богꙑни 'goddess', поустꙑни
'desert', ладнн (алъдни) 'ship'.
Masculine: владꙑка 'ruler', балнн 'healer', сѫдни (сѫдьн, сѫди)
'judge'.
In the following paradigms the endings are separated from the
stem by hyphens.

Singular
Hard stems

N.	глав-а	рѫк-а	ног-а
G.	глав-ы	рѫк-ы	ног-ы
D.	глав-ѣ	рѫц-ѣ	ноѕ-ѣ
A.	глав-ѫ	рѫк-ѫ	ног-ѫ
V.	глав-о	рѫк-о	ног-о
I.	глав-оѭ	рѫк-оѭ	ног-оѭ
L.	глав-ѣ	рѫц-ѣ	ноѕ-ѣ

Soft stems

N.	доуш-а	богъıй-и	сѫди-и (сѫди)
G.	доуш-ѧ	богъıй-ѧ	сѫди-ѩ
D.	доуш-и	богъıй-и	сѫди-и
A.	доуш-ѫ	богъıй-ѫ	сѫди-ѭ
V.	доуш-е	богъıй-е	сѫди-и (сѫди)
I.	доуш-еѭ	богъıй-еѭ	сѫди-ѥѭ
L.	доуш-и	богъıй-и	сѫди-и

Dual
Hard stems

N. A. V.	глав-ѣ	рѫц-ѣ	ноѕ-ѣ
G. L.	глав-оу	рѫк-оу	ног-оу
D. I.	глав-ама	рѫк-ама	ног-ама

Soft stems

N. A. V.	доуш-и	богъıй-и	сѫди-и
G. L.	доуш-оу	богъıй-ю	сѫди-ю
D. I.	доуш-ама	богъıй-ама	сѫди-ꙗма

Plural
Hard stems

N.	глав-ы	рѫк-ы	ног-ы
G.	глав-ъ	рѫк-ъ	ног-ъ
D.	глав-амъ	рѫк-амъ	ног-амъ
A.	глав-ы	рѫк-ы	ног-ы
V.	глав-ы	рѫк-ы	ног-ы
I.	глав-ами	рѫк-ами	ног-ами
L.	глав-ахъ	рѫк-ахъ	ног-ахъ

Soft stems

N.	доуш-а	богъін-а	сѫди-ѩ
G.	доуш-ь	богъін-ь	сѫди-и
D.	доуш-амъ	богъін-амъ	сѫди-ѩмъ
A.	доуш-а	богꙑ́н-а	сѫди-ѩ
V.	доуш-а	богъін-а	сѫди-ѩ
I.	доуш-амн	богъін-амн	сѫди-ѩмн
L.	доуш-ахъ	богъін-ахъ	сѫди-ѩхъ

(*a*) The velar consonants are palatalized in the stems of рѫка, нога, &c., when followed by ѣ [*ě*] according to § 30.1.

(*b*) The suffix -ꙑни (богъіни) goes back to -*yn'a*-, and derives feminine nouns from either masculine or feminine abstract nouns: господꙑни 'mistress', крьстиꙗнꙑни 'Christian woman', поганꙑни 'heathen woman', рабꙑни 'slave woman', самарѣнꙑни 'Samaritan woman', сѫсѣдꙑни '(female) neighbour', ꙗлинꙑни 'Greek (Hellenic) woman', магдалꙑни 'Magdalene', благꙑни 'goodness', гръдꙑни 'pride', льгꙑни 'consolation', правꙑни 'justice', простꙑни 'simplicity, stupidity', поустꙑни 'desert', свѧтꙑни 'holiness, sanctuary'.

(*c*) The nouns in -и represent old -*ija*- stems. They are either feminine: алъдни 'ship', млънни 'lightning', алъннн 'hind', крабин 'small basket', or masculine (ending in -ни, -чни or archaic -н, -чн): вѣтни 'speaker', балин (бали) 'healer', кънигъчни 'learned man', шаръчни 'painter', кръмъчни 'pilot', сокачни 'cook', самъчни 'overseer', левѣни (= левгни) 'Levi'.

(*d*) The vocative of the masc. -н(н) nouns is identical with the nom.: сѫди(н), вѣти(н).

(*e*) The fem. nouns of this category often by analogy join the -*ja*- fem. nouns: млъннꙗ on the analogy of змнꙗ 'dragon', землꙗ 'earth'; Манаснꙗ (Gr. Μανάσσης) for Манасни.

(*f*) The OCS texts show examples of nouns of this class which differ from the original forms. So the instrumental ending -*ojǫ*/-*ejǫ* appears contracted to -*ǫ*/-*jǫ*: силѫ (Ps. Sin. 40.12) for силоѭ; землѭ (Zogr., Mt. v. 35), земꙑѭ (Supr.) for землеѭ; доушѫ for доушеѭ, &c. The contracted forms are more frequent in Supr., they are absent in the Kiev Miss. and they appear sporadically in

Ass., Mar., Zogr., Savv. Kn. They may be explained by dissimilation of the ending -*ejeję* > -*eję* (cf. N. van Wijk, *Geschichte der altkirchenslavischen Sprache*, 1931, 179): гадидеіѫ < гадидеіеіѫ. In later texts of the Middle Bulgarian recension the instrumental ending appears as -оѫ, -еѫ (-оѧ, -еѧ) (§ 32.5).

(*g*) Masc. proper names of Greek origin take the masc. ending in the instrumental: Нієрелиита, instr. Нієрелиіелѣ, Нсаита, instr. Нсаиелѣ.

(*h*) Masc. nouns in -*a*-: вдижика 'fellow-creature', владꙑка 'ruler, Lord', прѣдътеча 'forerunner', сдоуга 'servant', сотона 'Satan', оувиица 'murderer', жжика 'relative', юнота, юноша 'young person', Каіафа 'Caiaphas', Нюда 'Judas', &c.

§ 40. II. The -*o*-/-*jo*- stems.

Masc.: рабъ 'servant', чдовѣкъ 'human being', доухъ 'spirit', вогъ 'god', коиь 'horse', вождь 'guide', краи 'limit, borderline', мѫжь 'man', отьць 'father', змии 'dragon'.

Neut.: мѣсто 'place', вѣко 'eyelid', подіе 'field', зналение 'sign, mark', срѣдьце 'heart', доже 'bed'.

I. MASCULINES
Singular
Hard stems

N.	раб-ъ	чдовѣк-ъ	вог-ъ	доух-ъ
G.	раб-а	чдовѣк-а	вог-а	доух-а
D.	раб-оу	чдовѣк-оу	вог-оу	доух-оу
A.	раб-ъ, -а	чдовѣк-ъ	вог-ъ, -а	доух-ъ
V.	раб-е	чдовѣч-е	вож-е	доуш-е
I.	раб-олѣ	чдовѣк-олѣ	вог-олѣ	доух-олѣ
L.	раб-ѣ	чдовѣц-ѣ	вос-ѣ	доус-ѣ

Soft stems

N.	мѫж-ь	вожд-ь	зми-и
G.	мѫж-а	вожд-а	зми-іа
D.	мѫж-оу	вожд-оу	зми-ю
A.	мѫж-ь, -а	вожд-ь	зми-и
V.	мѫж-оу	вожд-оу	зми-ю
I.	мѫж-елѣ	вожд-елѣ	зми-іелѣ
L.	мѫж-и	вожд-и	зми-и

Dual
Hard stems

N. A. V.	раб-а	чловѣк-а	бог-а	доүх-а
G. L.	раб-оү	чловѣк-оү	бог-оү	доүх-оү
D. I.	раб-ома	чловѣк-ома	бог-ома	доүх-ома

Soft stems

N. A. V.	мѫж-а	вожд-а	зми-ꙗ
G. L.	мѫж-оү	вожд-оү	зми-ю
D. I.	мѫж-ема	вожд-ема	зми-ѥма

Plural
Hard stems

N.	раб-и	чловѣц-и	бos-и	доүс-и
G.	раб-ъ	чловѣк-ъ	бог-ъ	доүх-ъ
D.	раб-омъ	чловѣк-омъ	бог-омъ	доүх-омъ
A.	раб-ы	чловѣк-ы	бог-ы	доүх-ы
V.	раб-и	чловѣц-и	бos-и	доүс-и
I.	раб-ы	чловѣк-ы	бог-ы	доүх-ы
L.	раб-ѣхъ	чловѣц-ѣхъ	бos-ѣхъ	доүс-ѣхъ

Soft stems

N.	мѫж-и	вожд-и	зми-и
G.	мѫж-ь	вожд-ь	зми-и
D.	мѫж-емъ	вожд-емъ	зми-ѥмъ
A.	мѫж-ѧ	вожд-ѧ	зми-ѩ
V.	мѫж-и	вожд-и	зми-и
I.	мѫж-и	вожд-и	зми-и
L.	мѫж-ихъ	вожд-ихъ	зми-ихъ

(a) The velar consonant of the stem is palatalized in V. sg. according to the rule of the first palatalization (§ 30.1), in L. sg., N., V., and L. pl. according to the rule of the second palatalization (§ 30.2).

(b) The spelling of the G. and D. sg., and of A. pl. of the soft stems varies: вожд-а but змн-ia; мѫж-оу and мѫж-ю; отьц-ю, отьц-оу; къназ-ю, къназ-оу; кои-a, мѫж-a, змн-ia.

(c) The G. of the nouns in -н may also be spelt with ѣ instead of -ia: змн-ѣ (§ 10).

(d) The original palatalized velar s [dz] (affricate) becomes a spirant з [z]: N. pl. боsн > возн.

(e) The Greek names in -αῖος, -εύς which in OCS have the ending -ѣн, -ен have in I. sg. and in D. pl. the endings -ѣомь, -ѣомъ: φαρισαῖος > фарнсѣн, I. sg. фарнсѣомь, D. pl. фарнсѣомъ (фарнсѣемъ); ἱερεύς > нерѣн, D. sg. нерѣовн, D. pl. нерѣомъ (§ 45) 'priest'.

(f) In the I. sg. the endings -омь, -емь are replaced, in isolated cases, by -ъмь, -ьмь; D. pl. -омъ is replaced by -ъмъ:гласъмь (Zogr., Mc. i. 26, L. xxiii. 46); съпьрьмь 'with the enemy' (Zogr., Mt. v. 25); мноѣмъ (Savv. Kn., Mt. xxvi. 60). The explanation of this replacement is either to be found in the confusion between o and ъ in strong position which already occurs in OCS (§ 33.1) or else it is due to the influence of West Slavonic (Moravian) where the -ъмь endings are normal. The later explanation seems to be supported by the Kiev Miss. which has only -ъмь in I. sg.

(g) Another factor which tended to encourage the substitution of -ъмь, -ьмь for -омь, -емь was the confusion of the -o- declension and -u- declension. The -u- category was eventually absorbed by the -o- category. As the original endings of the -u- declension were characterized by the ъ element (I. sg. -ъмь, D. pl. -ъмъ, L. pl. -ъхъ, I. pl. -ъмн) (§ 42) the interplay of analogy confused the endings of the two nominal categories.

(h) The above explanation is also supported by the fact that other case endings of the -u- declension appear with nouns of the -o- declension: D. sg. бог-овн (Zogr., Mar., Cloz., Ass., Ps. Sin., Euch. Sin., Supr.): бог-оу, доухові:доухоу, чловѣкові: чловѣкоу, мѫжеві:мѫжоу, цѣсареві:цѣсарю.

(i) The -o- stem endings are replaced by -u- stem endings also in L. sg. дароу 'in the gift', дѫвоу 'in the oak tree', ледоу 'in the ice',

рѧдоу 'in the line' (Supr.), &c., instead of дарѣ, джвѣ, ледѣ, рѧдѣ.

(*j*) I. sg. съньлль 'with the sleep', слоухъль 'with the hearing' (Zogr.), образъль 'with the picture' (Kiev Miss.), сънъмъ 'with sleep', трепетъмъ 'with the trembling' (Supr.), &c., instead of съноль, слоухоль, образоль, трепетоль. In Old Russian texts the regular ending is -ъль. The soft stems may have -*ĭmĭ*: отьцьль 'with the father', ножьль 'with the knife', сжпьрьль 'with the adversary', въпльль 'with the call'.

(*k*) N. pl. попове 'priests' (Euch. Sin., Supr.), доухове 'spirits' (Supr.), грѣхове 'sins' (Supr.), змиеве 'dragons' (Supr.), &c., instead of попи, доуси, грѣси, змии, &c.

(*l*) G. pl. грѣховъ, даровъ, зминевъ (Supr.), &c., instead of грѣхъ, даръ, зоии, &c.

(*m*) I. pl. грѣхъли (Cloz.), апостолъли 'with the apostles' (Supr.), даръли (Euch. Sin.) instead of грѣхъ, апостолъ, даръ.

(*n*) L. pl. даръхъ (Ps. Sin., Euch. Sin.) instead of дарѣхъ, дарохъ (Euch. Sin.) < даръхъ, жидохъ (Supr.) < жидѣхъ (§ 33. 1).

The frequency of the -*u*- stem endings in -*o*- stems varies from text to text, but it is clear that later texts (Supr.) show a greater number of -*u*- stem endings: G. sg. дльгоу (Supr.); the G. sg. лироу, родоу, рѧдоу which occur in Supr. may also represent old -*u*- stems.

(*o*) The V. sg. of the nouns in -*ĭcĭ* is in -*če*: отьць, V. отьче 'father', коупьць, V. коупьче 'merchant'. From кънѧзь 'prince' the V. is кънѧже; Supr. has also кънѧзоу. These vocatives were formed from the stems: *otĭk-, *kupĭk-, *kŭněg- before the working of the third palatalization (§ 30. 1), or they are analogical formations.

(*p*) The masc. -*o*- stems gen. sg. of persons functioned as accusative: да раздроушиши врага и местьника (Ps. viii. 2) 'that thou mightest still the enemy and the avenger'; она же абие оставьша корабь и отьца своего (Mt. iv. 22) 'and they (two) immediately left the ship and their father'.

2. NEUTERS

Singular

Hard stems		Soft stems		
N.	мѣст-о	вѣк-о	знамени-ѥ	сръдьц-е	лож-е
G.	мѣст-а	вѣк-а	знамени-ꙗ	сръдьц-а	лож-а
D.	мѣст-оу	вѣк-оу	знамени-ю	сръдьц-оу	лож-оу
A.	мѣст-о	вѣк-о	знамени-ѥ	сръдьц-е	лож-е
V.	мѣст-о	вѣк-о	знамени-ѥ	сръдьц-е	лож-е
I.	мѣст-омь	вѣк-омь	знамени-ѥмь	сръдьц-емь	лож-емь
L.	мѣст-ѣ	вѣц-ѣ	знамени-и	сръдьц-и	лож-и

Dual

Hard stems		Soft stems		
N. A. V.	мѣст-ѣ	вѣц-ѣ	знамени-и	сръдьц-и	лож-и
G. L.	мѣст-оу	вѣк-оу	знамени-ю	сръдьц-оу	лож-оу
D. I.	мѣст-ома	вѣк-ома	знамени-ѥма	сръдьц-ема	лож-ема

Plural

Hard stems		Soft stems		
N.	мѣст-а	вѣк-а	знамени-ꙗ	сръдьц-а	лож-а
G.	мѣст-ъ	вѣк-ъ	знамени-и	сръдьц-ь	лож-ь
D.	мѣст-омъ	вѣк-омъ	знамени-ѥмъ	сръдьц-емъ	лож-емъ
A.	мѣст-а	вѣк-а	знамени-ꙗ	сръдьц-а	лож-а
V.	мѣст-а	вѣк-а	знамени-ꙗ	сръдьц-а	лож-а
I.	мѣст-ы	вѣк-ы	знамени-и	сръдъц-и	лож-и
L.	мѣст-ѣхъ	вѣц-ѣхъ	знамени-ихъ	сръдьц-ихъ	лож-ихъ

(a) The neuter nouns have identical forms for N. A. V. in each. of the three numbers.

(b) Stems ending in a velar are very rare in the neuter category, and the changes of the velars conform to the second palatalization.

The more frequent suffixes of the neuter -o- stems are: -ло (expressing the idea of the instrument for the accomplishment of the action denoted by the verbal stem): дѣло 'work', масло 'oil', село 'village, settlement', гребло 'oar' (§ 48.4.5); -ьство (forming abstract nouns): божьство 'divinity', чловѣчьство 'humanity', рождьство 'birth', оубииство 'murder'; -ьствие, -ие (forming abstract nouns): пришьствие 'arrival', цѣсарьствие 'kingdom', питие 'drinking', обьштие community', начѧтие 'beginning' (§ 48.3); -иште (denoting places or instruments associated with the meaning of the stem): съборище 'assembly place, synagogue', съньмиште 'id.', съкровиште 'chamber, room, treasure', пристаниште 'harbour, refuge', топориште 'axe-handle'; -ьце (forming diminutives): срьдьце 'heart', слъньце 'sun', чѧдьце 'child' (§ 48.2).

(c) The ending -ие is a development of an older -ье (§ 33.3), and it is often spelt -ье or -ие, -ѥ, -ье in the nom. and in other cases: N. пѣние 'singing', моленье, молене 'prayer' (§ 48.1); I. sg. -ьелнь, -инлнь, -имнь, -ьимнь: дѣланьелнь, блисцанилнь (Cloz.) 'by glittering', хотѣньлнь (Cloz.) 'by the will', обѣданиилнь (Supr.) 'by overeating'; I. pl. цѣсарьствиими (Supr.) 'with the kingdoms', знамении (Zogr.) 'with the signs' are analogous to the adjectival declension (§ 56); L. pl. -иихъ may be contracted to -ихъ: моленихъ; D. pl. -иемъ is replaced in isolated cases by -нимъ: начѧтнимъ 'to the beginnings'.

(d) The neuter -o-/-jo- category adopts, in a very few cases, the endings of the neuter -s- stems of the type слово, G. словесе (§ 38. v. 3; § 44.3): лице, G. личесе instead of лица which prevails in the texts. However, the trend of development is in the other direction, the -s- stems often take the endings of the -o-/-jo- stems (§ 44.3f.).

(e) The endings of the -u- declension penetrated into isolated cases: D. sg. мореви for морю 'sea', D. зьданиеви for зьданю 'building'; I. sg. господьствъмь for господьствомь 'rule, lordship'.

(f) In G. pl. an isolated case shows the ending -еи:врачеи (Ass.) from врачь 'healer' developed from врачьи [vračji] (§ 33.1).

(g) In D. pl. словъмъ occurs once for словомъ (§ 33.1).

(h) In I. pl. the ending -ими appears in: оучениими

'with learning', орѫжьлми 'with weapons', цѣсарьствнилми 'with kingdoms'.

§ 41.

The masculine *-o-/-jo-* stems include a group of nouns with a mixed declension. These nouns are formed by means of the suffixes: (1) [*-ěninŭ*] -ганинъ, -ѣнинъ, -анинъ, -инъ denoting association with a locality or membership of a class of people; (2) [*-telĭ, -arĭ*] -тель, -арь denoting the agent. They decline in the singular according to the *-o-/-jo-* stems, but have the N. pl. in *-e* according to the consonantal stems (§ 44.2.5). The ending [*-ěninŭ*, *-aninŭ*] is reduced in the plural to [*-jane, -ane*]. Nouns of these categories are numerous in OCS texts:

граждднинъ 'citizen'	оучитель 'teacher'
издрдилитѣннинъ 'Israelite'	дѣлатель 'labourer'
болгаринъ 'nobleman'	благодѣтель 'benefactor'
поганинъ 'pagan'	жатель 'reaper'
роумлинъ 'Roman'	хранитель 'guardian'
исполинъ 'giant'	родитель 'parent'

мꙑтарь 'publican'
цѣсарь 'king'
винарь 'vine-labourer'
рꙑбарь 'fisher'
гръначарь 'potter'
вратарь 'janitor'

Plural

N.	гражддне	оучителе	мꙑтаре, мꙑтари
G.	гражданъ	оучитель,-телъ	мꙑтарь, цѣсаръ
D.	гражданелⷨъ	оучителемъ,-лмлъ	мꙑтарелⷨъ,-рьлⷨъ
A.	гражданꙑ	оучителѧ	мꙑтарѧ
V.	гражддне	оучителе	мꙑтаре
I.	гражданꙑ	оучителꙑ	мꙑтаръ, мꙑтари
L.	гражданехъ	оучителехъ,-ихъ	мꙑтарихъ

(a) The A. and I. pl. of the nouns in *-ěninŭ, -aninŭ, -tel'ĭ, -ar'ĭ* have the endings of the *-o-* stems; the *-emŭ* in D. pl. and *-exŭ* in L. pl. are probably on the analogy of the N. The nouns in *-inŭ*

vary in the plural forms: болгаринъ, N. pl. болгаре, G. pl. болгаръ,
D. pl. болгаромъ; воинъ, оилинъ 'warrior', N. pl. вои (Euch.
Sin.), воини, оили (Supr. 90.30), G. pl. воинъ, вои, A. pl.
воинъы, воіа, I. pl. вои.

(b) The singular людинъ (Euch. Sin. 103a, 24) has a pl. людие
'people, folk' (§ 43.a). The nouns крьстигавинъ and поганинъ
have alternative adjectival forms крьстигавъ and поганъ used
as nouns, and form the plural крьстигави, погани. The plural
from господинъ 'master' is господые (-дие), from жидовинъ
'Jew', pl. жидове, жидови; чловѣчинъ appears for чловѣкъ (Supr.
358. 25, 365. 13).

§ 42. III. The -u- stems.

This class consists only of a few masculines whose case-endings
show considerable confusion with those of the -o- stems. In the
course of the later development of the language the -u- stem class
was completely absorbed by the -o- stems: съинъ 'son', волъ 'ox',
врьхъ (врѣхъ) 'top, upper end', домъ 'house', медъ 'honey',
полъ 'half', станъ 'camp', чинъ 'order', гадъ 'poison', ледъ
'ice', санъ 'office, rank'.

	Singular		*Plural*
N.	съин-ъ		съин-ове
G.	съин-оу		съин-овъ
D.	съин-ови		*съин-ъмъ, съин-омъ
A.	съин-ъ		съин-ъі
V.	съин-оу		съин-ове
I.	*съин-ъмь, съин-омь		съин-ъми
L.	съин-оу		*съин-ъхъ, съин-охъ

	Dual
N. A. V.	съин-ъі
G. L.	съин-овоу
D. I.	съин-ъма

(a) In the texts many nouns of this category show the endings
of the -o- stems: V. sg. съине, G. sg. съина, D. sg. съиноу,

L. sg. сꙑнѣ, N. pl. сꙑни, G. pl. сꙑнъ, I. pl. сꙑнꙑ, N. A. V.
du. сꙑна, G. L. du. сꙑноу. In I. sg. and D. pl. -*omĭ*, -*omŭ* have
superseded -*ŭmĭ*, -*ŭmŭ*. Of some old -*u*- stems the texts record
only isolated cases; in only a few instances has the full paradigm
been preserved.

(*b*) -*o*- stem nouns sometimes show endings from the -*u*- stem
category: G. sg. родоу, G. pl. родовъ (Ass., Supr.) from родъ
'birth'; G. sg. гласоу (Ps. Sin.), I. sg. гласъмь (Zogr., Ps. Sin.,
Euch. Sin.) from гласъ 'voice'; N. pl. доухове (Supr.) from доухъ
'spirit'; G. pl. врачевъ (Zogr., Savv. Kn., Supr.) from врачь
'healer, magician', &c. Such examples are numerous and it is
sometimes difficult to tell whether a particular noun is an original
-*u*- or -*o*- stem. Probable old -*u*- stems are: чинъ 'order, rank',
станъ 'camping place', санъ 'rank, dignity', гроздъ, грознъ
'grapes', оудъ 'limb, member', садъ 'garden, plantation', даръ
'gift', грѣхъ 'sin', врачь 'healer', гнои 'dung', змии 'dragon'.

(*c*) The -*u*- stem endings, being more distinctive, have, in some
Slavonic languages, replaced the endings of the other groups.
This tendency is already apparent in OCS. In Ps. Sin. the N. pl.
-ове appears as -ови, by contamination with the -и of the -*o*-
declension: N. pl. сꙑнови, волови.

§ 43. IV. The -*i*- stems.
   This group contains a small number of masc. nouns of the type:
боль 'sick man', гвоздь 'nail', голѫбь 'pigeon', господь
'master, Lord', гость 'guest', грътань 'throat', дръколь 'stick',
звѣрь 'animal', зать 'son-in-law', лакъть 'elbow', медвѣдь
'bear', ногъть 'nail', огнь 'fire', печать 'seal', пѫть 'way,
journey', тать 'thief', тьсть 'father-in-law', чрьвь 'worm',
ѫгль 'coal'. The fem. nouns are very numerous: блѧдь 'error',
вьсь 'village', вѣдь 'science', двьрь 'door', мꙑшь 'mouse',
рѣчь 'speech', соль 'salt', тварь 'creation', мꙑсль 'thought',
дѣтѣль 'action, deed', кѫпѣль 'bath', брань 'fight', болѣзнь
'disease', пѣснь 'song', зависть 'envy, hatred', кость 'bone',
масть 'ointment', съмрьть 'death', страсть 'suffering', чьсть
'honour', чѧсть 'part', юность 'youth', &c.

Singular

	Masculine	Feminine
N.	гост-ь	кост-ь
G.	гост-и	кост-и
D.	гост-и	кост-и
A.	гост-ь	кост-ь
V.	гост-и	кост-и
I.	гост-ьмь,-емь	кост-ыѭ,-иѭ
L.	гост-и	кост-и

Dual

N. A. V.	гост-и	кост-и
G. L.	гост-ью,-ию	кост-ью,-ию
D. I.	гост-ьма	кост-ьма

Plural

N.	гост-ые,-ию	кост-и
G.	гост-ьи,-ии,-еи	кост-ьи,-ии
D.	гост-ьмъ,-емъ	кост-ьмъ,-емъ
A.	гост-и	кост-и
V.	гост-ые,-ию	кост-и
I.	гост-ьми	кост-ьми
L.	гост-ьхъ,-ехъ	кост-ьхъ,-ехъ

(*a*) The plural form люд-ию, -ье 'people' belongs to this declension. The endings of the -*i*- stem nouns tend to fuse with those of the -*jo*- stem declension (§ 40). Thus огнь has a G. sg. огнѣ, огнꙗ alongside огни; господь has a G. sg. господѣ, господа, D. sg. господю, господоу alongside D. sg. господи, V. господи; the forms господа, господоу are from an -*o*- stem господъ. Радость 'gladness' has I. pl. радостьми, but also an adverbial form радоштами 'in gladness'.

(*b*) The endings G. L. du. -ию, I. sg. -иѭ, N. masc. pl. -ие, G. pl. -ии have alternative forms: -ью, -ыѭ, -ье, -ьи. The last appears also as -еи, or contracted to -и. For the explanation of и:ь see § 12.3.

(*c*) In I. masc. sg., D. and L. pl. the reduced vowel *ĭ*, in strong position, is vocalized to *e* (§ 33.1).

(d) One single word of this declension has three genders: masc. трие (трье) 'three', fem. три (трии), neut. три, which decline like -i- stems (§ 59).

(e) The -i- stem declension was absorbed in the later development of the language by the -jo- stems, but some of its endings survived, and so in late OCS texts we already find N. pl. мжжие, G. pl. мжжии, I. pl. мжжьлии for мжжи, мжжь, мжжи.

(f) A few masc. nouns of this declension form some of their cases according to the consonant stems: лакъть 'elbow', G. pl. лакътъ (Zogr., Mar., Ass., Supr., Savv. Kn.), I. pl. лакъты (Supr.); печать 'seal', N. pl. печате (Supr.); D. pl. печатомъ (Cloz.) follows the -o-stems (§ 44.4.c).

§ 44. V. The consonant stems.

1. -v- stems. This declension is divided into several groups according to the final consonant of the stem. The -v- or -ŭv- stems are from the historical point of view long -ū- stems, because their nominative ending goes back to an IE -ūs. From the Slavonic point of view this group has a consonant stem in -v-, and declines like the other consonant stems. It contains only fem. nouns: свекры 'mother-in-law', неплоды 'sterile', брады 'axe', боукъ 'letter', жрьны, жрьны 'millstone', локы 'pool, marshland', любы 'love', смокы 'fig', хоржгы 'flag', црькы 'church', цѣлы 'healing, cure'. In CS *kry 'blood' belonged to this class. In OCS the N. sg. is кръвь or кровь, with vocalized reduced vowel in strong position; the G. sg. кръве shows the ending of the consonant stems, all other cases are those of the fem. -i- stems (§ 43):

	Singular			Dual	
N.	црьк-ы, црък-ы	кръвь	N. A. V.		црькъв-и
G.	црькъв-е,-и	кръв-е,-и	G. L.		црькъв-оу
D.	црькъв-и	кръв-и	D. I.		црькъв-ама
A.	црькъв-ь	кръв-ь			
V.	*црьк-ы	*кръвь			
I.	црькъв-ыж,-иж	кръв-ыж			
L.	црькъв-е	кръв-и			

Plural

N.	цръкъв-и	кръв-и
G.	цръкъв-ъ	кръв-ьи,-ии,-ъ,-ъі
D.	цръкъв-амъ	кръв-ьмъ,-емъ
A.	цръкъв-и	кръв-и
V.	*цръкъв-и	*кръв-и
I.	*цръкъв-ами	кръв-ьми
L.	цръкъв-ахъ	кръв-ьхъ

(*a*) The following alternative endings are found in cases where there is a reduced vowel in strong position: A. цръковь, L. pl. кръвехъ.

(*b*) In the later development of the language the A. цръковь, цръкъвь replaced the N. цръкъі, on the analogy of the -*i*- stems.

(*c*) In the G. sg. the ending -ве is replaced, in isolated cases, by -ви: цр҃къвьви; the same replacement takes place in L. sg. цр҃къвьви.

(*d*) The G. sg. in -ве is used in some texts as A. (Supr.); this function was acquired probably on the analogy of the -*o*- stems, which use the G. of personal nouns as A., and was influenced also by the -*r*- stems, in which group матере and дъштере are used as A. (Ps. Sin., Savv. Kn., Supr.). So, on the pattern of богъ любитъ отьца и матере, съіна и дъштере, the -*v*- stem G. свекръве also acquired an A. function (§ 38.4).

(*e*) The plural had been remodelled on the fem. -*i*- stem pattern in the N., and on the fem. -*a*- stems in the D., I., and L. taking the endings -и, -амъ, -ами, -ахъ.

(*f*) In the G. pl. appear the forms любъ, прълюбъ (for любъвъ, пръ́любъвъ) isolated in the expression не пр́ѣлюбъ д́ѣи 'thou shalt not commit adultery'.

2. -*n*- *stems*. The -*n*- stems have the nominative endings -ъі, -ень for the masc., and -а for the neut. nouns. The ending of the G. is -ен-е. The -*o*- stems in -́книнъ, -анинъ also decline in the plural according to this pattern (§ 41) as well as дьнь 'day' in most of its cases. Masc. nouns in -*n*- are камъі 'stone', пламъі 'flame'; all other -*n*- stems have replaced the N. by the A.: ремень 'strap',

степень 'degree', юлень 'stag', сѧжень 'fathom', корень 'root', прьстень 'finger-ring', ѩчьмень 'barley', also N. камень, пламень. Neut. nouns in -*men*- > -мѧ: имѧ 'name', брѣмѧ 'burden', врѣмѧ 'time', писмѧ 'letter', племѧ 'tribe', сѣмѧ 'seed', чисмѧ 'number', слѣмѧ 'wooden beam', тѣмѧ 'skull, top of the skull'.

Singular

	Masculine			Neuter
N.	кам-ъı, -ень	корен-ь / *кор-ѧ	дьн-ь	им-ѧ
G.	камен-е,-и	корен-е	дьн-е,-и	имен-е
D.	камен-и	корен-и	дьн-и	имен-и
A.	камен-ь	корен-ь	дьн-ь	им-ѧ
I.	камен-ьмь, -емь	корен-ьмь, -емь	дьн-ьмь, -емь	имен-ьмь, -емь
L.	камен-е	корен-е	дьн-е,-и	имен-е

Dual

N. A. V.	камен-и	*корен-и	дьн-и	имен-ѣ,-и
G. L.	*камен-оу	*корен-оу	дьн-оу / дьнь-ю	*имен-оу
D. I.	камен-ьма	*корен-ьма	дьн-ьма	имен-ьма

Plural

N.	*камен-е	*корен-е	дьн-е,-иѥ	имен-а
G.	камен-ъ	*корен-ъ	дьн-ъ	имен-ъ
D.	камен-ьмъ, -емъ	*корен-ьмъ, -емъ	дьн-ьлıъ, -емъ	имен-ьмъ, -емъ
A.	камен-и	*корен-и	дьн-и	имен-а
I.	камен-ьми	*корен-ьмь	дьн-ьми, -ъı	имен-ъı
L.	камен-ьхъ, -ехъ	*корен-ьхъ, -ехъ	дьн-ьхъ, -ехъ	имен-ьхъ,

(a) The N. A. -ъı appears only in камъı and пламъı (in Supr.).

(b) The N. *корѧ, though non-existent in OCS, may be reconstructed on the basis of corresponding OR forms.

(c) In G. sg. -є is replaced, in isolated cases, by -и:врѣмєни (Mar., Mat. xxvi. 16). Also L. sg. in -и instead of -є appears in many texts:имєни (Zogr., Mar., Ass., Savv. Kn., Supr.).

(d) The N. pl. masc. in -є is preserved only in дьнє and in the type граждане, оучитєлє (§ 41). From дьнь there is a pl. form дьнью, дьниѥ; also камъı and корень have a collective form for pl.: камєн-иѥ (-ьѥ), корєн-иѥ (-ьѥ) (§ 48.1).

(e) In G. pl. дьнь has alternative forms: дєнъ, дьньи, дьнєн, дьнии. For the explanation of these forms, as well as for the forms of the I. sg., D., L. pl. see § 12.3, § 33.1; in I. sg. there appears once (Supr.) дьниѩ 'by day' alongside нощтиѩ 'by night'.

(f) In G., L. du. appear also дьнью, дьнию, ѥлєнию.

(g) In the Ps. Sin. there occur a few forms without the vowel є in the stem or with ь for є: L. sg. камни (Ps. xxxix. 3), N. pl. врѣмна (Ps. ciii. 19), G. sg. камьньѣ (Ps. ciii. 12) from камєниѥ.

3. -s- stems. All nouns of this group are neuter and have in the N. sg. the ending -o. The other cases add to the stem the derivative element -es-: слов-о 'word', G. слов-єс-є. Because of the identity of the N. ending with the neuter -o- stems, these -s-stems were absorbed by the -o- stem type. The OCS texts still distinguish clearly between the two types: диво 'miracle', дѣло 'work', дрѣво 'tree', коло 'wheel', люто 'misdeed, vehemence', нєбо 'sky, heaven', тѣло 'body', чюдо 'miracle', око 'eye', оухо 'ear', истєса N. pl. 'kidneys' has no sing. *исто, but appears in du. N. истєсѣ (Ps. Sin. 15. 3–7 in a marginal gloss); from a vanished *liko, replaced by the -jo- stem лицє, there exist -s- forms: G. личєсє, &c. Each of these nouns also appears in the texts with endings from the -o- declension.

	Singular	*Plural*
N.	слов-о	словєс-а
G.	словєс-є, -и	словєс-ъ
D.	словєс-и	словєс-ьмъ, -ємъ
A.	слов-о	словєс-а
V.	слов-о	словєс-а
I.	словєс-ьмь, -ємь	словєс-ъı
L.	словєс-є, -и	словєс-ьхъ, -єхъ

Dual

N. A. V.   словес-ѣ, -и
G. L.   словес-оу
D. I.   *словес-ьма

(a) The nouns око and оухо seldom form a plural, they occur more frequently in a -i- stem dual form:

N. A. V.	очи	оуши
G. L.	очию, очью	оушию, оушью
D. I.	очима	оушима

(b) In the G. sg. the ending -и appears in Ass., Ps. Sin., Euch. Sin., and in later texts.

(c) In the L. sg. the ending -и appears alongside the ending -е in the older texts; -и predominates in Euch. Sin. and in Ps. Sin.; Ass., Supr. have only -и forms.

(d) For the explanation of the alternative forms in I. sg., D. pl., L. pl. see § 33.1.

(e) The N. A. du. in -и appears in Supr.

(f) As a result of the mixing of the -s- and -o- neuters we find in the texts hybrid forms: N. pl. слова (Zogr., Supr.), D. pl. тѣломъ, instead of тѣлесьмъ, are found in Euch. Sin. and in Supr., D. sg. небоу (Zogr., Mar., Supr., Savv. Kn.), I. sg. неболь (Mar., Zogr.), D. sg. словоу (Ass., Supr.), D. sg. оухоу (Zogr., Mar., Ps. Sin.), G. sg. ока (Ass., Ps. Sin.), I. sg. околь (Mar., Zogr., Ps. Sin., Euch. Sin.), L. sg. оцѣ (Mar. Zogr.), &c.

(g) Because of this interpenetration of the two declensions it is sometimes difficult to establish the original class of a noun, e.g. дѣло, which appears in G. дѣлесе and дѣла, I. дѣлесемь and дѣломь, D. pl. дѣлесемъ and дѣломъ, &c., could be an original -o- stem which entered the -s- declension.

(h) Other -o- nouns which appear in texts with endings of the -s- type declension are: иго 'yoke', N. pl. ижеса, чрѣво 'stomach', N. pl. чрѣвеса, &c.

4. -nt- stems. The neut. -nt- stems have in the N. the ending -ѧ, in the other cases the stem ends in -ęt- < -ent-. The nouns of this group designate young living creatures and are diminutives. Recorded in the texts are: отрочѧ 'child', агнѧ 'lamb',

жрѣба 'foal', клюса 'transport animal', козьла 'kid', овьча 'lamb', осьла 'donkey'.

	Singular	Plural
N.	отроч-а	*отрочат-а
G.	отрочат-е	отрочат-ъ
D.	*отрочат-и	*отрочат-ьлїъ, -емъ
A.	отроч-а	*отрочат-а
V.	отроч-а	*отрочат-а
I.	*отрочат-ьлїь, -емь	*отрочат-ы
L.	отрочат-е, -и	*отрочат-ьхъ, -ехъ

	Dual
N. A. V.	*отрочат-ѣ
G. L.	*отрочат-оу
D. I.	*отрочат-ьма

(a) Most of the cases (I. sg., the du., the pl.) are reconstructed on the analogy of the other consonant stems; they do not occur in the texts.

(b) In later Slavonic texts the G. sg. in -и appears instead of the OCS -е. Also a L. sg. in -и appears in later OCS texts.

(c) Some nouns in -ть belonging to the -i- stem declension show cases of the -et- stems: G. pl. лакътъ from лакъть 'elbow', N. pl. печате from печать 'seal', L. sg. десате, N. pl. десате, G. pl. десатъ, I. pl. десаты from десать 'ten' (§ 43.ƒ).

5. -r- stems. This declension comprises two fem. nouns: мати 'mother' and дъшти 'daughter'.

	Singular	Plural
N.	мат-и	матер-и
G.	матер-е, -и	матер-ъ
D.	матер-и	матер-ьлїъ, -емъ
A.	матер-ь, -е	матер-и
V.	мати	матер-и
I.	матер-ыж, -иж	матер-ьлїи
L.	*матер-и	*матер-ьхъ, матер-ехъ

Dual

N. A. V.	*матер-и	*дъшер-и
G. L.	*матер-оу	дъшер-ью (late form)
D. I.	*матер-ьма	дъшер-ьма

(a) The declension of these fem. nouns became intermingled with the fem. declension of the -*i*- stems: e.g. in I. and L. sg.

(b) The G. sg. in -и appears in Supr., Ps. Sin., Euch. Sin. Some texts (Ps. Sin., Savv. Kn., Supr.) use the G. in the function of the A. sg.: чьти отьца и матере (Savv. Kn., Mt. xix. 19).

(c) In the G. pl. there appears a form дъштереı, i.e. дъштерьи (Ps. Sin. cv. 38) on the analogy of the -*i*- stems.

(d) The numeral четъıре follows this declension: N. masc. четъıре, fem., neut. четъıри, G. четъıръ, четъıрь (Supr., Zogr., Ass., Savv. Kn.), D. четъıремъ, A. четъıри, I. четъıрьмь, L. четъıрехъ (§ 59.1).

(e) The declension of дъшти, G. дъштере follows the paradigm of мати.

DECLENSION OF NAMES OF GREEK ORIGIN

§ 45. The Greek text of the Bible presented the translator with numerous proper names, many of them indeclinable. As a rule these Greek names entered a Slavonic declension: those ending in -ος were declined as -*o*- stems, e.g. Πέτρος > Петръ, G. Петра; 'Αβραάμ > Авраамъ, G. Авраама; the ending -ιος was assimilated by the -*jo*- stems, e.g. Γρηγόριος > Григории, G. Григориıа; The original gender was usually preserved, as shown by the preceding example, and by the following: 'Ελισάβετ > Ѥлисаветь according to the fem. -*i*- stems; Εὐδοκία > Ѥвдокиıа.

The Greek names in -εύς and -αῖος are generally rendered as -*jo*- stems which, however, also present some forms of the hard category: ἱερεύς > ниереи, нереи, G. sg. ниереа, D. sg. ниереови, D. pl. ниереомъ; архнереи < ἀρχιερεύς, G. sg. архиереа, (-ѣа); 'Ιουδαῖος > июдѣи, июдеи; φαρισαῖος > фарисѣи, фарисеи. The V. is either in -е or in -ю: фарисею; Ζακχαῖος > Закхѣи, V. Закхѵе = Ζακχαῖε.

The names in -*as* enter the -*a*- declension while preserving the original masc. gender: Ιούδας > Июда, Καϊάφας > Каиѧфа, Σατα-νᾶς > Сотона. In later texts we sometimes find these nouns as -*o*- stems: 'Ανίνας > Анина, Анинъ (Ps. Sin.), 'Αγρίππας > Агрипа, Агрипъ (Supr.). The names in -*ιas* take the ending -*ja*: Ζαχαρίας > Захарига, Μεσσίας > Месига; 'Ησαΐας > Исанга. The declension, however, is not consistent with the paradigm. Endings of the -*o*-/-*jo*- or -*u*- stems appear in many cases: I. Исаиемь; 'Ιερεμίας > Іеремига, I. Іеремиемь; D. Андрькови: Андрька < 'Ανδρέας.

The names in -*ηs* take the ending -*и* and have a mixed declension: Μωυσῆς > Мюси (Мюнсин), G. Моська, Мосеа, D. Москови, Москеви, Москю, Мосею, A. Мюси, Мюнсиж, I. Москемь, Мосеемь, Москомь, L. Моськи, Мосии.

The names in -*ιs* are treated as masc. -*ija*- stems (§ 39) of the type сждьи, сждии: Λευείς, λευί 'Levi' > леуѣин (= левгин), A. леуѣниж; the ħ = *g'* represents the soft velar of the Greek form λευγίς; Δεκάπολις is attested in G. Декаполька (Zogr.), Декаполѣ (Zogr., Ass.), Декаполига (Savv. Kn.), L. Декаполи (Zogr.).

Fem. nouns in -*a*, -*ía*, -*aía*, which are indeclinable in Greek, enter the -*a*-/-*ja*- declension and take the endings of this declension: γέεννα > ħеона (= геона), A. sg. ħеонж, &c.; Ἄννα > Анна, G. Анны; ἐν Σινά > въ Синѣ. Examples which show endings of the -*ja*- stems are explained by the Greek oblique cases in which -*a* is replaced by -*η*: Σμύρνα, G. Σμύρνης: L. sg. въ Змурнии. The word Кана < Κανᾶ is not declined in OCS because it was considered as the first part of a compound name: Κανᾶ Γαλιλαίας.

Greek names, containing -*λ* in the ending, have a soft *l'* or a hard *l*, and are accordingly declined as -*jo*- or -*o*- stems: Ἄβελ > Авель, Авелъ; 'Ισραήλ > Издраиль, Израиль; Даниилъ, Гавриилъ, Михаилъ (§ 40.1).

The feminine nouns in -*η*, -*ή* take the ending -*ии* (§ 39.*b*): παρασκευή > параскевьħии 'the day before the Sabbath', Μαγδαληνή > Магдалыйни, Магдалинйи.

Greek common nouns follow the same general rule by fitting into one of the OCS paradigms: σκάνδαλον > скандалъ 'offence,

temptation'; πραιτώριον > преторъ 'palace'; χρῖσμα > хризма
'oil, ointment'; θυμίαμα > тьмиꙗнъ 'incense'; εὐαγγέλιον >
еваньгелиѥ 'Gospel'.

NOMINAL ENDINGS

§ 46. The following equations of the case-endings are to be re-
garded as a hypothetical attempt at explaining the Slavonic flexional
system in relation to the IE prototype (cf. O. Hujer, *Slovanská
deklinace jmenná*, 1891).

1. *Nominative singular.*

-а, -ꙗ < -ā, -i̯ā (жен-а, доуш-а, земл-ꙗ) correspond to an
original -ā which appears also in other IE languages: Gr.
θεά 'goddess', Lat. *equa* 'mare', Lith. *rankà* 'hand, arm', Gr.
μυῖα 'fly', χώρα 'country'.

-ь < -i (кост-ь, пѫт-ь) corresponds to an original -*is*: Gr. πόλις
'city', Lat. *ovis*, Skt *áviḥ* 'sheep'.

-ъ < -u (сꙑн-ъ, вол-ъ) corresponds to an original -*us*: Lat.
manus 'hand', Lith. *sūnùs* 'son', Goth. *sunus* id., Skt *sūnúḥ*
id., Gr. πῆχυς 'the fore-arm'.

-и, -ьи < -ī/-i̯ā (богꙑн-и fem., лад-ьи fem., сѫд-ьи masc.,
несѫшт-и fem. pr. part., несъш-и fem. p. part., мьньш-и fem.
comp.) corresponds to an original -*ī*: Goth. *frijōndi* fem.
'friend', Lith. *patì* 'wife, mistress, woman', Skt *bhárantī*:
OCS верѫшти, Skt *vidúšī*: OCS ведъши.

-ꙑ < -ū (свекр-ꙑ, *kry) corresponds to an original -*ūs*: Skt
śvaśrūḥ 'husband's mother', Lat. *socrūs* 'mother-in-law', Skt
krū-ráḥ 'bloody', Gr. ῦς 'swine, wild boar'.

-ꙑ (кам-ꙑ, пламꙑ). The origin of this ending is not
clear. It may go back to a IE -*ons* (< *kamōns*) (cf. acc. pl.
of the -*o*- stems), or to an IE -*ōn* (cf. Gr. ἀηδών, -ονος 'the
nightingale', Lat. *homo, hominis*), or to an IE -*ēn* (cf. Gr.
ποιμήν, ποιμένος 'shepherd'). The difficulty inherent in this
explanation lies in the unusual equation *ōn:y*. This also
appears, however, in the case of the pr. part. act. вер-ꙑ: Gr.
φέρων, but here we may postulate a base *bherōnt-: Gr. φέροντ-,
in which case the ending is -*ōnts* (cf. Goth. *frijōnds* friend').

-ъ, -ь (-и) < -*us* < -*os*, -*ios*; -о, -ѥ < -*os*, -*on*, -*ion* (рав-'ь, мѫж-ь, кра-и; дѣл-о, мор̑-е, слов-о). These endings should be explained together because they form one morphological category. Their origin is complicated and not entirely clear. The corresponding IE forms are: OLat. *serv-os* 'slave' (Classical Lat. *servus*), Gr. λύκ-ος 'wolf', Lith. *vil̃kas* 'wolf', Skt *vr̥'kaḥ* 'wolf', Lat. *al-ius* 'other'; Lat. *verb-um* 'word', Gr. ἔργον 'work', Lat. *init-ium* 'beginning', Lat. *gen-us*, Gr. γένος 'race, stock'. The difficulty of explaining these endings consists in the fact that in the masculine -*ŭ* and in the neuter -*o* correspond to an original -*os* (cf. Gr. κλέϝος 'rumour': CS *slovo*). The other neuter type in -*on* (cf. Gr. ἔργον 'work', Lat. *verbum*) should result in Slavonic -*ŭ* (cf. aor. ἔλαβον: OCS ведъ). In order to explain these difficulties it has been assumed that the neuter cases in Slavonic were formed by analogy with the pronoun *to, ta* and that the masculine endings represent the regular development. The explanation by analogy with the pronoun, however, is not entirely satisfactory, and the regularity of the masculine ending is obscured by the fact that -*os* in nom. and -*om* in acc. underwent the same treatment: -*ŭ* (cf. S. Agrell, *Zur Geschichte des idg. Neutrums*, 1926).

-ъ < -*us*, -въ < -*ṷus* (нес-ъ, дѣла-въ): Skt *vidúš*: Sl. вѣд-ъ (p. part. act.); Skt *babhūvúš* (part. pf.): OCS бꙑвъ (p. part. act.).

·-ѧ < -*en* (сѣм-ѧ), -ѧ < -*ent*-, -*int*- (агн-ѧ, хвал-ѧ) which may go back to an IE -*n̥*-, -*n̥t*-: Lat. *sēmen* 'seed', Skt *nā́ma* 'name', Goth. *namō*, Gr. φέρον, -τος, Gr. κοράσιον 'a little girl, maiden' < -*n̥t-iion*.

-и (мат-и, дъшт-и) very probably represents an original -*ē* with a falling intonation as appears from Lith. *mótė* 'wife', *duktė̃* 'daughter', Skt *mātā́* 'mother', *duhitā́* 'daughter'. The Slavonic, Baltic, and Skt forms postulate a prototype without the -*r*- suffix, whereas other IE languages presuppose forms with the -*r*- suffix: Lat. *mater*, Gr. θυγάτηρ 'daughter', Goth. *daúhtar*.

2. Nominative plural.

-ъı, -ıѧ = acc. plur. (жєн-ъı, доүш-ѧ, зємłѧ-ıѧ). The original ending was *-ās* (cf. Skt *aśvās*) parallel to the consonant stems, or a secondary diphthong in Latin and Greek (*terrae*, χῶραι). Because of the difficulty of explaining the development of Sl. *-y* < *-ās*, the nom. plur. of the *-ā-* stems has been explained as an original accusative (§ 46.6). A similar difficulty arises in the explanation of the ending *-i-* in the nom. plur. of the *-o-* stems.

-и < *-oi̯* (раб-и, крѧ-и) is of pronominal origin. The IE ending was *-ōs* (masc.), *-ās* (fem.). This ending appears in Teutonic nouns (cf. Goth. *wulfōs* 'wolves') and in Skt adjectives (cf. *brāhmaṇās* 'belonging to a Brahman'). In Slavonic these endings would have been reflected by *-ās* (§ 6.1.2). The ending *-oi̯* has been taken over from the demonstrative pronouns (cf. Gr. τοί 'those', OCS ти, они 'these'); this pronominal ending appears in Slavonic, Lat., Gr., Celtic with nouns (cf. Lat. *lupī* < **lup-oe* 'wolves', Gr. λύκοι 'wolves') and in Teutonic with adjectives (cf. Goth. *blindai* 'blind'). (Cf. A. Meillet, *Le slave commun*, 1934, 408.)

-є, -ıє, -овє, -ѧнє, -ѧрє, -єлє (пѧтъ-ıє, съıн-овє, грѧжд-ѧнє, мъıт-ѧрє, оүчит-єлє). The ending *-e* in all these suffixes corresponds to IE *-es/-i̯es*: Lat. *hostēs*, Gr. ἡγεμόνες 'leaders', Skt *sūnávaḥ* 'sons'. The consonant stems and the pr. part. act. take the same ending: мѧтєрє : Lat. *matres*, вєдѧшт-є : Lat. *laudantes*, трнıє 'three' < IE **trei̯es* (cf. Skt *tráyaḥ*).

-и (кост-и). The ending of the fem. *-i-* stems is explained as an original accusative ending in the same way as the nom. pl. of the *-ā-* stems (§ 46.2.6).

-ѧ < *-ā* (мѣст-ѧ, словєс-ѧ, имєн-ѧ, тєлѧт-ѧ) is the same ending that we find in the nom. sg. of the *-ā-* stems. The neut. pl. form is in origin a collective feminine noun.

3. Nominative and accusative dual.

-ѧ < *-ō* (влькк-ѧ, раб-ѧ). The same ending appears in Gr. λύκω 'two wolves', Lat. *duo, ambo*, Vedic *vŕkā*, Lith. *vilkù* < *-ő* 'two wolves'.

-ъ̈к < -o*i̯* < -o-+-*i̯* (мѣ̈ст-ъ̈к). The ending -o*i̯* represents the final stem vowel of the neuter -o- and the ending -*i*. The same diphthongal origin is suggested by Skt *jugé* 'both yokes'.

-ъ̈к < -a*i̯* < -ə*i̯* (жен-ъ̈к). The ending -ə*i̯* represents the reducea grade of -ā*i̯*. The ending -*ě* of the du. fem. could hardly represent the diphthong -o*i̯* of the masc. nouns. Lithuanian too has different endings in the two categories: *ranki* 'two hands' and *gërëji* 'two drinkers'. There is a difficulty also in deriving this -*ě* directly from the diphthong -a*i̯* because of its rising intonation as shown by Lith. *rankì* (§ 10.2). Therefore, as in the case of -*ě* in the masc. nouns, it seems that this ending represents a combination of the du. -*i* ending of the consonantal stems (see below) added to the final -*a* of the stem, i.e. to its reduced grade -ə*i̯*.

-и < -*i* (кост-и, гост-и). This ending appears also in corresponding forms of other IE languages: Lith. *avì*, Skt *ávī* 'both sheep'.

-ъı < -*ū* (съ̈ıн-ъı). This ending appears only in isolated examples, because the -*ū* stems have been assimilated to the -o stems: съ̈ınа 'both sons' (§ 42.*a*).

-и (камен-и, дьн-и). In view of the fact that other IE languages do not have this ending in the masc. and fem. consonantal nouns, this -*i* is considered as being an analogical formation from the -*i* nouns. In the corresponding noun category Greek has the ending -*e* (Gr. πόδε 'two feet', μητέρε 'two mothers') which represents the IE ending of the consonantal stems in the dual. The neuter consonantal nouns have the ending -*i* or -*ě*: имени or именѣ̈. The -*ě* has been taken over from the -o stems. The -*i* ending appears also in очи, оүши (§ 44.3).

4. Vocative singular.

-е < -*e* (рав-е, вож-е). The ending is of IE origin: Lat. *domine*, Gr. λύκε 'wolf'.

-оү < -o*u̯* (кра-ю, мжж-оү). This ending has been taken over from the -*u*- stem nouns (съ̈ıноү). It is of diphthongal origin (cf. Lith. *sūnaũ*, Skt *sūnő*, Goth. *sunau*).

-и < -ei̯ (кост-и) seems to be also of diphthongal origin if it is compared with other IE cognates: Lith. akẽ 'eye', Skt ágnē.

-о < -a (жен-о). Latin and Greek have in this case the ending -a: poeta, νύμφα (§ 7). In the plur. and dual the voc. is identical with the nom.

5. Accusative singular.

-ж < -ām (жен-ж, доүш-ж) which appears also in other IE languages: Lat. equam, Gr. θεάν, Lith. rañką (§ 13.3).

-ь < -im (гост-ь) compares with Lat. turrim 'tower', Gr. πόλιν 'city'.

-ъ < -um (сын-ъ, вол-ъ) compares with Skt sūnúm 'son', Lat. portum 'harbour'.

-ь < -m̥ (свекр̑ъв-ь). Long -ū- developed, in these stems, into -ŭu̯-, which changed in Slavonic into -ŭv-. The acc. *svekrŭu̯m̥ became svekrŭvǐ. The same origin accounts for the ending -ь in the acc. of consonantal stems (камень, матерь) which compare with Lat. matrem, hominem, Gr. μητέρα, ἄκμονα 'anvil', Skt mātáram, áśmānam 'stone', Lith. móteri̯, akmeni̯ 'stone' (§ 16.3).

-ъ < -um < -om (раб-ъ) compare with Lat. servum < servom, Gr. ἵππον 'horse', Skt áśvam 'horse'. When the preceding vowel was short the -m disappeared.

-ь < -im or -i̯um (кра-и, кон-ь). The ending of the soft stems is ambiguous. It may go back to -im, as -ь of the nom. may go back to -is, or it may represent -i̯um > -i̯ŭ > -i̯ĭ. The difficulty which complicates the latter development is of a chronological nature, namely -i̯um could not represent a development of -i̯om because this should have changed into Slavonic i̯ę (§ 46.6), as shown also by кра⟨ѩ⟩ (acc. pl.) < *krajons or by морѥ < *morjom, before having reached the stage -i̯um. The working of analogy may also have played some part in this process.

6. Accusative plural.

-ы < -ūs < -ons (влък-ы, жен-ы) (§ 9.2). The ending -ons is attested by Gr. (Cretan) λυκονς (Attic λύκους), Lat. lupōs < *lupons, Goth. wulfans, OPr deiwans, Lat. deos (§ 9.2).

-ъı < -ūs < -ųs < -ūns < -ŭns (съın-ъı), cf. Goth. *sununs*
Skt *sūnūn* 'sons' (§ 9.2).

-и < -is < -įs < -ins < -ĭns (пѫт-и, камен-и), cf. Gr. (Cretan)
πόλινς 'cities', Skt *agnīn* 'lambs'.

-ѧ < -jons (кон-ıѧ, зеѧıл-ıѧ). After *j* the treatment of -ons was
different from that described in § 9.2. The development of
this group is reconstructed by the following stages: *jens* >
-*jęns* > -*ję* (§ 14.3). In a dialectal area (Western and Eastern
Slavonic) the nasalization disappeared and so the ending -*ě*
arose in acc. pl. and gen. sg.: OR кон'ѣ, доуш'ѣ, OCz *dušě*.

-a (словес-a, мѣст-a): see nom. pl. endings (§ 46.2).

7. *Genitive singular.*

-ъı < -ōns (жен-ъı). For the development of -ons see § 9.2.
The probability of this origin of the gen. ending is supported
by its presence in other IE languages: Lat. *serm-ōnis, reg-iōnis*,
Goth. *tugg-ōns* 'tongue'. The ending has been taken over
from the -*n*- stem nouns. Some of the -*a*- stems are original
-*n*- stems: *voda* (cf. Skt *udán-*, G. *udn-áḥ*), *žena* (cf. Goth.
quinō, G. *quinōns*).

-ѧ < -jōns (доуш-ѧ). The explanation of the origin of -ъı from
-ōns applies also to this ending. Attempts have been made to
explain the -ъı as a continuation of -*ās* in view of the fact that
the accusative has the ending -*ām*, and of the existence of
gen. -*ās* ending in other IE languages (cf. Lat. (*pater*) *familiās*,
Skt *dēvyāḥ* 'goddess', Lith. *rañkos* 'hand', Gr. χώρᾱς 'country').
The ending -*ę* of the soft stems argues against this explanation.
Some authorities consider it analogical to A. pl. (cf. A. Meillet,
Le slave commun, 1934, 398).

-a, -ıа < -*ād* < -*ōd* (раб-a, крa-ıа). The genitive has been
explained as representing an original ablative (cf. Skt ablative
vṛkāt, vṛkād 'wolf'; Lat. *lupō* < **lupōd, eō* < OLat. *eōd*). The
origin of the ending -*ōd* (-*ōt*) is not clear. It may be an original
preposition. In other stems too the genitive was originally
identical with the ablative; so: пѫти, полоу, имене continue
IE genitive-ablative forms.

-е < -es/-os (камен-е, словес-е, матер-е, телат-е) represents the IE genitive-ablative ending of the consonantal stems in the e grade (cf. Gr. πατρός, Lat. *hominis*).

-и < -eis/-ois (пѫт-и) represents the stem vowel -*i*- which was originally followed by -s (cf. Lat. *pont-is* 'bridge').

-оү < -eus/-ous (сꙑн-оү, доли-оү) represents the IE -*eu̯/-ou̯* which was followed by -s (cf. Lith. *sūnaũs* 'son', Goth. *sunaus* 'son', Lat. *manūs* 'hand'.

8. Genitive plural.

-ъ, -ь < -*um* < -*om* (раб-ъ, мѫж-ь, жен-ъ, доүш-ь, сꙑн-ов-ъ, пѫть-и [*pǫti̯-ji̯*], камен-ъ, матер-ъ). All stems have the same ending -*u* which changes into -*i* after *j*. The other IE languages, however, show a long ending: Gr. θεῶν, Lat. *deūm*, Lith. *vilkũ*, Skt *vŕ̥kām*. The Slavonic short vowel is difficult to explain because there are no other examples of a shortened vowel in this position. The attempt to account for the shortening of -*ōm* by its falling intonation is not supported by other cases. One may suppose that in IE a short ending existed alongside the long one, as posited also by OPr -*an* (*grikan* 'of the sins'), Lat. -*om* (*Romanom, Romanum* 'of the Romans'), and by Irish (*maqua* 'of the sons') (A. Meillet, *Le slave commun*, 1934, 394).

9. Genitive and locative dual.

-оү < -au, -ou, -eu (раб-оү, рѫк-оү, ноштъ-ю, сꙑнов-оү, камен-оү). The same ending appears in the Lith. preposition (originally a gen. loc.) *pusiaũ* 'between' from *pùsė* 'half', just as OCS междоү is an original loc. du. from межда 'boundary'.

10. Dative singular.

-ѣ, -и < -*āi̯* (жен-ѣ, доүш-и). The origin of this ending is clear. It goes back to the diphthong which appears in Lat. *terrae*, Gr. θεᾷ, Lith. *rañkai*. The soft stems have the corresponding ending -*i*.

-оү < -*ōi̯* (раб-оү). On the analogy of the preceding fem. ending it has been accepted that the masc. ending also represents

a diphthong—that attested by Gr. θεῷ, OLat. *populoi*, Lith. *vilkui*. Though the postulated development -*ōi̯* > -*ōü* > -*ōu̯* > -*ou̯* > -*u* is unusual, it might be confirmed by the development of the instr. plur. ending -*y* < -*ōi̯s* (§ 46.14).

The explanation of this ending by analogy from the loc. of the -*u*- stems is not probable in view of the fact that there are no other cases of the working of analogy between these two categories in the prehistoric period, and that the fusion of the two nominal categories is a phenomenon of late date.

-и < -*ai̯* (пѫт-и, кост-и, сынов-и, камен-и, матер-и, словес-и). The origin of this ending is not clear. It might have been taken over from the consonantal stems (which have acc. sg. in -*ĭ*, identical with the acc. of the -*i*- stems) just as the Lat. *ov-ĭ* has taken its ending from the consonantal stem *homin-ĭ*, or it may represent an original diphthong. The latter derivation presents difficulties because the other IE languages have the ending -*ei̯*/-*ai̯* (parallel to -*eu̯*/-*ai̯* of the -*u*- stems) which should develop into Slavonic -*ĭji*. To meet this difficulty haplology of the two diphthongs, in the IE period, has been suggested (A. Meillet, *Le slave commun*, 1934, 418); thus we might postulate: **kostei̯ai̯* > **kostei̯ei̯* > **kostei̯* > *kosti*; **sūneu̯ai* > *synovi* (cf. Lat. *senatui*, Skt *sūnáve* 'son', Skt *agnaye* 'lamb').

11. Dative plural.

-мъ (доуша-мъ, рабо-мъ, кость-мъ, камень-мъ). To the ending -*bhos*, -*bhi̯os* (cf. Lat. -*bus*, Celtic -*bo*, Skt -*bhias*) corresponds in Slavonic (and also in Baltic and Germanic) an original ending -*mos*. However, in view of the fact that the development -*os* > -*ŭ* is no more than a hypothesis (§ 46.1), the explanation of -*mŭ* from -*mos* is not entirely satisfactory. Therefore the existence of an original ending -*mon* (-*mom*) alongside -*mos* has been assumed. A dative ending with a nasal appears in Skt -*bhi̯ām* (dat., abl., instr., du.) and this ending could justify a prototype -*mom* for the Slavonic dialect (cf. матерьмъ : OCeltic *matre-bo(s)*, Lat. *matri-bus*; влькомъ, Lith. *vilkams*, Skt *vŕ̥kebhyaḥ*).

12. Dative and instrumental dual.

-ма (жена-ма, ра́бо-ма, кость-ма). This ending may go back to -mā, -mō, -mās, -mōs; it has the consonant m, like the Baltic languages (cf. Lith. *rañkoma*: OCS ржкама, to which in Skt corresponds -bh-: Skt *vṛkābhjām*, OCS влькома, Lith. *vilkam̃*).

13. Instrumental singular.

-ОІѪ < -oi̯ām (ржк-оіѪ, доүш-еіѪ, кост-ьіѪ, мъ̈н-оіѪ, т-оіѪ). This ending represents a contamination of the pronominal ending -ojǫ < -oi̯ām -oi̯ā (cf. Skt *táyā*) with the nominal ending -ǫ < -ām (cf. Lith *rankǭ* < *ronkấm). The old instr. in -ǫ < -ām has been replaced in OCS by the instr. in -ojǫ. A similar development is illustrated by Skt *áśvajā* for Vedic *áśvā*. The forms in -ǫ of the OCS texts of the type ржкѪ are new formations by contraction of the ending -ojǫ, or they are archaisms.

-мь < -mi (ра́бо-мь, съінъ-ль, пѫть-мь, словесь-мь). The origin of this ending is not clear. It goes back to -mi, but the -o- stems of other IE languages have an original ending -ṓ: Lith. *vilkù*, Goth. *wulfa*, Avesta *vəhrka*. The -mi appears in Lith. -i- stems (*naktimì* 'with the night') and -u- stems (*sūnumì* 'with the son') and corresponds to -bhi in Greek (ἶ-φι 'with strength') and Armenian (*marb* 'with the mother' < *mātṛ-bhi).

14. Instrumental plural.

-ми < -mī (жена-ми, съінъ-ми, пѫть-ми, матерь-ми). The ending -mī or -mīs is postulated also by Lithuanian which forms the instr. pl. in -mis (except from the -o- stems): *rañkomis*: *rǫkami*, *sūnumis*: *synŭmi*. To -m- corresponds -bh- in Skt *mātṛ́bhiḥ*, Irish *māthraib*, Armenian *marbkʻ* 'with the mothers' (§ 46.11).

-ъі, -и < -ōis (ра́б-ъі, кра-и, моѯ̂-и, словес-ъі, имен-ъі, гра́жда́н-ъі). To the Slavonic -y corresponds in Baltic -ais and in Skt -āis (in the -o- stems), in Lat. -is, in Gr. -ois (cf. Lith. *vilkaĩs*, Skt *vṛkaiḥ*, Lat. *lupīs*, Gr. λύκοις). The development -ōis > -y presents difficulties; generally the development

-ōis > ūis (> ūu̯s) > -ūs > y has been postulated. Hujer suggests the possibility of explaining the instr. plur. of the hard -o- stems (rab-y) on the analogy of the soft -jo- stems (kraj-i), the -i being a normal development of -ois. A. Meillet (Le slave commun, 1934, 153) explains the development -ōis > y as being parallel to the development -ons > y (§ 9.2).

15. Locative singular.

-ѣ, -и < -ai̯ < -a- + -i (жен-ѣ дроуш-и). This ending appears also in Lat. loc. Romae, Gr. θεᾷ (dat. sg.) (§ 46.10).

-ѣ, -и < -oi̯ (раб-ѣ, кра-и). The corresponding Greek case is οἴκοι 'at home', Lith. vilkė 'wolf', Skt vŕ̥ke id., Lat. domi 'at home' (§ 10.2, § 23.1).

-и < -ēi̯ (пѫт-и, кост-и). The same ending appears in Homeric Gr. πόληι.

-оу < -ēu̯, -ōu̯ (дом-оу, съін-оу). This ending appears in Lat. noctū, Goth. sunau, Skt sūnáu.

-e (дьн-e, небес-e, цръкъв-e). This category of nouns had originally a loc. form with zero ending: *nebes like Gr. αἰές, αἰέν = Attic αἰεί 'always'. The ending -e, of obscure origin, has been added to the stem. We find the same ending in Lith. loc. sg. of the -ā- stems rañkoj-e 'in the hand' < *rankāi+e.

16. Locative plural.

-хъ < -su (жена-хъ, рабѣ-хъ, гости-хъ, съін-хъ, камень-хъ, матерь-хъ) (§ 10.2). This ending is common to the Indo-Iranian, Slavonic, and Baltic languages (Old Lithuanian -su, Modern Lithuanian -se), Gr. -si: Skt náktiṣu, vŕ̥keṣu, Lith. rañkosu, rañkose, Gr. (Homer) λύκοισι. For the change s > x see § 22.1. Forms with s have been preserved in locatives of Czech names of tribes like Lužas from Lužane, Pol'as from Poljane for Lužanexŭ, Poljanexŭ.

FORMATION OF NOUNS

§ 47. The vocabulary was largely increased by means of composition and of suffixal derivation. A great number of compound nouns are translations of Greek compounds: благословлѥнниѥ 'blessing' =

εὐλογία, жестокосръдиіе 'hardness of the heart, stubbornness' = σκληροκαρδία, малодоушніе 'timidity' = μικροψυχία, дльго-тръпѣниіе 'long-suffering, patience' = μακροθυμία, законо-оучитель 'law-teacher' = νομοδιδάσκαλος, пѫтьшьствиіе 'journey' = ὁδοιπορία, рѫкопьсаниіе 'handwriting, bond' = χειρόγραφον.

Of Teutonic origin are the compounds: малъжена 'wife' (cf. MHG māl-wîp 'wife', māl = 'agreement'), оусерагъ, оусерѧсь 'ear-ring' < Goth. *ausariggs < T *ausan (Goth. ausō) 'ear'+T *hringa 'ring', MHG öserinc 'a coin'.

From the point of view of the constituent elements and their endings there are different types of compound nouns.

The most productive type is that in which the first element is represented by a noun showing the -o- stem vowel: водоносъ, водоносъ 'water-pot, urn', кръвопролитиіе 'blood-shedding', виноградъ 'vineyard', Богородица = Gr. Θεοτόκος, рѫкотворенъ 'made by hand' = Gr. χειροποίητος, воіеводѧ 'war-leader' = OHG heri-zogo, G Herzog, which is a translation of Byzantine Greek στρατηλάτης 'army-commander'.

The first part of the compound could be an adjective: соухорѫкъ 'with a dried hand', маломоштъ 'weak', тѧжькосрѧдъ 'low-spirited, stupid' = Gr. βαρυκάρδιος.

The first part of the compound could show a case-ending: медвѣдь 'bear' = 'honey eater', домоузаконикъ 'master of the house' = οἰκονόμος, братоучѧдъ 'nephew'.

In a few compounds the first part is a verbal stem: неіасытъ 'pelican' (= 'who does not take satiety'), неіавѣръ 'unbeliever' (= 'who does not accept belief'), невѣгласъ 'ignorant' (= 'one who does not understand the voice; does not learn').

The first part may be a numeral, an adverb, a pronoun: четврѣ-ногъ '(on) four feet', четвръто-дьньнъ (adj.) 'on the fourth day, lasting four days' = Gr. τετραήμερος, триименьнъ (adj.) 'with three names', пакыбытиіе (neut.) 'rebirth' = παλιγγενεσία, вьседръжитель (masc.) 'Almighty' = Gr. παντοκράτωρ, велѣлѣпота (fem.) 'splendour' = Gr. μεγαλοπρέπεια.

Numerous are the compounds whose first part is a negation, a preposition, a particle: неправьда 'injustice', неприіазнь (fem.)

'evil; devil', Безмлъвнїе (neut.) 'silence', прадѣдъ (masc.) 'great grandfather', оубогъ (adj.) 'poor', сѫсѣдъ (masc.) 'neighbour', ждолиїе (neut.) 'valley', съблазнь (fem.) 'temptation, offence' = Gr. σκάνδαλον, съвадьникъ (masc.) 'contentious, disputatious (person)', распѧтиїе (neut.) bifurcation, cross-road', сънѣдь (fem.) 'meal', снитиїе (neut.) 'the going down' = Gr. κατάβασις, зависть (fem.) 'envy', проказа (fem.) 'leprosy; intrigue'.

The formation of nouns and adjectives by means of suffixes (§ 48) is a very productive process throughout the history of OCS. The derivative suffixes are not recognized in the language unless they are opposed by corresponding words without suffixes, e.g. отьць, срѣдьце, овьца have no forms without suffix, though they are nouns derived by means of a -k- suffix, whereas the derivation of длъжьникъ (masc.) 'debtor' by means of the suffix -ĭn-ik-ŭ, and of длъжьнъ (adj.) by means of the suffix -ĭn-ŭ, from длъгъ (masc.) 'debt' is apparent.

Nouns are derived from verbal stems by means of the masc. endings -ъ, -ь or by means of the fem. endings -а, -ь: сънь мѧ сѧ 'I come together' — сънь мъ (masc.) 'gathering', метѫ 'I throw' — подъметъ (masc.) 'fringe, border, end', приложити 'to add' — прилогъ 'addition', глаголати 'to speak' — глаголъ 'the word'; оградити 'to enclose, to fortify' — ограда 'enclosure', похвалити 'to praise' — похвала 'the glory', вѣдѣти 'to know' — вѣдь 'the knowledge', ꙗсти 'to eat' — ꙗдь 'meal, food', водити 'to lead' — вождь (masc.) 'leader'.

Some deverbative formations alternate the thematic vowel: събьрати 'to bring together' — съборъ 'gathering', творити 'to make' — твар (fem.) 'creation, creature', цвисти, цвьтѫ 'to flourish' — цвѣтъ 'flower' (§ 37).

By means of the same ending -ь are formed abstract feminine nouns from adjectives: зълъ 'bad' — зьль 'evil' (also зъло (neut.)), твръдъ 'hard' — твръдь (fem.) 'solidity', чрьнъ 'black' — чрьнь (fem.) 'blackness'. The same suffix derives collective nouns: чадо 'child' — чадь 'retinue', дѣтꙗ 'child' — дѣть 'children', скждѣлъ 'roof-tiles, tiled roof' — скждѣль 'bricks' (coll.).

§ 48. Denominal and Deverbative Suffixes

1. *Vocalic suffixes.*

-a, -ra derives feminine nouns: дроугъ (masc.): дроуга (fem.) 'friend', рабъ (masc.): раба (fem.) 'servant', коупити: коупла 'trade', красти 'to steal': кражда 'theft'.

-ю derives neuter nouns: ложе 'bed' < *log-je (cf. по-ложити 'to lay out, to set').

-нга derives nouns with collective meaning: братрига, братига 'brethren'.

-ние is very productive and derives neuter collectives and abstracts: връвние 'willow trees': връба, камение 'stones', съдравие 'health', безоумие 'ignorance', безмлъвие 'silence'; also some with concrete meaning: подъножие 'footstool', подроужие 'marriage'.

-ии derives masculine nouns: балии 'healer': балгати 'to speak', сждии 'judge': сждъ 'judgement', гвоздии 'nail': гвоздь id. These nouns decline like the feminine nouns in -ija- (§ 39.c).

-ѣи, -аи derive masculine nouns: обычаи: обыкнжти 'to get accustomed', приключаи 'good chance': приключити сѧ 'to happen'.

-ѣга, -ага derive feminine nouns: лажага 'brooding hen': лешти, лѧгж 'to sit down, to brood'.

2. *-k- suffixes.*

These suffixes appear under different forms owing to palatalization and to the addition of other suffixal elements.

-къ, -ъкъ, -нъкъ, -тъкъ: мракъ 'darkness', камыкъ 'stone', остатъкъ 'remnant', начатъкъ 'beginning', съвитъкъ 'paper-roll, volume'.

-акъ, -ика, -икъ, -ъка, -окъ, -ьникъ, -ыка: тѧжакъ 'labourer': тѧжати 'to pull', инакъ (pron.) 'of another kind': инъ 'one, the other', инокъ 'monk', владыка 'ruler': власти, владж 'to rule', дѣвъка 'girl', ближика 'neighbour': близъ (adj.) 'near', оученикъ 'disciple': оученъ 'learned', грѣшьникъ 'sinner': грѣхъ 'sin'.

-ьць, a very productive suffix deriving *nomina agentis*, diminutives, nouns from adjectives: жьрьць 'sacrificer, priest': жрѫти 'to sacrifice', ловьць 'hunter': ловити 'to hunt', корабиць 'small boat', агньць 'lamb': агнѧ, id., старьць 'old man': старъ (adj.).

-ьца, derives masculine nouns from verbs: оубиица 'murderer', гадьца 'great eater'; diminutives: мъишьца 'arm, muscle of the arm, biceps', овьца 'sheep'.

-ица, -ьница, derive feminine nouns, diminutives, nouns from adjectives: цѣсарица 'empress', въдовица 'widow', пига-ница 'drunkard', рыбица 'small fish', мъишица, моушица 'small fly', десница 'right hand', троица 'trinity', грѣшьница 'sinner' (fem.), тьмьница 'prison', кънижьница 'library'.

-ьце derives neuter diminutives: чадьце 'baby': чадо 'child', имѣньце 'small possession': имѣние 'possession', cf. also слъньце 'sun', срѫдьце 'heart', ганьце 'egg'.

-чь, -ачь, -ъчии, -ьчии : бичь 'whip': бити 'to beat', копачь 'vine-dresser' : копати 'to dig', кънигъчии 'scribe' : кънигы 'book', кръмьчии 'pilot': кръма 'rudder, helm'.

-иште < *iskjo (§ 21.2.b) derives neuter nouns which designate place-names: сѫдиште 'tribunal': сѫдъ 'judgement', гробиште 'cemetery': гробъ 'grave', сънмиште 'synagogue': сънъмъ (сънѧти, сънмѫ) 'gathering'.

3. -t- suffixes.

-ть, -остъ, -тва, -ьство, -ьствие, -ота, -юта derive abstract nouns: власть 'rule, power': власти, владѫ 'to rule', вѣсть 'news': вѣдѣти 'to know', мошть 'power': мошти 'to be able', благость 'goodness' : благъ 'good', сладость 'sweetness': сладъкъ (adj.) 'sweet', молитва 'prayer': молити сѧ 'to pray', жрѫтва 'sacrifice' : жрѫти 'to sacrifice', богатьство 'richness' : богатъ 'rich', отьчьство, отьчьствие 'fatherland': отьць 'father', чловѣчьство 'humanity' : чловѣкъ 'man', цѣсарьствие 'kingdom': цѣсарь 'emperor', чистота 'cleanness' : чистъ 'clean', великота 'greatness' : великъ 'great', соуюта 'vanity': соуи 'vain'.

-иштъ < *itjĭ* (§ 21.2.*a*) derives nouns for young creatures: отрочиштъ 'infant':отрокъ 'child' (=отъ+решти, рекѫ 'to speak'), дѣтиштъ 'boy':дѣтѧ 'child', козлиштъ 'kid': козьлъ 'wether, ram'.

The -*t*- suffix has the same semantic function in the -*nt*- stems (§ 44.4): козьлѧ, G. козьлѧте 'kid' : козьлъ, отрочѧ, G. отрочѧте 'baby':отрокъ, дѣтѧ, G. дѣтѧте 'child', жрѣбѧ 'foal', G. жрѣбѧте.

-тель derives *nomina agentis* from verbs: дѣлатель 'worker': дѣлати 'to work', съвѣдѣтель 'witness':съвѣдѣти 'to know', оучитель 'master':оучити 'to teach'.

-(а)таи designates agents: ратаи 'ploughman':орати, ходатаи 'intermediary':ходъ 'going', возатаи 'driver':возъ 'cart'.

4. -*d*- suffixes.

-ьда derives abstract nouns: правьда 'justice':правъ 'right', вражьда 'animosity':врагъ 'enemy'.

-ло < -*dlo*: derives names of instruments: рало 'plough':орати 'to plough', рыло 'mattock, spade':рыти 'to dig', кадило 'censer':кадити 'to burn incense'.

5. -*l*- suffixes.

-ло, -сло derive mainly abstract nouns: дѣло 'work':дѣгати 'to work', начало 'beginning':начати 'to begin', число 'number': чьтѫ 'I count'; but also concrete nouns: гребло 'oar':гребѫ 'I row', масло 'grease':мазати 'to grease'.

-лъ, -ьль, -ль, -ѣль, -елъ: ѫзълъ 'tie, bond':ѫза 'tie, bond', прибыль 'gain, profit':прибыти 'to come to, to increase', новорасль 'new plant' : расти 'to grow', гъыбѣль 'loss': погыбнѫти 'to perish', дѣтѣль 'action':дѣгати 'to act', безоумьль 'fool' : безъ оума 'without intelligence', плѣвелъ 'weed':плѣва 'chaff'.

6. -*n*- suffixes.

-нь, -снь, -знь derive feminine nouns from verbs: дань 'tribute':дати 'to give', пѣснь 'song':пѣти 'to sing', жизнь 'life':жити 'to live'.

-ина is a productive suffix and derives nouns from nouns and from adjectives: истина 'truth':истъ 'the same, real',

тишина 'quietness': тихъ 'quiet, silent', пажчина 'spider-web' : пажкъ 'spider', храмина 'house' : храмъ 'house', звѣрина 'wild animal' : звѣрь id.

-изна: главизна 'chapter' : глава 'head', оукоризна 'scorn, derision' : оукорити 'to despise, to scorn'.

-ьна: вечерьна 'even-tide, vespers' : вечеръ 'evening'.

-ыни derives feminine nouns from masculine, and abstract nouns from adjectives: рабыни 'servant-woman' : рабъ, поганыни 'heathen woman' : поганъ, сжсѣдыни 'neighbour (female)' : сжсѣдъ, Магдалыни 'Magdalen', Самарꙗныни 'woman of Samaria', благыни 'goodness' : благъ, поустыни 'wilderness' : поустъ 'desert' (§ 38.1. I).

-инъ, -анинъ, -ꙗнинъ, -ѣнинъ, the first of these suffixes appears only in singular and dual. It has a singularizing function. The second suffix derives names of inhabitants of a locality or country: господинъ 'master' : Господь 'Lord', людинъ 'a man, a layman' : людиѥ (pl.), Роулинъ 'Roman' : Роумꙑ (I. pl.) (Supr.), поганинъ 'heathen' : поганъ 'heathen', гражданинъ 'citizen' : градъ 'city', Галилѣанинъ 'Galilean', Назарѣнинъ (§ 41).

7. -b- suffixes.

-обь, -оба: зълобь 'wickedness', зълоба 'wickedness' : зълъ 'bad', жтроба 'intestines' : жтрь 'insides'.

-ьба: алъчьба 'hunger' : алъкати 'to be hungry', мольба 'prayer, demand' : молити сѧ, слоужьба 'service' : слоуга 'servant'.

8. -v- suffixes.

-во: пиво 'drink' : пити 'to drink', сѣчиво 'axe' : -сѣкати 'to cut'.

-ва, -ꙗва: клѧтва 'curse' : клѧти 'to curse', дръжава 'holding, power' : дръжати 'to hold', кричава 'shouting, cry' : кричати 'to shout'.

9. -g- suffixes.

-огъ: острогъ 'hedge, fortified place' : остръ (adj.) 'sharp'.

-ежь: мѧтежь 'trouble, tumult' : мѧсти, мѧтж 'to disturb'; the origin of this suffix is not clear.

10. *-r- suffix.*

-ар҄ь is a borrowed suffix (cf. Lat. *-ārius* in *librārius*, Goth. *-areis* in *bokareis*) and derives names of professions or occupations: вратар҄ь 'porter':врата 'door', гръньчар҄ь 'potter': грънъ 'vessel', мытар҄ь 'toll-gatherer':мыто 'gift, gain' (§ 41), воукар҄ь 'scribe':воукъ 'book'.

ADJECTIVES

DECLENSION OF THE NOMINAL FORMS OF ADJECTIVES

§ 49. The adjectives appear in two forms, a simple, short, or nominal form, and a form with a pronominal suffix, called the compound, long, or pronominal form (§ 56). The two forms fulfilled different syntactical functions and had different declensions.

The simple adjectives have the endings and declensions of the noun (§ 38. I. II):

> Masc. добръ, fem. добра, neut. добро 'good', decline like masc. рабъ 'servant', fem. глава 'head', neut. мѣсто 'place'.
>
> Masc. ништь, fem. ништа, neut. ниште 'poor' decline like masc. вождь 'leader', fem. доуша 'soul', neut. ложе 'bed'.

The soft adjectives could have the ending -ии, -иꙗ, -ие:

> Masc. божии, fem. божиꙗ, neut. божие 'divine' which decline like masc. змии 'dragon', fem. змиꙗ 'snake', neut. знамение 'sign'.

Hard stems

Singular

	Masculine		Neuter	Feminine
N.	добр-ъ		добр-о	добр-а
G.		добр-а		добр-ы
D.		добр-оу		добр-ѣ
A.	добр-ъ, добр-а		добр-о	добр-ѫ
V.	добр-е		добр-о	———
I.		добр-омь		добр-оѭ
L.		добр-ѣ		добр-ѣ

Plural

	Masculine	Neuter	Feminine
N.	добр-и	добр-а	добр-ы
G.	добр-ѣ		добр-ъ
D.	добр-омъ		добр-амъ
A.	добр-ы	добр-а	добр-ы
V.	добр-и	добр-а	добр-ы
I.	добр-ы		добр-ами
L.	добр-ѣхъ		добр-ахъ

Dual

	Masculine	Neuter	Feminine
N. A. V.	добр-а	добр-ѣ	добр-ѣ
G. L.	добр-оу		добр-оу
D. I.	добр-ома		добр-ама

Soft stems

Singular

	Masculine	Neuter	Feminine
N.	ништ-ь	ништ-е	ништ-а
G.	ништ-а		ништ-ѧ
D.	ништю, -оу		ништ-и
A.	ништ-ь, ништ-а	ништ-е	ништ-ѫ
V.	——	ништ-е	——
I.	ништ-емь		ништ-еѭ
L.	ништ-и		ништ-и

Plural

	Masculine	Neuter	Feminine
N.	ништ-и	ништ-а	ништ-ѧ
G.	ништ-ь		ништ-ь
D.	ништ-емъ		ништ-амъ
A.	ништ-ѧ	ништ-а	ништ-ѧ
V.	ништ-и	ништ-а	ништ-ѧ
I.	ништ-и		ништ-ами
L.	ништ-ихъ		ништ-ахъ

Dual

	Masculine	Neuter	Feminine
N. A. V.	ннɯт-а	ннɯт-и	ннɯт-и
G. L.	ннɯт-ю, -оүʼ		ннɯт-ю, -оүʼ
D. I.	ннɯт-ема		ннɯт-ама

(*a*) The stem of the adjectives could end in any consonant: слѣп-ъ, слѣп-а, слѣп-о 'blind'; нов-ъ, нов-а, нов-о 'new'; ръдр-ъ, ръдр-а, ръдр-о 'red'; вѣрьн-ъ, вѣрьн-а, вѣрьн-о 'faithful'; пророчьск-ъ, -а, -о 'prophetic'; тѧжьк-ъ, -а, -о 'heavy'. Velar consonants change before the front vowels of the endings according to the rules noted in § 30.

(*b*) When the stem was soft the endings changed accordingly: пѣɯ-ь, -а, -е 'on foot'; лъж-ь, -а, -е 'lying'; отьч-ь, -а, -е 'of the father, paternal'; обьɯт-ь, -а, -е 'common'; боүʼ-н, -а, -ѥ 'foolish'.

(*c*) The hard masc. adjective shows in some cases the ending -*e* in voc. sg., but more frequently the voc. sg. is the pronominal form of the adjective in nom. (§ 56).

FORMATION OF ADJECTIVES

§ 50. (*a*) By means of the endings -овъ, -евъ, -инъ, -ьнь, -ь, -ин [-*ijĭ*] possessive adjectives are formed from nouns: Авраам-овъ 'of Abraham' : Авраамъ; Исоүʼс-овъ 'of Jesus' : Исоүʼсъ; Мосѣ-овъ 'of Moses': Мосѣн; Издраил-евъ 'of Israel': Издраиль; ĸесар-евъ, ĸесар-овъ 'of Caesar': ĸесарь; льв-овъ 'of the lion': львъ; —Ион-инъ 'of Jonah': Иона; Июд-инъ 'of Judas': Июда; Моис-инъ 'of Moses': Моисин; —Господ-ьнь 'of the Lord': Господь; братр-ьнь 'of the brother': братръ; дроүж-ьнь 'of the friend': дроүгъ; —Авраам-ль 'of Abraham': Авраамъ; кънѧж-ь 'of the prince': кънѧзь; пророч-ь 'of the prophet': пророкъ; овьч-ь 'of the sheep': овьца; —враж-ин 'of the enemy': врагъ; вел-ин 'big': вел-икъ. The ending -ин represents an original -*ijĭ* (§ 33.3.4).

(*b*) Adjectives derived by means of the suffix -ьнь (masc.), -ьна (fem.), -ьнѥ (neut.) express place or time: выш-ьнь 'upper, highest': въс-окъ; ниж-ьнь 'low, lower': низ-ъ (adv.) 'lowly'; древ-

ьнь (дрєв-ьнни), дрєв-льнь 'old'; въняⲧр-ьнь 'inside':въняⲧрь
(adv.). Enlarged by -ѕ̌- the suffix fulfils the same function:
вьчєрⴰ-шьнь 'of yesterday':вьчєрⴰ (adv.); дьнь-шьнь 'of today':
дьнь 'day', дьньсь 'today'; домⴰ-шьнь, домⴰ-шⲧьнь 'belonging
to the home':домⲧ 'house'.

(c) The suffix -ьнⲧ derives adjectives, expressing potentiality,
from the p. part. pass. (§ 77): прнꙗⲧ-ьнⲧ 'agreeable':прнꙗⲧⲧ
'received'; нєпосⲧрⴰдⴰн-ьнⲧ 'unbearable':посⲧрⴰдⴰнⲧ 'exhaus-
ted'; хвⴰл-ьнⲧ 'praiseworthy' for хвⴰлєн-ьнⲧ:хвⴰлнⲧн 'to praise'.
This suffix is very productive in deriving adjectives from nouns:
дьн-ьнⲧ 'daily':дьнь; зⴰпⴰд-ьнⲧ 'western':зⴰпⴰдⲧ; огн-ьнⲧ
'fiery':огнь 'fire'.

(d) In a few compound adjectives -ьнⲧ is replaced by -ⲧ, in
later texts: бєзряк-ⲧ (13th century) 'without hands':бєзряч-
ьнⲧ; вєлємяⲣдр-ⲧ 'magnanimous':вєлємяⲣдр-ьнⲧ; вєлєглⴰв-ⲧ
'with a big head':глⴰв-ьнⲧ 'principal'.

(e) The endings -ⲧ̈нⲧ, -ꙗнⲧ added to the stem of a noun form
adjectives which indicate the material expressed by the stem:
дрⲧ̈в-ⲧ̈нⲧ 'wooden':дрⲧ̈во 'tree'; льн-ⲧ̈нⲧ 'linen':льнⲧ 'flax';
рожⴰнⲧ 'of horn':рогⲧ 'horn'; можⴰⴰнⲧ '(full) of marrow':мозгⲧ
'marrow'.

(f) Adjectives expressing the category of the noun from which
they are formed show the ending -ьскⲧ: жєньскⲧ 'feminine':
жєнⴰ; дⲧ̈ⲧьскⲧ 'childish':дⲧ̈ⲧь; словⲧ̈ньскⲧ 'Slavonic':словⲧ̈нє
(nom. pl.); чловⲧ̈чьскⲧ 'human':чловⲧ̈кⲧ; госпⴰдьскⲧ 'belonging
to a master': Господь 'master, Lord'.

(g) The ending -ивⲧ, -ьливⲧ forms adjectives expressing the
quality associated with the meaning of the word from which they
derive: лⲧжнвⲧ 'lying':лⲧжь 'lie'; прⴰвьднвⲧ 'rightful':прⴰвьдⴰ
'justice, truth'; послоушьлнвⲧ 'obedient':послоушⴰⲧн 'to obey',
зⴰвнсⲧьлнвⲧ 'envious':зⴰвнсⲧь 'envy'.

(h) The endings -ⴰⲧⲧ, -нⲧⲧ, -ⴰвⲧ form adjectives to express the
possession of the quality contained in the basic word: богⴰⲧⲧ
'rich':оубогⲧ 'poor' < *baga- 'share, destiny'; крнлⴰⲧⲧ 'winged':

крило; именитъ 'famous':имѧ; плодовитъ 'fruit-bearing': плодъ; тинавъ 'muddy':тина; кръвавъ 'cruel':кръвь 'blood'.

(i) The endings -акъ, -икъ form pronominal adjectives: единакъ 'of one kind', инакъ 'of another kind', толикъ 'such' (§ 55.5).

(j) The endings -окъ, -ъкъ, -ькъ derive adjectives from original -u- stems: высокъ 'high', тяжькъ 'heavy', сладъкъ 'sweet' (cf. Lith. saldùs 'sweet', Gr. ἡδύς, Skt svāduḥ).

(k) The ending -ръ appears in бъдръ 'vigilant':бъдѣти 'to watch'; мокръ 'wet':мочити 'to wet'; the ending -нъ appears in желѣзнъ 'of iron':желѣзо 'iron'.

COMPARATIVE FORMS OF ADJECTIVES

§ 51. The IE suffix of the comparative is: $-ies-/-ios-/-is-$ (cf. Lat. *alt-ior, alt-ius, mag-is*). The CS result of these suffixes is: $-ios-, -ies- >$ $-je$; $-is- > -jĭs-+i$ (fem. ending) $> -jĭx+i$ (§ 22) $> -jĭši- =$ -ьши. The formation of the comparative in OCS is obscured by the addition of a secondary $-jĭ$. The comparative suffix -ии ($< -je- +$ $-jĭ$) could be enlarged by adding $-ě-$ to form -ѣи (masc.), -ѣиши (fem.), -ѣѩ (neut.).

These processes gave rise to the following types of comparative forms which decline like soft stems (§ 49, § 52.3) with some differences:

1. A short comparative form in -ии (masc.), -е, -ѩ (neut.), -ьши (fem.):

(a) The endings are attached to the adjectival stem:

	Masculine	Neuter	Feminine
грѫбъ 'rough'	грѫбли	грѫбле, -лю	грѫбльши
драгъ 'dear'	дражии	драже	дражьши
лихъ 'exceeding'	лишии	лише	лишьши
лютъ 'violent'	люштии	люште	лютьши
хоудъ 'bad'	хоуждии	хоужде	хоуждьши
твръдъ 'hard'	твръждии	твръжде	твръждьши

(*b*) The adjectives ending in a secondary suffix -ъкъ, -ькъ, -окъ drop this suffix in the comparative:

	Masculine	*Neuter*	*Feminine*
въісокъ 'high'	въішнн	въіше	въішьшн
глѫбокъ 'deep'	глѫблнн	глѫблѥ, -лѥ	глѫбльшн
сладъкъ 'sweet'	слаждни	слажде	слаждьшн
крѣпъкъ 'strong'	крѣплнн	крѣплѥ, -лѥ	крѣпльшн

(*c*) Comparative forms without positive bases:

Masculine	*Neuter*	*Feminine*	
болнн 'bigger'	болѥ, -лѥ	большн	велнн, великъ 'big'
вѧштнн 'larger, more'	вѧште	вѧштьшн	мъногъ 'many'
мьнн 'smaller'	мьнѥ	мьньшн	малъ, 'small'
лоучнн 'better'	лоучѥ	лоучьшн	благъ, добръ 'good'
оунн 'better'	оунѥ оунѣѥ	оуньшн	
соулнн, соулѣн 'better'	соулѥ соулѣѥ	соульшн соулѣишн	
горнн 'worse'	горѥ	горьшн	зълъ 'bad'
рачнн 'better'	рачѥ	рачьшн	

(*d*) Adverbial comparative forms:

паче (adv.) 'more'   пакъі (adv.) 'again'

далѥ (adv.) 'further'   далечѥ (adv.) 'far'

нижѥ (adv.) 'lower'   низъ 'low'

лишѥ (adv.) 'bigger, more'   лихъ 'abundant'

хоуждѥ (adv.) 'less'   хоудъ 'small'

2. A long comparative form in -ѣн (-ıан, -ан), -ѣѥ, -ѣншн:

	Masculine	*Neuter*	*Feminine*
новъ, -о, -а 'new'	новѣн	новѣѥ	новѣншн
старъ, -о, -а 'old'	старѣн	старѣѥ	старѣишн

чистъ, -о, -а 'pure'	чистѣи	чистѣю	чистѣиши
мъногъ, -о, -а 'many'	мъножаи	мъножаю	мъножаиши
добль, -е, -ꙗ 'valiant'	доблꙗи	доблꙗю	доблꙗиши
соухъ, -о, -а 'dry'	соушаи	соушаю	соушаиши
оубогъ, -о, -а 'poor'	оубожаи	оубожаю	оубожаиши

(a) There are isolated instances of comparatives formed from adjectives in -ъкъ (§ 51.1.b) by means of the suffix -ѣи attached to the secondary stem:

	Masculine	Neuter	Feminine
горьк-ъ, -о, -а 'bitter'	горьчаи, горіни	горъчѣю	гор(ь)чаиши
тьнък-ъ, -о, -а 'tender'	*тьнъчаи	тънъчаю	*тьнъчаиши
кротък-ъ, -о, -а 'tame'	крот(ъ)чаи	*кротъчаю	крот(ъ)чѣиши

(b) There is no precise criterion to indicate which comparative ending is taken by an adjective. The adjectives ending in a secondary -k- suffix (§ 51.1.b) and the adjectives without a basic degree (§ 51.1.c) take, as a rule, the ending -ии (masc.), -ю (neut.), -ьши (fem.). Other adjectives form the comparative with the ending -ѣи (masc.), -ѣю (neut.), -ѣиши (fem.).

3. The superlative is formed by the prefix наи- and the comparative form; this form of superlative occurs only in adverbs: наивꙑше, наиновѣю, наипаче 'the most'. More frequently the superlative is indicated by the genitive of comparison. The context shows the meaning, e.g. вьсѣхъ мьнии 'the smallest of all'.

The absolute superlative, which does not express a comparison, is expressed by means of adverbs: ѕѣло 'very' or by the prefix прѣ-: прѣсвѧтъ, прѣвеликъ.

4. The comparatives have a nominal and a pronominal declension (§ 57). With the exception of N.A.V. sg., masc. and neut., the declension is based on the feminine stem in -ьш- or -ѣиш- to which are added the case-endings of the soft adjectives:

Declension of short comparative forms

Singular

	Masculine	Neuter	Feminine
N. V.	въіш-ии	въіш-е	въішьш-и
G.	въішьш-а		вꙑшьш-ѧ
D.	въішьш-оу, -ю		въішьш-и
A.	въіши-и, -шьшь въішьш-а	въіш-е	въішьш-ѫ
I.	въішьш-емь		въішьш-еѭ
L.	въшьш-и		въішьш-и

Plural

N.	въішьш-е, -и	въішьш-а	вꙑшьш-ѧ
G.	въішьш-ь		въішьш-ь
D.	въішьш-емъ		въішьш-амъ
A.	въішьш-ѧ	въішьш-а	въішьш-ѧ
I.	въішьш-и		въішьш-ами
L.	въішьш-ихъ		въішьш-ахъ

Dual

N. A. V.	въішьш-а	въішьш-и	въішьш-и
G. L.	въішьш-оу, -ю		вꙑшьш-оу, -ю
D. I.	въішьш-ема		въішьш-ама

Declension of long comparative forms

Singular

N. V.	старѣ-и	старѣ-ѥ	старѣиш-и
G.	старѣиш-а		старѣиш-ѧ
D.	старѣиш-оу, -ю		старѣиш-и
A.	старѣ-и старѣиш-а	старѣ-ѥ старѣ-ише	старѣиш-ѫ, -ѭ
I.	старѣиш-емь		старѣиш-еѭ
L.	старѣиш-и		старѣиш-и

Plural

	Masculine	*Neuter*	*Feminine*
N.	старѣйш-е, -и	старѣйш-а	старѣйш-ѧ
G.	старѣйш-ь		старѣйш-ь
D.	старѣйш-емъ		старѣйш-амъ
A.	старѣйш-ѧ	старѣйш-а	старѣйш-ѧ
I.	старѣйш-и		старѣйш-ами
L.	старѣйш-ихъ		старѣйш-ахъ

Dual

	Masculine	*Neuter*	*Feminine*
N. A. V.	старѣйш-а	старѣйш-и	старѣйш-и
G. L.	старѣйш-оу, -ю		старѣйш-оу, -ю
D. I.	старѣйш-ема		старѣйш-ама

(a) The expected form of the N. sg. masc. is *vyšī, *bol'ī, &c. The secondary -jī (vyšī́jī = въішни) is of obscure origin; it may be analogous with the pronominal ending (§ 56), supported also by the -ѣи ending of the enlarged comparative.

(b) The fem. ending -i is that of the fem. -i- stems in -yn'i (§ 39).

(c) The nom. pl. masc. -e is the ending of the consonantal stems.

(d) The soft endings -ѩ, -ю, -ѩ, &c., alongside the hard -а, -оу, -ѫ, &c., are explained in § 31.

DECLENSION OF NOMINAL FORMS OF PARTICIPLES

§ 52. 1. The following participles are declined like hard or soft stem adjectives (§ 49, § 56):

(a) pr. part. pass. in -мъ, -ма, -мо: несомъ (masc.), несома (fem.), несомо (neut.) (§ 74).

(b) p. part. pass. in -нъ, -на, -но: движенъ (masc.), движена (fem.), движено (neut.) (§ 77).

(c) p. part. pass. in -тъ, -та, -то: пѧтъ (masc.), пѧта (fem.), пѧто (neut.) (§ 77).

(d) p. part. act. in -лъ, -ла, -ло: молилъ (masc.), молила (fem.), молило (neut.) (§ 70).

2. *The present participle active* (§ 73). These participles are

originally consonantal stems formed by means of the derivative
suffix -nt- (cf. Lat. *lauda-ns, lauda-nt-is*). In N. sg. masc. neut.
these participles added the suffix -o- and developed into Slavonic
-o-nt-s > -ъı [-y] (§ 9.2). In the other cases they added the suffix
-jo-, -ja- and declined like -jo- stems (masc. and neut.) or like
-ja- stems (fem.). The N. pl. masc. has the ending -e of the
consonantal stems.

Verbs of conjugations I, II, and V

Singular

	Masculine		Neuter	Feminine
N.	ид-ъı		ид-ъı	идѫшт-и
G.		идѫшт-а		идѫшт-ѧ
D.		идѫшт-оү		идѫшт-и
A.	идѫшт-ь		идѫшт-є	идѫшт-ѫ
I.		идѫшт-емь		идѫшт-еѭ
L.		идѫшт-и		идѫшт-и

Plural

	Masculine		Neuter	Feminine
N.	идѫшт-є		идѫшт-а	идѫшт-ѧ
G.		идѫшт-ь		идѫшт-ь
D.		идѫшт- емъ		идѫшт-амъ
A.	идѫшт-ѧ		идѫшт-а	идѫшт-ѧ
I.		идѫшт-и		идѫшт-ами
L.		идѫшт-ихъ		идѫшт-ахъ

Dual

	Masculine		Neuter	Feminine
N. A.	идѫшт-а		идѫшт-и	идѫшт-и
G. L.		идѫшт-оү		идѫшт-оү
D. I.		идѫшт-ема		идѫшт-ама

Verbs of conjugations III and IV

Singular

	Masculine	Neuter	Feminine
N.	зна-ıѧ, мол-ѧ		знаıѫшт-и, молѧшт-и
G.	знаıѫшт-а, молѧшт-а		знаıѫшт-ѧ молѧшт-ѧ

further, like идъı

(a) In A. sg. neut., and in other cases, forms appear in -ѫштє, -ѧштє derived from the fem. stem.

(b) The N., A. fem. pl. ending -ѩ of these participles represents: *-jens* > *-ję* and *-ins* > *-ję* (§ 14.3).

3. *The past participle active 1* (§ 75). The endings of the past part. act. 1 are -ъ (masc., neut.), -ъши (fem.) for the hard stems ending in a consonant, and -въ (masc., neut.), -въши (fem.) for the hard stems ending in a vowel. The verbs of the second conjugation attach the ending to the primary stems, dropping the infix *-ne-*. The soft stems of the verbs of the fourth conjugation take the ending -ь (masc., neut.), -ьши (fem.); the former is replaced, in later texts, by -ивъ:

Masculine	Neuter	Feminine
несъ		несъши
подвигъ		подвигъши
знавъ		знавъши
моль, моливъ		мольши, моливъши

In all other cases, except in the N. sg. masc. and neut., the stem is characterized by -š- (fem.). The masc. and neut. decline like -*jo*-stems. The masc. regularly has in the N. pl. the ending -*e* of the cons. stems. The fem. forms decline like the fem. nouns in -*yňa*- (богꙑйи) (§ 39).

Singular

	Masculine	Neuter	Feminine
N.	нес-ъ, знав-ъ, мол-ь, мол-ивъ		нес-ъши, знавъ--ши, мол-ьши
G.	несъш-а, знавъш-а, мольш-а, моливъш-а		несъш-ѧ, знавъш--ѧ, мольш-ѧ
D.	несъш-оу, -ю, &c.		несъш-и, &c.
A.	несъш-ь, &c.	несъш-є, &c.	несъш-ѫ, &c.
I.	несъш-емь, &c.		несъш-еѭ, &c.
L.	несъш-и, &c.		несъш-и, &c.

Plural

	Masculine	*Neuter*	*Feminine*
N.	несъш-е, &c.	несъш-а, &c.	несъш-ѧ, &c.
G.	несъш-ь, &c.		несъш-ь, &c.
D.	несъш-емѷ, &c.		несъш-амѷ, &c.
A.	несъш-ѧ, &c.	несъш-а, &c.	несъш-ѧ, &c.
I.	несъш-и, &c.		несъш-ами, &c.
L.	несъш-ихъ, &c.		несъш-ахъ, &c.

Dual

	Masculine	*Neuter*	*Feminine*
N. A.	несъш-а, &c.	несъш-и, &c.	несъш-и, &c.
G. L.	несъш-оу, -ю, &c.		несъш-оу, -ю, &c.
D. I.	несъш-ема, &c.		несъш-ама, &c.

INDECLINABLE ADJECTIVES

§ 53. The OCS texts contain examples of invariable adjectival forms in -ь:

испльнь 'full': дъва на десѧте коша испльнь (-лънь) (Mar., Mat. xiv. 20) 'twelve baskets full', скръби испльнь сръдъца ваша (Zogr., J. xvi. 6) 'your hearts (are) full of sorrow';

различь 'varied': многоу и различь гнѣвоу (D. sg. masc.) (Supr. 303.4) '(to) a great and varied anger';

свободь 'free': свободь бѫдете (N. pl. masc.) (Zogr., Mar., Ass., J. viii. 33, 36) 'you shall be free';

соугоубь 'double': соугоубь . . . . пришьствие (N. sg. neut.) (Supr. 449. 1) 'double (is) the presence';

оудобь 'easy': не оудобь естъ . . . . вьнити (Zogr., Mar., Mk. x. 24) 'hard is it . . . . . to enter';

прѣпростъ 'plainly': житие прѣпростъ (Supr. 272.5) 'the life, the biography'.

In some examples these adjectival forms could be conceived also as adverbs. In general, adjectives of this category have an adverbial form (§ 54) or are themselves adverbs (§ 99).

ADVERBIAL FORMS

§ 54. The adverbial form of an adjective is, as a rule, identical with the neuter sg. of the adjective: горько 'bitter', мъного 'much', добле 'heroically', влште 'more' (§ 99.2).

Some adjectives show the adverbial form by means of the ending -ѣ: добрѣ 'well', сладьцѣ 'sweetly, agreeably', горъцѣ 'bitterly' (§ 99.1).

The adjectives in -ьскъ show the adverbial form in -ьскꙑ: словѣньскꙑ 'in Slavonic', пьсьскꙑ 'doglike', вьсачьскꙑ 'by all means' (§ 99.5).

Many adjectives form the adverbial form in -ь: правь (право, правѣ) 'right', исплънь 'fully' used also as adjective; the same ending also forms adverbs from nouns: опѧть 'again' (пѧта 'heel'), отънѫдь 'entirely, altogether' (cf. нѫжда 'compulsion, violence', нѫдити 'to compel, to force') (§ 99.2).

PRONOUNS

FORMATION AND DECLENSION OF THE PRONOMINAL CATEGORIES

§ 55. The pronouns can be divided into two categories: (1) pronouns having a single form for the three genders and (2) pronouns with a different ending for each gender. To the first category belong the personal and the reflexive pronouns; to the second the demonstrative, the relative, the possessive, and a great number of pronominal adjectives.

1. Personal and reflexive pronouns

Singular

	1st person	*2nd person*	*Reflexive (3rd pers., sg., du., pl.)*
N.	азъ 'I'	тꙑ 'thou'	
G.	мене	тебе	себе '(of) oneself'
D.	мьнѣ, ми	тебѣ, ти	себѣ, си
A.	мѧ, мене	тѧ, тебе	сѧ, себе
I.	мъноѭ	тобоѭ	собоѭ
L.	мьнѣ	тебѣ	себѣ

Dual

	1st person	2nd person
N.	вѣ	ва, вы
A.	на, ны	ва, вы
G. L.	наю	ваю
D. I.	нама (D. на)	вама (D. ва)

Plural

	1st person	2nd person
N.	мы	вы
G.	насъ	васъ
D.	намъ, ны	вамъ, вы
A.	ны, насъ	вы, васъ
I.	нами	вами
L.	насъ	васъ

(a) For the 3rd person is used the demonstrative pronoun онъ, она, оно (§ 55. 2).

(b) The dative forms ми, ти, си are used only enclitically. The enclitics are used in unstressed positions and never after a preposition.

(c) The accusative forms мѧ, тѧ, сѧ, ны, вы are used as stressed independent words at the beginning of a sentence and as enclitics. The last function developed in opposition to the use of the gen. forms (мене, тебе, себе) as acc. forms.

(d) The D. pl. ны and вы appear as enclitics in Supr., Euch. Sin., Cloz. In the Kiev Miss. нъи appears regularly in the 1st pers. N. pl.

(e) The variants ны, вы:на, ва in A. du., вы:ва in N. du. are supposed to be of dialectal origin. Mar., Zogr., Ass. use ны, вы; Savv. Kn. has ны, вы and на, ва.

(f) For G. sg. мене appear also мне, м'не which could be conceived as dialectal variations created under the influence of the D. мьнѣ > *m'ně > mne.

(g) For the N. азъ there appears once ѣзъ (Mar., Mk. xi. 29) which is postulated by all the modern Slavonic forms, with the

exception of Bulgarian, which has азъ. The origin of азъ, compared with Lat. *ego*, Gr. ἐγώ, is not clear. In Ps. Sin. 38. 13 we find
а 'I', which is probably a mistake.

2. Demonstrative, possessive, and pronominal adjectives

The pronominal declension is characterized by the ending -*go*
in gen. sg. masc. neut., which is added to the hard stem by means
of the liaison vowel -*o*- and to the soft stem by -*e*-; and by the
ending -*xŭ* in gen. pl., which is added to the hard stem by -*ě*- and
to the soft stem by -*i*-. The other case endings are built on the
nominal endings of the -*a*-/-*ja*- and -*o*-/-*jo*- stems (§ 39, § 40).

I. Hard stems

онъ, она, оно 'that'; тъ, та, то 'that'; инъ, ина, ино 'another';
овъ, ова, ово 'this, that'; къжьдо 'everyone'; самъ, сама, само
'alone, oneself'; тъжде, тажде, тожде 'the same'; юдинъ,
юдина, юдино 'one'; a number of pronominal adjectives ending
in -акъ, -икъ: такъ, така, тако 'such'; гакъ, гака, гако 'of what
kind'; гакъже, гакаже, гакоже id.; вьсакъ 'everyone, each';
сикъ 'such'; селикъ 'so much'; юликъ 'however much'; коликъ
'so much'; толикъ 'so big'; мъногъ 'much, many'; the numerals
дъва 'two' and ова 'both' have only dual forms according to
this declension (§ 59.1).

Singular

	Masculine		Neuter	Feminine
N.	он-ъ		он-о	он-а
G.		он-ого		он-ога
D.		он-омоу		он-ои
A.	он-ъ, он-ого		он-о	он-ж
I.		он-ѣмь		он-огж
L.		он-омь		он-ои

Dual

	Masculine		Neuter	Feminine
N. A.	он-а		он-ѣ	он-ѣ
G. L.		он-ою		он-ою
D. I.		он-ѣма		он-ѣма

Plural

	Masculine	Neuter	Feminine
N.	он-и	он-д	он-ъі
G.	он-ѣхъ		он-ѣхъ
D.	он-ѣмъ		он-ѣмъ
A.	он-ъі	он-д	он-ъі
I.	он-ѣми		он-ѣми
L.	он-ѣхъ		он-ѣхъ

(*a*) Instead of тъ (N. sg. masc.) we may find тъі in the texts, instead of ти (N. pl. masc.) we may find тии, instead of тъі (N. pl. fem.) тъіа. These secondary forms are on the analogy of the pronominal adjectives (§ 56).

(*b*) The suffixes -же, -жде, -жьдо are added to the inflected pronominal forms: N. тъжде, G. тогожде, D. томоужде.

(*c*) къжьдо (къжьде), G. когожьдо has one single form for masc. and fem. and has no plural forms.

II. Soft stems

сь, сии, се 'this'; the possessive pronouns: мои, моа, мое 'my', твои, твоа, твое 'thy', свои, своа, свое 'his' (refl.), нашь, наша, наше 'our', вашь, ваша, ваше 'your'; the pronominal adjectives: сиць, сица, сице 'such', вьсь, вьса, вьсе 'all'; the collective numerals: дъвое 'group of two', обое 'both', трое 'three'; the relative pronoun иже, аже, еже 'who'; the anaphoric *и- preserved in G. sg. masc., neut. его 'his', fem. еіа 'her', D. sg. masc., neut. емоу 'to him', fem. еи 'to her', &c.

Singular

	Masculine	Neuter	Feminine
N.	сь, сии	се	си
G.	сего		сеіа
D.	семоу		сеи
A.	сь, сего	се	сиѭ (сьѭ)
I.	симь		сеѭ
L.	семь		сеи

Dual

	Masculine	Neuter	Feminine
N. A.	сиꙗ	си, сии	си
G. L.		сею	сею
D. I.		сима	сима

Plural

	Masculine	Neuter	Feminine
N.	сии, си	си	сиꙗ (сыꙗ)
G.		сихъ	сихъ
D.		симъ	симъ
A.	сиꙗ (сыꙗ)	си	сиꙗ (сыꙗ)
I.		сими	сими
L.		сихъ	сихъ

Singular

	Masculine	Neuter	Feminine
N.	мо-и	мо-ѥ	мо-ꙗ
G.		мо-ѥго	мо-ѥꙗ
D.		мо-ѥмоу	мо-ѥи
A.	мо-и, мо-ѥго	мо-ѥ	мо-ѭ
I.		мо-имь	мо-ѥѭ
L.		мо-ѥмь	мо-ѥи

Dual

	Masculine	Neuter	Feminine
N. A.	мо-ꙗ	мо-и	мо-и
G. L.		мо-ѥю	мо-ѥю
D. I.		мо-има	мо-има

Plural

	Masculine	Neuter	Feminine
N.	мо-и	мо-ꙗ	мо-ꙗ
G.		мо-ихъ	мо-ихъ
D.		мо-имъ	мо-имъ
A.	мо-ꙗ	мо-ꙗ	мо-ꙗ
I.		мо-ими	мо-ими
L.		мо-ихъ	мо-ихъ

(*a*) With the particle -жде, added to the flexional form, an enlarged demonstrative is obtained: сьжде 'this' (emphasized).

(*b*) There are three demonstrative pronouns in OCS: сь for

the nearer object, онъ for the farther object, and the general demonstrative тъ. Apart from these forms there exist the correlative demonstrative овъ . . . окъ 'this . . . that', овъ . . . ннгъ 'this (here) . . . the other (there)'.

(c) The secondary form снн (сен) of the N. sg. masc. appears in later texts (Euch. Sin., Supr.).

(d) The variants with н for ь can be explained according to § 33. 3.

(e) In N. A. sg. neut. there appears also сне, in very few cases (Euch. Sin., Supr.).

(f) The reflexive-possessive pronoun свон, своfa, своie is used with all three persons.

(g) The possessive relation in the third person is expressed by the genitive of the anaphoric pronoun: отьць ieifa 'her father', мати iero 'his mother', слава нхъ 'their glory', or by the dative of the personal pronoun: сънъ тн 'thy son'.

(h) In G. sg., D. L. sg., I. sg. fem., and G. L. du. contracted forms appear frequently in the texts: моifa, твоifa, своifa; мон, твон, свон; моifж, твоifж, своifж; мою, твою, свою, &c.

(i) The vowel of the pronominal endings, in the soft and in the hard declension, varies according to regular correspondences: to a hard stem -o- corresponds a soft stem -e (того : сего); to a hard stem -ě- corresponds a soft stem -i- (тѣлгъ : снмгъ); to a hard stem -y- corresponds a soft stem -ę- (онъі : снifa) (§ 37.6).

(j) The origin of the G. ending -go is obscure, the other endings can generally be found in the nominal declension:

The N. A. sg. masc. -ъ, -ь is the ending of раб-ъ, мжж-ь.

The N. A. sg. neut. -o continues an IE -od (cf. Lat. istud).

The D. sg. masc., neut. has the ending -оу of the nouns supported by an -m- of obscure origin.

The I. sg. masc., neut. has the ending -мь of the nouns added to a stem in -oį-, -eį-: *onoį-mi, *seį-mi.

The origin of the ending -мь in the L. sg. masc., neut., added to the -o- or -e- stem, is not clear: оно-мь, се-мь.

The vocative case of the pronouns is identical with the nominative.

The -н ending of N. sg. сн is the same as that which we find in some -*ija*- stems (§ 39.I.*c*).

The N. A. pl. neut., N. sg. fem. have the same ending as in the nominal declension: лѣта, ложа; глава, доуша.

The -хъ ending of the G. L. pl. goes back to IE -*su* which changed into -хъ, after the diphthongs -*oi̯*-, -*ei̯*- were monophthongized: *onoi̯-su*, *sei̯-su* > онѣхъ, сихъ (§ 22).

3. Interrogative and indefinite pronouns

N.	къ-то 'who?, anybody'	чь-то 'what?, anything'
G.	кого	чесо
D.	комоу	чесомоу
A.	кого	чьто
I.	цѣмь	чимь
L.	комь	чемь

Singular

	Masculine		Neuter	Feminine
N.	къıн 'which'		кою	каıа
G.		коıего		коıеıа
D.		коıемоу		коıен
A.	къıн, коıего		кою	кѫѭ
I.		къıнмь		коıеѭ
L.		коıемь		коıен

Dual

	Masculine			Feminine
N. A.	(каıа)			цѣн
D. I.	къıнма			къıнма

Plural

	Masculine		Neuter	Feminine
N.	цʰн		каıа	къıнѧ
G.		къıнхъ		къıнхъ
D.		къıнмъ		къıнмъ
A.	къıѧ		каıа	къıѧ
I.		къıнмн		къıнмн
L.		къıнхъ		къıнхъ

(*a*) The interrogative pronouns may have an undefined meaning and they are used as indefinite pronouns. The pronoun къто has one single form for masc. and fem., and there are no plural forms.

(*b*) The I. цѣмь is the regular phonetical development according to § 30.2, but it shows a tendency to be replaced by къинлиь, which restores the initial к to this form.

(*c*) The G. чесо is the only form preserving the IE -*so* ending, **čego* does not appear in OCS texts; the D. челиоу for чесолиоу appears once in Supr. There are secondary forms: G. чесого, чьсо(-го), D. чьсолиоу, L. чесолиь.

(*d*) The declension of къин is followed by: нѣкъин, нѣкала, нѣкоіе 'someone', никъинже, никалаже, никоіеже 'none', G. нѣкоіего, никоіегоже, &c.

(*e*) In N. sg. masc. there appears also къı, in G. коіа for коіеіа, D. кои for коіен, in A. коіж for кжіж, in I. коіж for коіеіж, in G. pl. конхъ for къинхъ.

(*f*) The prefix нѣ- gives the word an indefinite meaning, the prefix ни- gives it a negative meaning: нѣкъто 'some one', нѣчьто 'something', никъто 'none', ничьто 'nothing'; никакъже, никакаже, никакоже 'of no kind', ниіединъже, ниіединаже, ниіединоже 'no one' decline like hard stems and the particle -же is added to the flexional form: G. никакогоже, &c.

The prefixes нѣ- and ни- are separated from their flexional form: нѣ оу кого 'with somebody', ни о колиьже неродиши 'thou dost not care for anybody'.

(*g*) The possessive-interrogative чин (чи) (masc.), чина (fem.), чиіе (neut.) 'whose' and the indefinite pronoun прочин, -чана, -чеіе 'remaining, all others' are declined like къин (§ 55.2. II), прокъин, -кала, -коіе id., которъин, котеръин, -рала, роіе 'which?, someone' are declined like pronominal adjectives (§ 56).

4. Relative and anaphoric pronouns

The relative иже, иаже, іеже is formed by the anaphoric pronoun of the 3rd pers. и- 'he, that', which has no independent nominative, and by the particle -же which is attached to each case in the declension. The nominative of the anaphoric pronoun, which fulfils the function of the 3rd pers. of the personal pronoun, is supplemented by the demonstrative тъ or онъ (§ 55.2). The other cases are identical with those of the relative pronoun without the suffix -же.

Singular

	Masculine		Neuter	Feminine
N.	иже		ѥже	ѣже
G.		ѥгоже, ѥго		ѥіаже, ѥіа
D.		ѥмоѵже, ѥмоѵ		ѥнже, ѥн
A.	иже, и, ѥго		ѥже, ѥ	іѫже, іѫ
I.		имьже, имь		ѥѫже, ѥѫ
L.		ѥмьже, ѥмь		ѥнже, ѥн

Dual

	Masculine		Neuter	Feminine
N. A.	ѣже		иже, и	иже, и
G. L.		ѥюже, ѥю		ѥюже, ѥю
D. I.		имаже, има		имаже, има

Plural

	Masculine		Neuter	Feminine
N.	иже		ѣже	іаже
G.		ихъже, ихъ		ихъже. ихъ
D.		имъже, имъ		имъже, имъ
A.	іаже, іа		ѣже, ѣ	іаже, іа
I.		иминже, имин		иминже, имин
L.		ихъже, ихъ		ихъже, ихъ

(*a*) In A. du. an anaphoric form ѣ, ѣ appears for the three genders.

(*b*) The A. sg. masc. form of the anaphoric pronoun и is used enclitically: избавитъ и 'he shall save him'.

(*c*) The relative and the anaphoric pronouns preceded by a preposition took over from the preposition a prothetic *n*: въ нь 'in him', въ ньже 'in which', къ нѥмоѵ 'towards him', на нѥмь 'on him', из нѥго 'from him', отъ нѥго 'from him'. It originated after the prepositions къ, въ, съ which had in IE a final -*n* (cf. съ : Lat. *cum*). This prothetic *n* spread also to cases where other prepositions preceded a pronoun: на, за, до, по, при, оѵ, из, безъ, въз, ов, отъ, прѣдъ, подъ, надъ, none of which ended originally in *n* or *m*. An epenthetic *n* appears also in verbal forms: въниде 'he went in', and also before adverbs: въ нѥгда 'when', доньдеже 'as long as' : доиндеже, въ нѫтрь 'inside' : въ ѫтрь.

5. Mixed declension of pronouns

The pronoun вьсь, вьста (вьса), вьсе 'entire, every' is a soft-stem pronoun. However, its inflexion shows some hard-stem endings: I. sg. -ѣмь, G. pl. вьсѣхъ, &c.

Singular

	Masculine		Neuter	Feminine
N.	вьсь		вьсе	вьса (вьста, -сѣ)
G.		вьсего		вьсеѩ
D.		вьсемоу		вьсеи
A.	вьсь		вьсе	вьсѫ (вьсіѫ)
I.		вьсѣмь		вьсеіѫ
L.		вьсемь		вьсеи

Plural

	Masculine		Neuter	Feminine
N.	вьси		вьса (вьста, -сѣ)	вьсѧ
G.		вьсѣхъ		вьсѣхъ
D.		вьсѣмъ		вьсѣмъ
A.	вьсѧ		вьса (вьс-та, -сѣ)	вьсѧ
I.		вьсѣми		вьсѣми
L.		вьсѣхъ		вьсѣхъ

(a) In some cases pronominal adjectives, whose stems end in a velar, show the pronominal endings in preference to their regular nominal endings: дроугъ 'other', ıеликъ 'how big', коликъ 'how much', толикъ 'so much', селикъ 'such,' мъногъ 'much'; I. sg. мъносѣмь: D. pl. мъноголи, мъногыми, G. pl. мъносѣхъ: G. pl. мъногъ, мъногъхъ, D. pl. дроугѣмъ: D. sg. дроуголоу, G. L. pl. колицѣхъ, ıелицѣхъ, &c.

Alongside the hard stem сикъ 'such', there appears сиць, G. сицего, A. sg. neut. сице, N. A. pl. neut. сица, N. sg. fem. сица, A. sg. fem. сицѫ.

(b) The adjective тоуждь (стоуждь, штоуждь), тоужда, тоужде 'foreign, alien' has a G. sg. тоуждего, штоуждего, L. sg. neut. въ тоуждемь.

(c) The pronominal adjectives ıетеръ, -ра, -ро 'some one', каковъ, -ва, -во 'of what kind', show only a nominal declension; таковъ, -а, -о 'such', сицевъ, -ва, -во 'such' show both declensions.

DECLENSION OF THE PRONOMINAL FORMS
OF ADJECTIVES

§ 56. Adjectives and participles also have a compound declension, called pronominal because the second element of this compound formation is a pronoun. In some cases the pronominal element is clearly recognizable, in other cases the formation is less clear. In general the pronominal (definite) form of the adjective or participle is obtained by adding the anaphoric pronoun to the adjective or participle: *dobrŭ+jĭ, dobra+ja, dobro+je* > добръı-и, добра-ıa, добро-ıе 'that good one', ништн-и, ништа-ıa, ниште-ıе 'that poor one', болн-и, больши-ıa, больше-ıе 'the bigger one', несъı-и, несѫшти-ıa, несѫште-ıе 'that one who is carrying', несъı-и, несъша-ıa, несъше-ıе 'that one who has carried', моль-и (моли-и), мольши-ıa, мольше-ıе 'that one who has prayed' (§ 9.3, § 33.3). Possessive adjectives (§ 50 *a*), adjectives in -ьскъ (§ 50 *f*), and adjectives in -ьнъ (§ 50 *c*) have, as a rule, no pronominal forms.

The original syntactical function of the pronominal, definite adjective is attributive; the short, indefinite adjective was used predicatively. So, чловѣкъ добръ = a good man, man is good; чловѣкъ добръıи = the good man, the man who is good. The last construction can be said to contain a relative clause which defines the noun. There is a difference in meaning between the two constructions: the first has a general, indefinite meaning: man is good; the second refers to a certain, definite category: the good man. In the history of the Slavonic languages the nominal adjectives tend to disappear and the pronominal forms take over their syntactic functions.

Hard stems

Singular

	Masculine	Neuter	Feminine
N. V.	добръı-и, -ръı, -рън, -рон	добро-ıе	добра-ıa, -аа
G.	добра-ıего, -аго, -го		добръı-ıѧ
D.	доброу-ıемоу, -оумоу, -моу		добрѣ-и
A.	= N., = G. (masc.)		добрѫ-ıѫ, -ѫ
I.	добръı-имь, -мь, -рѣимь		добрѫ-ıѫ, -роıѫ
L.	добрѣ-ıемь, -мь, -ѣмь, -амь		добрѣ-и

Dual

	Masculine	Neuter	Feminine
N. A. V.	добра-ꙗ, -а	добрѣ-и	добрѣ-и
G. L.		доброу-ю	
D. I.		добры-има, -ꙗ, -рꙑима	

Plural

	Masculine	Neuter	Feminine
N. V.	добри-и	добра-ꙗ, -а	добры-ꙗ
G.		добры-ихъ, -хъ, -рꙑихъ	
D.		добры-имъ, -мъ, -рꙑимъ	
A.	добры-ꙗ	добра-ꙗ, -а	добры-ꙗ
I.		добры-ими, -ми, -рꙑими	
L.		добры-ихъ, -хъ, -рꙑихъ	

Soft stems

Singular

	Masculine	Neuter	Feminine
N. V.	ништи-и, -ти, -тьи, -теи	ниште-ѥ	ништа-ꙗ, -а
G.	ништа-ѥго, -аго, -го		ништꙗ-ꙗ
D.	ништю-ѥмоу, -оумоу, -моу		ништи-и
A.	= N., = G. (masc.)		ништѫ-ѭ
I.	ништи-имь, -мь		ништѫ-ѭ, -теı
L.	ништи-имь, -мь		ништи-и

Dual

	Masculine	Neuter	Feminine
N. A. V.	ништа-ꙗ, -а	ништи-и	ништи-и
G. L.		ништю-ю	
D. I.		ништи-има, -ма	

Plural

	Masculine	Neuter	Feminine
N. V.	ништи-и	ништа-ꙗ, -а	ништꙗ-ꙗ
G.		ништи-ихъ, -хъ	
D.		ништи-имъ, -мъ	
A.	ништꙗ-ꙗ	ништа-ꙗ, -а	ништꙗ-ꙗ
I.		ништи-ими, -ми	
L.		ништи-ихъ, -хъ	

(a) In G., D., I. sg. fem. the original endings *-jeję, -jeji, -jejǫ* have been reduced to -ѩ, -и, -ѭ.   In G. L. du. ѥю has been reduced to -ю.   In the soft declension the ending -ѥмь of the L. sg. masc. and neut. has been replaced by -имь.

(b) In some cases (I. sg. masc., neut., D. pl. masc., fem., I. pl. fem., L. pl., D. I. du.) an analogical stem has been adopted: добры-, ништи- which recalls the G. sg. fem., A. pl. masc. of the nominal declension.

(c) The contracted forms in G., D. sg. masc., neut. (§ 32.5) occur frequently in the texts. They are more recent forms and their use varies from text to text.

(d) In the L. sg. masc., neut. some texts (Ass., Zogr., Supr.) present isolated variants with the endings: -ѣмь, -ѣꙗмь, -ѣѣмь: новѣѣмь, &c.

§ 57.

Declension of the Pronominal Forms of
Comparatives

Singular

	Masculine	Neuter	Feminine
N.	въиши-и, -шьи	въишьше-ѥ, въише-ю	въишьши-ꙗ
	старѣ-и	старѣише-ю, -рѣю	старѣиши-ꙗ
G.		въишьша-ѥго	въишьша-ѩ
		старѣиша-ѥго	старѣиша-ѩ
D.		въишьшоу-ѥмоу	въишьши-и
		старѣишоу-ѥмоу	старѣиши-и
A.	= G. (masc.), = N.		въишьшѫ-ѭ
			старѣишѫ-ѭ
I.	въишьши-имь		въишьшѫ-ѭ, -шеѭ
	старѣиши-имь		старѣишѫ-ѭ, -шеѭ
L.	*въишьши-ѥмь		въишьши-и
	*старѣиши-ѥмь		старѣиши-и

Dual

	Masculine	Neuter	Feminine
N. A.	въ̑ишьша-ꙗ	въ̑ишьши-и	въ̑ишьши-и
	старѣиша-ꙗ	старѣиши-и	старѣиши-и
G. L.	въ̑ишьшоу-ю		въ̑ишьшоу-ю
	старѣшоу-ю		старѣишоу-ю
D. I.	въ̑ишьши-ма,		въ̑ишьши-ма
	старѣиши-ма		старѣиши-ма

Plural

N.	въ̑ишьши-и	въ̑ишьша-ꙗ	въ̑ишьша-ꙗ
	старѣиши-и	старѣиша-ꙗ	старѣиша-ꙗ
G.	въ̑ишьши-ихъ		въ̑ишьши-ихъ
	старѣиши-ихъ		старѣиши-ихъ
D.	въ̑ишьши-имъ		въ̑ишьши-имъ
	старѣиши-имъ		старѣиши-имъ
A.	въ̑ишьша-ꙗ	въ̑ишьша-ꙗ	въ̑ишьша-ꙗ
	старѣишѣиша-ꙗ	старѣша-ꙗ	старѣиша-ꙗ
I.	въ̑ишьши-ими		въ̑ишьши-ими
	старѣиши-ими		старѣиши-ими
L.	въ̑ишьши-ихъ		въ̑ишьши-ихъ
	старѣиши-ихъ		старѣиши-ихъ

(*a*) In N. sg. masc. the pronominal form is practically identical with the nominal form of the adjective: старѣи, въ̑ишии, мъножаи, мьнии (§ 51).

(*b*) The N. A. sg. neut. is formed regularly from the fem. stem in -š-, but one finds also forms without š: въ̑ишеіе, болеіе, мьнеіе, &c.

(*c*) Here also, as in § 56 *c*, forms appear with contracted groups of vowels: G. -аго for -аіего, &c.

(*d*) The cases in which the initial vowel of the ending is preceded by a final -н- of the stem present, in isolated instances, -ен- instead of -нн-: N. sg. masc. въ̑ишьнеи (Ps. Sin.) 'the highest',

G. pl. чаѩштеїхъ (Zogr.) 'of those who are waiting', L. sg. каѭштеїмь (Zogr.) 'in that one who repents', &c.

(e) The N. pl. masc. has the ending -шнн instead of the expected -шеи.

§ 58.
DECLENSION OF THE PRONOMINAL FORMS OF PARTICIPLES

1. Present participle active

Singular

	Masculine	Neuter	Feminine
N.	идъı-и	идѫште-ю	идѫшти-ѣ
	знаѩ-и	знаѩжште-ю	знаѩжшти-ѣ
	молѧ-и	молѧште-ю	молѧшти-ѣ
G.	идѫшта-юго		идѫштѧ-ѩ
	знаѩжшта-юго		знаѩжштѧ-ѩ
	молѧшта-юго		молѧштѧ-ѩ
D.	идѫштоу-юмоу		идѫшти-и
	знаѩжштоу-юмоу		знаѩжшти-и
	молѧштоу-юмоу		молѧшти-и
A.	идѫшти-и	идѫште-ю	идѫштѫ-ѭ
	идѫштъ-и		
	знаѩжшти-и	знаѩжште-ю	знаѩжштѫ-ѭ
	знаѩжштъ-и		
	молѧшти-и	молѧште-ю	молѧштѫ-ѭ
	молѧштъ-и		
I.	идѫшти-имь		идѫштѫ-ѭ
			идѫште-ѭ
	знаѩжшти-имь		знаѩжштѫ-ѭ
			знаѩжште-ѭ
	молѧшти-имь		молѧштѫ-ѭ
			молѧште-ѭ
L.	идѫшти-имь		идѫшти-и
	знаѩжшти-имь		знаѩжшти-и
	молѧшти-имь		молѧшти-и

Dual

	Masculine	Neuter	Feminine
N. A.	идѫшта-ꙗ	идѫшти-и	идѫшти-и
	знаѭшта-ꙗ	знаѭшти-и	знаѭшти-и
	молѧшта-ꙗ	молѧшти-и	молѧшти-и
G. L.	идѫштоу-ю		идѫштоу-ю
	знаѭштоу-ю		знаѭштоу-ю
	молѧштоу-ю		молѧштоу-ю
D. I.	идѫшти-ма		идѫшти-ма
	знаѭшти-ма		знаѭшти-ма
	молѧшти-ма		молѧшти-ма

Plural

	Masculine	Neuter	Feminine
N.	идѫште-и, -штии	идѫшта-ꙗ	идѫшта-ѩ
	знаѭште-и, -штии	знаѭшта-ꙗ	знаѭшта-ѩ
	молѧште-и, -штии	молѧшта-ꙗ	молѧшта-ѩ
G.		идѫшти-ихъ	
		знаѭшти-ихъ	
		молѧшти-ихъ	
D.		идѫшти-имъ	
		знаѭшти-имъ	
		молѧшти-имъ	
A.	идѫшта-ѩ	идѫшта-ꙗ	идѫшта-ѩ
	знаѭшта-ѩ	знаѭшта-ꙗ	знаѭшта-ѩ
	молѧшта-ѩ	молѧшта-ꙗ	молѧшта-ѩ
I.		идѫшти-ими	
		знаѭшти-ими	
		молѧшти-ими	
L.		идѫшти-ихъ	
		знаѭшти-ихъ	
		молѧшти-ихъ	

(*a*) Some texts (Ass., Supr.) prefer the ending -ии, -и in N. pl. masc.: идѫштии, -шти. In the other cases there occur isolated forms with -еи- for -ии-: ведѫште-ихъ, &c.

2. Past participle active 1

Singular

	Masculine	Neuter	Feminine
N.	несъі-и, несъ-и	несъше-ю	несъши-ꙗ
	моли-и, моль-и	мольше-ю	мольши-ꙗ
G.	несъша-юго		несъша-ꙗ
	мольша-юго		мольша-ꙗ
D.	несъшоу-юмоу		несъши-и
	мольшоу-юмоу		мольши-и
A.	несъши-и, -шьи	несъше-ю	несъшѫ-ѭ
	мольши-и, -шьи	мольше-ю	мольшѫ-ѭ
I.	несъши-имь		несъшѫ-ѭ, -шеѭ
	мольши-имь		мольшѫ-ѭ, -шеѭ
L.	несъши-имь		несъши-и
	мольши-имь		мольши-и

Dual

N. A.	несъша-ꙗ	несъши-и	несъши-и
	мольша-ꙗ	мольши-и	мольши-и
G. L.		несъшоу-ю	
		мольшоу-ю	
D. I.		несъши-ма	
		мольши-ма	

Plural

	Masculine	Neuter	Feminine
N.	несъше-и, -шии	несъша-ꙗ	несъша-ꙗ
	мольше-и	мольша-ꙗ	мольша-ꙗ
G.		несъши-ихъ	
		мольши-ихъ	
D.		несъши-имъ	
		мольши-имъ	
A.	несъша-ꙗ	несъша-ꙗ	несъша-ꙗ
	мольша-ꙗ	мольша-ꙗ	мольша-ꙗ
I.		несъши-ими	
		мольши-ими	
L.		несъши-ихъ	
		мольши-ихъ	

(*a*) In N. sg. masc. variants with secondary endings appear: -ъі, -ои; -еи (§ 33.1, § 56), e.g. оумьръі 'the dead one', оумерои (Mar., J. xii. 1) 'the dead one', сътворен (Ass., Mt. xix. 4; L. x. 37) 'one who has done'.

(*b*) In this declension too (§ 56, § 57) the vocalic groups -аіе-, -оуіе- are contracted into -аа-, -а-; -оуоу-, -оу-, and in G. and D. sg. forms appear like: несъшааго, несъшаго, моль̈шааго, моль̈шаго; несъшоуоумоу, несъшоумоу, later несъшоомоу, несъшомоу. The phonetic change is based on the assimilation of *je*, *ju* to the preceding *a*. The various OCS texts behave differently as to the use of these variants. In N. pl. masc. there also appear forms in -ии: несъшии.

(*c*) The pr. part. pass. in -мъ, -ма, -мо (§ 74), the past part. pass. in -нъ, -на, -но and -тъ, -та, -то (§ 77) decline as adjectives and have definite (pronominal) and indefinite (nominal) inflexions. The past part. act. 2 in -лъ, -ла, -ло (§ 76) is, as a rule, declined as an indefinite adjective and used regularly in sing. and plur. in the formation of the compound tenses: perfect, pluperfect, future perfect; conditional.

NUMERALS

§ 59. Formation and Declension of the Numeral Categories

1. Cardinal numerals

The cardinal numerals from 1 to 4 are adjectives and they agree in case, number, and gender with the noun. The numerals 5–10 are quantitative (collective) fem. -*i*- stems (§ 43), and the object counted takes the G. pl. The numerals 11–19 are compound forms of units added to ten. The object counted agrees with the first element of the compound form, i.e. the unit. Therefore, after 11 the noun takes the singular, after 12 the dual, after 13 and 14 the plural, after 15–19 the G. pl. Similarly, after 20, 30–100, and 1,000 the noun takes the G. pl.

1. ѥдинъ masc., ѥдина fem., ѥдино neut.
   G. ѥдиного masc., neut., ѥдиноѩ fem. (§ 55.2).

2. дъва masc., дъвѣ fem., дъвѣ neut. (du. form). G. L.
   дъвою, D. I. дъвѣма; оба masc., обѣ fem., neut. 'both'
   (§ 55.2).

3. трию, трьѥ masc., три fem., три neut.
   G. трии, D. трьмъ, A. три, I. трьми, L. трьхъ.
   The declension follows that of the masc. -i- stems (§ 43).

4. четъіре masc., четъіри fem., четъіри neut.
   G. четъіръ (-рь), D. четъіремъ, A. четъіри, I. четъірь-
   ми, L. четъірьхъ. The declension follows in general
   the pattern of a consonant -r- stem (§ 44.5).

5. пать, G. пати ⎫
6. шесть, G. шести ⎪
7. седмь, G. седми ⎬ decline like fem. -i- stems (§ 43).
8. осмь, G. осми ⎪
9. девать, G. девати ⎭

10. десать, G. десати declines like пать, but has also cases
    according to consonant stems: G. десати, D. десати,
    A. десать, I. десатыⰶ, L. десате, десати, du. N. A.
    десати, G. L. десатоу, D. I. десатьма, plur. N.
    десате, десати, G. десатъ (десатии), D. десатьмъ,
    A. десати, I. десаты, L. десатьхъ.

11. ѥдинъ на десате masc., ѥдина на десате fem., ѥдино
    на десате neut. G. ѥдиного на десате раба 'of the
    11 servants', ѥдиноѩ на десате дѣвъі 'of the 11 girls',
    ѥдиного на десате лѣта 'of the 11 years', &c.

12. дъва на десате masc., дъвѣ на десате fem., neut.
    G. дъвою на десате рабоу, дѣвѣ, лѣтѣ 'of the twelve
    servants, girls, years' (du.).

13. трию на десате masc., раби '13 servants', три на десате
    fem., neut., дѣвъі, лѣта '13 girls, years'. G. трии на
    десате рабъ 'of the 13 servants', &c.

14. четъіре на десате masc., раби '14 servants', четъіри на
    десате дѣвъі, лѣта, 14 girls, years'. G. четъіръ
    на десате рабъ 'of the 14 servants', &c.

15. пать на десате рабъ, дѣвъ, лѣтъ '15 servants, girls,

years'; G. пати на десате рабъ, дѣвъ, лѣтъ 'of the 15 servants, girls, years', &c.

16. шесть на десате.

17. седмь на десате.

18. осмь на десате.

19. девать на десате.

20. дъва десати, G. дъвою десатоу, D. дъвѣма десатьма. Both parts decline as duals.

30. трніе десате, три десати, G. трни десатъ, &c. Both parts decline.

40. четыре десате, четыри десати, G. четыръ (-рь) десатъ. Both parts decline.

50. пать десатъ (G.), G. пати десатъ, &c. The first part declines as an -i- stem, the second part is invariable.

60. шесть десатъ ⎫
70. седмь десатъ ⎪
                 ⎬ decline like пать десатъ.
80. осмь десатъ ⎪
90. девать десатъ ⎭

100. съто neut., G. съта declines as a neuter hard -o- stem noun (§ 40.2).

200. дъвѣ сътѣ, G. дъвою сътоу, &c. Both parts decline as duals.

300. три съта, G. трни сътъ. Both parts decline according to the appropriate paradigms (§ 40.2, § 43).

400. четыри съта. Declines like 300 (§ 40.2, § 44.5).

500. пать сътъ (G.). The first part declines like a -i- stem, the second part remains unchanged.

600. шесть сътъ ⎫
700. седмь сътъ ⎪
               ⎬ decline like пать сътъ.
800. осмь сътъ ⎪
900. девать сътъ ⎭

1,000. тысѫшти, тысашти. It declines like a fem. -ỹa- stem of the type богыни (§ 39 b): G. тысѫшта, D. тысѫшти, A. тысѫштѫ, etc.

2,000. дъвѣ тысѫшти.

3,000. три тысѫшта.

4,000. четыре тысѫшта.

5,000. ПѦТЬ ТЪІСѦШТЬ, &c.

10,000. ДЄСѦТЬ ТЪІСѦШТЬ or ТЪМА 'darkness, myriad', which declines like an -a- stem (§ 39).

(a) Alongside ІЄДИНЪ there also appears in Supr. the form ІЄДЬНЪ, ІЄД'НЪ, ІЄДИНЪ.

(b) The numeral ДЄСѦТЬ is a fem. -i- stem noun, which in some cases has the endings of a consonantal stem (L. sg., N. G. I. pl., G. L. du.) (§ 44). So L. sg. ДЄСѦТЄ is used for the formation of numerals from 11 to 19 by means of the preposition НА 'on, upon': ІЄДИНЪ НА ДЄСѦТЄ, whereas L. sg. ДЄСѦТИ is used otherwise in a true locative-function: О ДЄСѦТИ ДѢВИЦЪ 'about the 10 girls' (Supr. 368.22).

(c) In the numerals 20–90 the noun ДЄСѦТЬ is counted like any other word: ДЪВА ДЄСѦТИ (masc. du.), ТРИІЄ ДЄСѦТИ (-ТЄ)(N. pl.), ПѦТЬ ДЄСѦТЪ (G. pl.). The units are added to the tens by the conjunction И or ТИ 'and': ДЄВѦТЬ ДЄСѦТЪ И ПѦТЬ = 95.

(d) For 10,000 and over there is no special numeral. An indefinitely great quantity is expressed by the noun ТЬМА, ТЪМА 'darkness', or НЄСЪВѢДА 'no knowledge'.

(e) In isolated cases the simple numerals take, like adjectives, the formative element of the definite form: ДЄСѦТИИ (Zogr., Mar., Mt. xx. 24) 'the ten'; СЄДМИІѦ (acc.) (Zogr., Mc. viii. 20) 'the seven'; ІЄДИНЪІ ЖЄ НА ДЄСѦТЄ ОУЧЄНИКЪ 'the 11 apostles' (Mar., Zogr., Ass., Savv. Kn., Mt. xxviii. 16).

(f) In numerals whose last component part is a unit, the noun counted agrees with the unit, which is declined with the noun: О ДЄВѦТИ ДЄСѦТЪ И ДЄВѦТИ ПРАВЄДЬНИЦѢХЪ (Mar., Lk. xv. 7) 'over ninety-nine just men'; ДЪВА ДЄСѦТИ І ПѦТЬ СТАДИІ '25 furlongs'.

2. Ordinal numerals

These numerals have adjectival forms in -Ъ, -ЬИ, -ТЪ, -ЬНЪ and occur regularly in the definite form, whereas some indefinite forms appear in adverbial expressions:

	Definite	*Indefinite*
1st	прьвы-и masc., прьвд-ѣ fem., прьво-ѥ neut.	прьв-ъ, -д, -о
		прьв-ъ, -д, -о
2nd	въторъ-и masc., -рдѣ fem., -рою neut., дроугы-и masc., &c.	въторъ-ъ, -д, -о
		дроуг-ъ, -д, -о
3rd	трети-и, треть-и masc., третнѣ-ѣ fem., третьне-ѥ neut.	трети-и, -ѣ, -ѥ
		треть-и, -ѣ, -ѥ
4th	четврьты-и masc., &c.	четбрьт-ъ, -д, -о
5th	пѧты-и	пѧт-ъ, -д, -о
6th	шесты-и	шест-ъ, -д, -о
7th	седмы-и	седм-ъ, -д, -о
8th	осмы-и	осм-ъ, -д, -о
9th	девѧты-и	девѧт-ъ, -д, -о
10th	десѧты-и	десѧт-ъ, -д, -о
11th	ѥдинъ-и на десѧте, ѥдинонадесѧты-и	ѥдинонадесѧтъ, прьвъ на десѧте
12th	въторы-и на десѧте	etc.

13th трети-и на десѧте; 14th четврьты-и на десѧте; 15th пѧты-и на десѧте; 16th шесты-и на десѧте; 17th седмы-и на десѧте, седмьдесѧтьны-и; 18th осмы-и на десѧте, осмонадесѧты-и; 19th девѧты-и на десѧте; 20th дъвадесѧтьныи; 30th тридесѧтьныи; 40th четыридесѧтьныи; 50th пѧтьдесѧтьныи; 60th шестьдесѧтьныи; 70th седмьдесѧтьныи; 80th осмьдесѧтьныи; 90th девѧтьдесѧтьныи; 100th сътьныи; 1000th тысѫштьныи.

(a) The ordinal numerals decline like adjectives. Apart from прьвъ and въторъ, they are formed by means of the derivative elements -to-, -mo-, -tŭŭ. The numerals for 1st and 2nd are old inherited IE forms comparable to Lat. *primus*, Lith. *pìrmas*, Goth. *fruma* to which in CS corresponds *prĭvŭ, Skt *pūrva-*. The first part of въторъ is not clear (§ 15.2). The other formations have their counterparts in other IE languages: пѧ-тъ: Lat. *quin-tus*,

Lith. *peñk-tas*, Gr. πέμπ-τος; ос-мъ: Lith. *aš-mas* < **ok't-mos*, Goth. *ahtāu* < **ok'tou-*.

(*b*) The ordinal numerals 11–19 are formed either with a derivative element attached only to the (unit figure) first part, retaining the cardinal number 10: шестъ на десяте, or by adding the derivative element at the end of the compound numeral, which is conceived as a unit: дъвадесятьнъ, дъводесятьнъ.

(*c*) The ordinal numerals 20–90 keep the cardinal units and attach to them десятъ or десятьнъ: дъвадесятьнъ, девятъ десятъ. The OCS texts contain few examples of ordinal numerals between the tens: седмьдесятъноѥ и девятоѥ 'the 79th' (Supr. 295.6). In later texts such numerals are expressed by the preposition междоу 'between': четврътыи междоу десятьми 'the 14th', or by a periphrasis: четврътыи третьиаго десяте 'the fourth of the third decade = the 24th'.

3. Collective (qualitative) numerals

The meaning '*a group, a quantity of* ' is expressed by adjectival forms derived from the stems of the cardinal numbers:

	Masculine	Feminine	Neuter
2.	дъвои	дъвоꙗ	дъвоѥ
	обои	обоꙗ	обоѥ
3.	трои	троꙗ	троѥ
4.	четворъ	четвора	четворо
	четверъ	четвера	четверо
5.	пяторъ	пятора	пяторо
	пятеръ	пятера	пятеро
6.	шесторъ	шестора	шесторо
7.	седморъ	седмора	седморо
8.	осморъ	осмора	осморо
9.	девяторъ	девятора	девяторо
10.	десяторъ	десятора	десяторо

(*a*) The first three forms (дъвои, обои, трои) decline like pronouns (§ 55. 2.II); the other forms have a nominal declension (§ 49).

(*b*) These numerals appear in the texts either in the plural (and also in the dual) for the three genders expressing several groups or categories of nouns: нынꙗ оубо трои сѫтъ пакости дѣѥжште

нами, сотона и доуѕъ и воievoda (Supr. 73.1) 'but now there are three (a group of three) who are doing evil to us: Satan, the Dux, and the military leader'; четворы во сѫтъ . . . (Supr. 370.11) 'there are namely (a group of) four (parables); веригами двонми (Supr. 146.5) 'with double chains'—or in neuter sing. expressing a multitude of individual objects as a unity: и примъ десаторо братриѧ (G.) (Supr. 279.15) 'and having received ten brothers'. So, дъвоі людье . . . пріdѫ (Cloz. 840 f.) 'people of two kinds . . . came'; нъ вино ново въ мѣхꙑ новꙑ вълнвалѫтъ, и обоie съблюдетъ сѧ (Mar., Zogr., L. 5.38) 'but new wine must be put into new bottles, and both are preserved'. Sometimes the meaning is that of a cardinal numeral: обои . . . пастѣ (Supr. 417.29) 'the two kinds . . . of Easter'.

4. Multiplicative numerals

The multiplicative meaning is expressed by the word кратъ, a noun derived from the same root as the verb чрьтати, чрьтаѭ 'to cut in, to scratch' (cf. Lith. *kertù, kir̃sti* 'to cut': *kar̃tas* '(two) times'); or by the word -шьди probably derived from the root of ходити, шьдъ meaning 'a "go"' § 94*l*, § 100):

дъва краты (du.) 'twice'	дъва-шьди, -шди
три краты (acc. pl.) 'three times'	три-шьди
*четыри краты 'four times'	четыри-шьди (четыри-шти)
пать кратъ (gen. pl.) (краты) 'five times'	шести-шьди
седмь кратъ (gen. pl.) 'seven times'	седми-шьди
седмь десатъ кратъ 'seventy times'	многы-шьдꙑ, многа-шьди, многꙑ-шти 'often'
девать десатъ кратъ 'ninety times'	
много краты 'many times'	

5. Fractions

There are no special forms to express fractions; nouns are used for that purpose: полъ 'half' (§ 42), третина 'the third part' occurs

in later texts after the OCS period, четврътъ 'quarter', десатина 'tithe'.

6. Nouns of number and adverbial numerals

Nouns and adjectives with numerical meanings are formed by composition and derivation:

(*a*) Feminine nouns are formed from ordinal, cardinal, or collective numerals by the addition of the suffix -ица: въторица 'couple', дъвоица, третьница (третиница) 'group of three', троица 'Trinity', четверица (четворица), пѧторица, седмица, съторица.

The instr. sg. (sometimes also the loc.) is used as an adverb expressing the idea of multiplication (§ 99.3):

дъвоицеѭ, въторицеѭ 'twice, again', третицеѭ, третицеи 'three times, the third time', седмицеѭ, седморицеѭ, седмькратицеѭ 'seven times'; съторицеѭ 'hundred times', сътократицеѭ id., единоѭ 'once', in later texts also единицеѭ.

(*b*) The suffix -гоѵбъ (соѵгоѵбъ 'double'), representing historically the same root which appears in the verb съ-гънѫти 'to bend, to fold', conveys, when attached to a numeral, the meaning of the English ending -*ble* in *double, treble*, Lat. -*plex* in *simplex, duplex*. These formations are rare and occur only in later texts: единогоѵбъ, дъвогоѵбъ, дъвоѥгоѵбъ, трьгоѵбъ, четврѣгоѵбъ. The nouns шестогоѵбьць, седмогоѵбьць are derived by means of a suffix -ьць. Also, a verb трьгоѵбити 'to treble' occurs in Euch. Sin.

(*c*) Numerals enter into the composition of a noun or adjective: трьзѫбьцѧ (Supr. 181.27) 'tridents', трьсвѧтъ 'thrice holy', четврѣногъ 'quadruped', въторъкъ, въторьникъ 'Tuesday' = second day of the week.

VERBS

Survey of Verbal Forms and Stems

§ 60. 1. *Verbal forms.* The verb has three simple tenses: present, aorist, and imperfect, and three compound tenses: perfect, pluperfect, and future perfect. Each of these forms is characterized by

special endings which distinguish three persons (1st, 2nd, 3rd), in singular, dual, and plural.

The nominal forms of the verb are: present participle active, present participle passive, past participle active 1, past participle active 2, past participle passive, and verbal noun.

The invariable verbal forms are: infinitive, supine, present gerund and past gerund.

Apart from the indicative, there exists an imperative mood (in origin an optative) and a conditional mood.

There are no special passive forms. When the passive concept is to be expressed a periphrasis (pr. part. pass.+auxiliary verb БЪІТН) or a reflexive verb is used (with the pronoun cѧ irrespectively of number and gender, like in Baltic).

2. *Verbal stems.* The various verbal forms are obtained by adding certain suffixes to the stem, which is the bearer of the meaning and which remains unchanged throughout the paradigm. The verbal system is based on two stems: one called the *infinitive-aorist stem* and the other the *present stem*: (*a*) from the infinitive-aorist stem are formed the aorist, the imperfect, the p. part. act. 1 and 2, the p. part. pass., and the supine; (*b*) from the present stem are formed the present tense, the present participles active and passive, the imperative, and in some cases the imperfect (§ 70). This duality of derivation is, however, obscured by phonetic changes in the stem, by analogical formations, and by other developments in the history of the language. Examples of regular infinitive and present stem forms:

Infinitive:	ЗЪВАТН	*Present*:	ЗОВѪ 'I call'
	'to call'		ЗОВЕШН
supine	ЗЪВАТЪ		'thou callest'
aorist	ЗЪВАХЪ	imperative	ЗОВН
	'I called'		
imperfect	ЗЪВААХЪ		
p. part. act. 1	ЗЪВАВЪ	pr. part. act.	ЗОВЪІ
p. part. act. 2	ЗЪВАЛЪ	pr. part. pass.	ЗОВОЛІЪ
p. part. pass.	ЗЪВАНЪ		

Infinitive:	брати 'to fight'	*Present*:	борѭ 'I fight' бориеши 'thou fightest'
supine	братъ	imperative	*бори
aorist	брахъ	pr. part. pass.	борелїъ
imperfect	брахомїъ сѧ (Supr., 1st. pl.)		
p. part. act. 2	брадлъ	pr. part. act.	борїѧ
p. part. pass.	бранъ боренъ	imperfect	бор҄еахъ

Infinitive:	жрѣти 'to sacrifice'	*Present*:	жьрѭ 'I sacrifice'
supine	жрѣтъ		жьреши 'thou sacrificest'
aorist	жрѣхъ, жрѣ (2nd & 3rd sg.)	imperative	жьри
imperfect	жьр҄еахъ		
p. part. act. 1	жьръ	pr. part. act.	жьръı
p. part. act. 2	жрѣлъ	pr. part. pass.	жьромъ
p. part. pass.	жьренъ, жрѣтъ		
verbal noun	жрѣтиѥ 'sacrifice'		

Infinitive:	плоути 'to swim, to float'	*Present*:	пловѭ 'I swim' пловеши 'thou swimmest'
supine	плоутъ		
aorist	плоухъ	imperative	плови
p. part. act. 1	плоувъ	pr. part. act.	пловъı
p. part. act. 2	плоулъ	pr. part. pass.	пловомъ
p. part. pass.	пловенъ	imperfect	плов҄еахъ

Infinitive:	бьрати 'to take'	*Present*:	берѭ 'I take' береши 'thou takest'
supine	бьратъ		

aorist	БЬрахъ	imperative	Бєрн
imperfect	БЬрддхъ		
p. part. act. 1	БЬрдвъ	pr. part. act.	Бєрꙑ
p. part. act. 2	БЬрдлъ	pr. part. pass.	Бєромъ
p. part. pass.	БЬрднъ		

The verbs with stems ending in -н have identical present and infinitive-aorist stems:

Infinitive:	молнтн	*Present:*	моліѫ
	'to demand'		'I demand'
supine	молнтъ		молншн
aorist	молнхъ		'thou deman-
imperfect	молꙗдхъ		dest'
p. part. act. 1	моль	imperative	молн
p. part. act. 2	молнлъ	pr. part. act.	молѧ
p. part. pass.	молѥнъ	pr. part. pass.	молнмъ

(*a*) The infinitive-aorist stem is obtained by dropping the ending -тн of the infinitive: глдголд-тн 'to speak', stem глдголд-; хвдлн-тн 'to praise', stem хвдлн-. However, the phonetic changes which took place in the history of the language obscured the actual stem; so пдс-тн 'to fall' has an actual infinitive stem пдс-, which goes back to *pad- (§ 29.10), and therefore the aorist is пдд-ъ or пдд-охъ; тєш-тн 'to run' is a development from *tek-ti and forms the aorist from the original stem тѣх-ъ or тєк-охъ.

(*b*) The infinitive-aorist stem is either identical with the root of the verb or is enlarged by a suffix which is -*a*-, -*ě*-, or -*i*-: нєс-тн, БЬр-д-тн, рдзоум-ѣ-тн, Боуд-н-тн (§ 61).

(*c*) The present stem is obtained by dropping the ending of the 2nd pers. sg. pr.: зовє-шн 'thou callest', stem зовє-; молн-шн 'thou demandest', stem молн-; коупоуѥ-шн 'thou buyest', stem коупоуѥ-.

(*d*) The present stem is derived from the root by the vocalic elements -*e*- (-*o*-), -*ne*- (-*no*-), -*je*- or -*i*-.

(*e*) There are four verbs which add the endings directly to the

root-stem without any of the above-mentioned derivative elements. These verbs are called athematic: Ꙗесмь 'I am', дамь 'I give, I shall give', вѣмь 'I know', ꙗмь 'I eat' (§ 61.V, § 98).

CLASSIFICATION OF THE VERBS

§ 61. The verbs are classified in five conjugations on the basis of the present stems (§ 60.2. c.d.). The infinitive-aorist stem is the criterion for the subdivisions within each conjugation (§ 60.2. a.b.). It should be borne in mind that this classification serves practical purposes and is not the only possible one. For practical purposes, too, each verb should be considered in its three main forms: inf., 1st sg. pr., and 2nd sg. pr.

I. The first conjugation (§ 94) contains verbs with present stem in -*e*- whose infinitive stem is either:

(*a*) the radical alone, i.e. without any suffix:
нес-ти 'to carry': pr. stem нес-е-ши; or

(*b*) enlarged by the suffix -*a*-:
бьр-а-ти 'to collect': pr. stem бер-е-ши,
зъв-а-ти 'to call': pr. stem зов-е-ши.

II. The second conjugation (§ 95) contains verbs which form the present stem by means of the suffix -*ne*-, and the infinitive stem by means of the suffix -*nǫ*- (cf. Gr. τέμνω 'I cut' 1st sg., τέμ-νο-μεν 1st pl., τέμ-νε-τε 2nd pl.). The root may end either in a vowel or in a consonant, and some verbal forms are derived directly from the root (aorist, participles, verbal nouns):

inf. двиг-нѫ-ти   2nd pers. двиг-не-ши   aor. двиг-ъ
'to move'

inf. ми-нѫ-ти   2nd pers. ми-не-ши   aor. ми-нѫ-хъ
'to pass by'

III. The third conjugation (§ 96) contains verbs which have a present stem in -*je*-. The infinitive-aorist stem either:

(*a*) is identical with the root (ending in a vowel):
inf. зна-ти 'to know'   2nd pers. зна-ю-ши
inf. грѣ-ти 'to warm'   2nd pers. грѣ-ю-ши; or

(b) ends in a consonant and is enlarged by the suffix -a- or -ova-:

    inf. пьс-а-ти 'to write'   2nd pers. пиш-е-ши

    inf. коуп-ова-ти 'to buy'   2nd pers. коуп-оуѥ-ши

The first group (a) of this conjugation also contains the verbs with radicals ending in a liquid diphthong of the type: борѭ, брати < *bor-ti 'to fight'; колѭ, клати < *kol-ti 'to stab'; мелѭ, млѣти < *mel-ti 'to grind'.

IV. The fourth conjugation (§ 97) contains verbs whose present stem is enlarged by the suffix -i-. The infinitive-aorist stem ends either:

    (a) in -i-, which is historically different from the present stem -i-:

    inf. мол-и-ти 'to demand' 2nd pers. мол-и-ши

                                          'thou demandest'

    inf. страш-и-ти 'to frighten' 2nd pers. страш-и-ши

                                          'thou frightenest'

or:

    (b) in -ě- (-a-):

    inf. сѣд-ѣ-ти 'to seat'   2nd pers. сѣд-и-ши

                                          'thou seatest'

    inf. вел-ѣ-ти 'to order'   2nd pers. вел-и-ши

                                          'thou orderest'

    inf. слъіш-а-ти 'to hear' 2nd pers. слъіш-и-ши

                                          'thou hearest'

    inf. сто-ꙗ-ти 'to be stand- 2nd pers. сто-и-ши

        ing'   'thou art standing'

This class of verbs is a new formation in Slavonic. Historically the -i- verbs represent a semithematic type which appears in the western IE languages (Albanian, Germanic, Italic, Celtic; cf. Chr. S. Stang, *Das slavische und baltische Verbum*, 1942, 23).

V. The fifth conjugation (§ 98) comprises four so-called athematic verbs whose stems show no suffix, and so the present tense stem is identical with the root of the verb:

    inf. бъі-ти 'to be'   1st pers. ѥс-мь

                                      2nd pers. ѥс-и

    inf. да-ти 'to give'   1st pers. да-мь

                                      2nd pers. да-си

inf. вѣдѣ-ти 'to know'   1st pers. вѣ-мь
                               2nd pers. вѣ-си
inf. ꙗс-, ѣс-ти 'to eat'   1st pers. ꙗ-мь
                               2nd pers. ꙗ-си

The verb имѣти 'to have' may form the present tense according to this conjugation: имамь, имаши, &c. Its regular forms follow the third conjugation: имѣѭ, имѣѥши, &c.

CHANGES IN THE VERBAL STEMS OF CONJUGATION I a

§ 62. The infinitive stem of the verbs of conjugation I a is identical with the radical of the verb. In the formation of this stem there occur apophonic changes of the thematic vowel (§ 37, § 94 c), and changes of the final consonant followed by -ти. These latter changes are explained by the phonetic tendencies described in § 29. The following main changes may arise:

1. A labial followed by the dental -t- is dropped (§ 29.11):
    чрьп-ѭ, чрьп-е-ши : чрѣ-ти < *čerp-ti 'to ladle, to draw (up)'
    съп-ѭ, съп-е-ши : соу-ти < *seup-ti 'to scatter, to spread'
        (the irregular s- for š- in the infinitive (*šuti < *sjuti § 8.2)
        is by analogy with the present)
    грєб-ѭ, грєб-е-ши : грети < *greb-ti 'to dig, to row'

2. A dental followed by another dental changes into -s- (§ 20.4, § 29.10):
    плет-ѭ, плет-е-ши : плес-ти < *plet-ti 'to plait'
    чрьт-ѭ, чрьт-е-ши : чрѣс-ти < *čert-ti 'to cut'
    блюд-ѭ, блюд-е-ши : блюс-ти < *bljud-ti 'to guard, to protect'
    влад-ѭ, влад-е-ши : влас-ти < *vold-ti 'to dominate'
    жлѣд-ѭ, жлѣд-е-ши : жлѣс-ти < *želd-ti 'to pay'
The spirant may, however, also represent an old spirant:
    пас-ѭ, пас-е-ши : пас-ти 'to graze' (cf. Lat. pascor)
    врьз-ѭ, врьз-е-ши : врѣс-ти 'to tie' with the IE *vr̥z-/*verz-
        (apophonic) alternation

3. When the radical ended in -r'-, metathesis opens the syllable (§ 10.4) and apophonic alternation is found in the stems (§ 17, § 37.5.d):
    мьр-ѭ, мьр-е-ши : мрѣ-ти < *mer-ti 'to die' < IE *mr̥'-

тьр-ѫ, тьр-е-ши:трѣ-ти (тьрⷮ-ти, трѫ-ти) < *ter-ti* 'to rub'

4. When the radical ended in -*m̥*-, this developed in the infinitive stem into a nasal (§ 14.1.2, § 15.2, § 18) which alternates with a reduced vowel followed by a nasal consonant in the present stem (§ 37.3):

дъм-ѫ, дъм-е-ши:дѫ-ти < *dom-ti* < IE *dhm̥-* 'to blow'
кльн-ѫ, кльн-е-ши:клѧ-ти < *klen-ti* 'to curse'

5. The velar consonants have been palatalized (§ 30.1 *b*): -*gti*, -*kti* > *šti*:

мог-ѫ, мож-е-ши:мош-ти < *mog-ti* 'to be able'
врьг-ѫ, врьж-е-ши:врѣш-ти < *verg-ti* 'to throw'
рек-ѫ, реч-е-ши:реш-ти < *rek-ti* 'to speak'
тлък-ѫ, тлъч-е-ши:тлѣш-ти < *telk-ti* 'to pull, to drag'

6. When the radical ended in a diphthong (*eu̯/ou̯*), the diphthong is monophthongized in the infinitive stem and changed in the present stem to -*ev*- > -*ov*- (§ 19.3):

слов-ѫ, слов-е-ши:слоути < *sleu̯-ti* < IE *k'leu̯-* (cf. Gr. κλέϝομαι) 'to be called'
ров-ѫ (рев-ѫ), ров-е-ши (рев-е-ши):роути (рюти) < *reu̯-ti* 'to roar'

7. A few irregular changes in the stems, for which it is difficult to account, are most probably due to analogy:

лаг-ѫ, лаж-е-ши:лешти < *leg-ti* 'to lie down'
сад-ѫ, сад-е-ши:сѣсти < *sěd-ti* 'to sit down'
ид-ѫ, ид-е-ши:и-ти < *i-ti* 'to go' (§ 94.2 *e*)
жив-ѫ, жив-е-ши:жи-ти < *ži(v)-ti* 'to live' (cf. Lith. *gyjù* 'I revive', *gývas* 'alive')
плѣв-ѫ, плѣв-е-ши:плѣ-ти < *pel-ti* 'to weed out'

Changes in the Verbal Stems of Conjugation I *b*·

§ 63. The verbs of conjugation I *b* show vocalic alternation in the root (-*ĭ*-/-*e*-, -*ĭ*-/-*i*-), and change in the stems the final diphthong -*eu̯* into -*ov* which alternates with -*ŭv*:

1. бер-ѫ, бер-е-ши:бьр-а-ти 'to take'

дер-ж, дер-е-ши : дьр-а-ти 'to tear apart'
пер-ж, пер-е-ши : пьр-а-ти 'to hit'
жид-ж (жьд-ж), жьд-е-ши : жьд-а-ти 'to wait'
зов-ж, зов-е-ши : зъв-а-ти 'to call'

2. Some verbs have the same vowel in the present and in the infinitive stem:

със-ж, със-е-ши : със-а-ти 'to suck'
тък-ж, тъч-е-ши : тък-а-ти 'to weave'
иск-ж, ишт-е-ши : иск-а-ти 'to seek'
ков-ж, ков-е-ши : ков-а-ти 'to forge'
ръв-ж, ръв-е-ши : ръв-а-ти 'to pull, to pluck out'
(о)-снов-ж, -снов-е-ши : -снов-а-ти 'to fix, to establish'
мет-ж, мет-е-ши : мет-а-ти 'to throw'

3. The verbs иск-а-ти, иск-ж and мет-а-ти, мет-ж also have forms that follow the third conjugation : иштж ; мештж or метаіж. гън-а-ти 'to drive': жен-ж is irregular. The verb мес-ти, мет-ж 'to sweep' belongs to conjugation I *a*.

CHANGES IN THE VERBAL STEMS OF CONJUGATION II

§ 64. The verbs of conjugation II show no alternation of the thematic vowel; the final consonant of the stem is subject to regular phonetic changes (§ 29):

1. въз-бъ-нж, -бъ-не-ши : -бъ-нж-ти < *bŭd-nǫ-ti 'to wake' (trans.): бъжд-ж, бъд-и-ши : бъд-ѣ-ти 'to be awake' (intrans.)

оу-ван-ж, -ва-не-ши : -ва-нж-ти < *vęd-nǫ-ti 'to wither'

оу-глъ-нж, -глъ-не-ши : -глъ-нж-ти < *glĭb-nǫ-ti 'to sink, to stick'

ка-нж, ка-не-ши : ка-нж-ти < *kap-nǫ-ti 'to drop' (cf. кап-а-ти)

рас-тръгн-ж, -тръг-не-ши : -тръг-нж-ти < *trŭg-nǫ-ti 'to tear to pieces'

2. In some examples the consonant that had been dropped reappeared; or had not been assimilated (§ 29.5):

гъіб-нж, гъіб-не-ши : гъіб-нж-ти and гъінж, &c. 'to perish'
о-слъп-нж, -слъп-не-ши : -слъп-нж-ти 'to become blind'

про-ꙁѧв-нѫ, -ꙁѧв-не-ши: -ꙁѧв-нѫ-ти 'to sprout, to germinate'

оу-глꙭв-нѫ, оу-глꙭв-не-ши: оу-глꙭв-нѫ-ти 'to sink, to stick'

3. The verb ста-ти, станѫ, ста-не-ши 'to get up' once belonged to the first conjugation. It inserted the -*n*- only in the present stem.

CHANGES IN THE VERBAL STEMS OF CONJUGATION III

§ 65. Conjugation III contains: (1) primary verbs, i.e. those formed from a radical by means of a suffix -*je*-, and (2) secondary verbs, i.e. those formed from nouns:

   1. би-ѭ, би-ѥ-ши: би-ти 'to beat'

   дѣ-ѭ (деждѭ), дѣ-ѥ-ши: дѣ-ти (дѣꙗти, дѣати) 'to make, to put'

   ши-ѭ, ши-ѥ-ши: ши-ти 'to sow'

   жьн-ѭ, жьн-ѥ-ши: жѧ-ти 'to harvest'

   кол-ѭ, кол-ѥ-ши: кла-ти 'to stab'

   вѣ-ѭ, вѣ-ѥ-ши: вѣ-ꙗ-ти 'to blow'

   плю-ѭ, плю-ѥ-ши: плюв-а-ти 'to spit'

   алч-ѭ, алч-е-ши: ал(ъ)к-а-ти 'to be hungry'

   жажд-ѭ, жажд-е-ши: жад-а-ти 'to be thirsty'

   чеш-ѭ, чеш-е-ши: чес-а-ти 'to comb'

   съ-рашт-ѭ, съ-рашт-е-ши: съ-рѣс-ти 'to meet'

The suffix -*je*- appears as -*e*- when the preceding consonant is a palatal spirant or affricate.

The primary character of some verbs cannot always be ascertained. They may be derived from nouns or from other verbs: глаголати 'to speak': глаголъ (n.); доухати, доушѫ, доушеши 'to breathe': доухъ; шьпътати, шьпъштѫ, шьпъштеши 'to whisper': шьпътъ; навъꙑцати, -въчѭ, -въꙑчеши 'to learn': навъꙑкнѫти, оучити; скакати, скачѫ, скачеши 'to jump': скочити, &c. Most of these verbs are imperfective-indeterminate (iterative).

2. The suffixes -*a*-, -*ě*- derive verbs either from nominal or from verbal stems: дѣл-а-ѭ, дѣл-а-ѥ-ши, дѣл-а-ти 'to act': дѣл-о (n.); ꙁнамен-а-ѭ, ꙁнамен-а-ѥ-ши, ꙁнамен-а-ти 'to mark': ꙁнамен-нѥ (n.); раꙁоум-ѣ-ѭ, раꙁоум-ѣ-ѥ-ши, раꙁоум-ѣ-ти 'to

understand':разоумі-ъ (n.); оумі-ѣ-ѭ, оумі-ѣ-ѥ-ши, оумі-ѣ-ти
'to know': оумі-ъ (n.); нариц-а-ѭ, нариц-а-ѥ-ши, нариц-а-ти
'to name':нареш-ти (v.); бъів-а-ѭ, бъів-а-ѥ-ши, бъів-а-ти 'to
be (habitually)':бъі-ти (v.); имѣ-ѭ, имѣ-ѥ-ши, имѣ-ти 'to
have':имі-а-лꙑ (v.).

3. The suffix -оу-, which appears in the infinitive stems as -ov-a-
and in the present stem as -u-je-, forms a great number of verbs
(§ 96.4): бесѣд-ов-а-ти, бесѣд-оу-ѭ, бесѣд-оу-ѥ-ши 'to speak':
бесѣд-а; наслѣд-ов-а-ти, наслѣд-оу-ѭ, наслѣд-оу-ѥ-ши 'to
inherit':слѣд-ъ; мин-ов-а-ти, мин-оу-ѭ, мин-оу-ѥ-ши 'to pass
by':мин-ѫ-ти; съваз-ов-а-ти, съваз-оу-ѭ, зъваз-оу-ѥ-ши
'to tie':съваз-а-ти. This category of verbs is particularly
prolific in some modern Slavonic languages.

CHANGES IN THE VERBAL STEMS OF CONJUGATION IV

§ 66. The verbs of conjugation IV have always, in the 1st pers.
sg. pr., a palatalized final stem consonant caused by the following *j*:
врати-ти, врашт-ѫ < *vort-jǫ, врати-ши 'to turn'; люби-ти,
любл-ѭ, люби-ши 'to love'; троуди-ти, троужд-ѫ, троуди-ши 'to
toil, to make an effort'; врьтѣ-ти, врьшт-ѫ, врьти-ши 'to turn';
видѣ-ти, вижд-ѫ, види-ши 'to see'; глѧдѣ-ти, глажд-ѫ, глѧ-
ди-ши 'to look at'; свьтѣ-ти, свьшт-ѫ, свьти-ши 'to light', &c.

When the infinitive stem ended in *j*, *č*, *ž*, *š*, *št*, (*žd*) +*ě*, the -*ě*-
changed into -*a*-:
боꙗ-ти сѧ, бо-ѭ сѧ, бои-ши сѧ 'to fear'; крича-ти, крич-ѫ,
кричи-ши 'to shout'; сътажд-ти, сътаж-ѫ, сътажи-ши 'to
attain'; слꙑша-ти, слꙑш-ѫ, слꙑши-ши 'to hear'; тъшта-ти,
тъшт-ѫ, тъшти-ши 'to hurry'.

One single verb has -*a*- after a non-palatal consonant: съпа-ти,
съплѭ, съпи-ши 'to sleep'. It forms the imperfect and all other
non-present forms from the stem съпа- (§ 97.*g*). This verb
represents all that remained of a numerous verbal category which
changed the fourth conjugation for the third.

PERSONAL ENDINGS

§ 67. It is assumed that in IE there existed primary endings for
the formation of the personal forms of the present tense, and

secondary endings with which the past tenses and the optative were formed. The Slavonic equivalents of the second group are: the aorist, the imperfect, and the imperative, which is the continuation of an IE optative. In the 1st and 2nd persons plur. and in all persons of the dual the primary and secondary OCS endings are identical.

1. *The primary endings* of the verbs of the athematic class differ from those of the other four classes:

		Athematic	Thematic
Sing.	1st	-мь	-ѫ (-іѫ)
	2nd	-си	-ши
	3rd	-тъ	-тъ
Plur.	1st	-мъ	-мъ
	2nd	-те	-те
	3rd	-атъ (-ѫтъ)	-ѫтъ (-іѫтъ), -атъ
Dual	1st	-вѣ	-вѣ
	2nd	-та	-та
	3rd	-те	-те

(*a*) The 1st pers. ending of the athematic verbs, -мь, continues the IE ending -*mi*, but the origin of the thematic ending -ѫ is not clear. One explanation (Leskien) connects it with the IE subjunctive -*ām* ending (cf. Lat. *ferām*), another (Kul'bakin) proceeds from $\bar{o}$ + secondary ending *m*.

(*b*) The 2nd pers. ending -си cannot continue the IE -*si* because this should have developed into -сь, and it did develop into -*sĭ* (= -сь) in other Slavonic languages, e.g. Old Polish *jeś* < *jesĭ*. The OCS -си is explained by Leskien (*Grammatik der altbulg. Spr.*, 1919, 191) as representing the IE ending of the middle voice *-sai* (cf. Prussian *assai, essei* = OCS *jesĭ*). The *š* in the ending of the 2nd pers. sg. pr. is analogical. It corresponds to IE *s*, but IE *s* changes in Slavonic into *x* only after *i, u, r, k* (§ 22). Thus *š* was phonetically possible only in the verbs of the fourth conjugation: -*i-+-si-* > -*xi* — *šī-* (§ 21). From this category of verbs the ending may have been generalized in the other thematic conjugations. However, this explanation remains a mere hypothesis. The

situation is that OCS has the endings -сн (athematic), -шн (thematic), while the other Slavonic languages have -šĭ (athematic and thematic).

(c) The 3rd pers. ending -тъ is not clear either. To IE -ti should correspond OCS *-тъ. Old Russian regularly has the ending -ть in this person, while OCS regularly shows -тъ, e.g. ѥс-тъ 'he is', and only exceptionally writes -ть:ѥс-ть (cf. Gr. ἐστί). A short form ѥ for ѥстъ occurs in Supr., Cloz., Savv. Kn. Otherwise forms without -тъ in the 3rd sg. and pl. occur very rarely in OCS.

(d) The 1st pers. pl. ending -мъ is a regular continuation of the IE -mos. When followed by the enclitic pronoun н [jĭ], the ending -мъ changed into -мъін (§ 33.4): ведемъін 'we lead him', or into -мон (§ 33.1):ведемон 'id.'. In modern Slavonic languages this ending appears as -m, -mo, -me. The ending -мъі occurs in Zogr., Supr.

(e) The ending -те in the 2nd pers. pl. is a regular continuation of the IE -te.

(f) The 3rd pers. pl. endings -ѫтъ, -атъ correspond to IE -nt- (after vowels), -n̥t- (after consonants). The verbs of the first and second conjugations attach this ending to the radical by means of the vowel -o-: -o- + -nt- > -ǫt- (§ 61.I.II); the ending -jǫtŭ of the verbs of the third conjugation (§ 61.III) is formed by analogy with that of the verbs of the first and second conjugations, because -je- + -nt- should have developed into -ęt- (§ 14). Also the -ętŭ ending of the verbs of the fourth conjugation is not the regular development from IE -i- + -nt-. The fourth conjugation represents historically an athematic and semi-thematic category of verbs (§ 61.4). The ending of the athematic verbs in the 3rd pl. is -ętŭ (with the exception of сѫтъ 'they are', имѫтъ 'they have'); the -ę- represents an IE n̥ (§ 14.2). In this person too, as in the 3rd sg., the hard -тъ has not been satisfactorily explained.

(g) In a few examples the -тъ is dropped: начьнѫ (for начьнѫтъ) искати (Supr. 16.18) 'they will (begin to) search'; сѫ (Supr.) 'they are'.

(h) In this person also (cf. 1st pers. pl.) the ending -тъ, followed

by an enclitic pronoun, changed into -тъι (§ 33.3), or sometimes developed into -то (§ 33.1): постдвитъι-н (Mar., Mt. xxiv. 47) 'he shall make him'; можето-сѧ (Mar., J. vi. 52) 'he can this'; емлетъι-н (Mar., L. ix. 39) 'he takes him'.

(*i*) The ending -вѣ of the 1st pers. du. is parallel to the personal pronoun of the 1st pers. (§ 55.1). The verbs of the first and second conjugations attach this ending to the radical by means of the vowel -*e*- instead of the expected -*o*- (cf. 3rd pers. pl.). This vowel, in -е-вѣ, is the result of analogy with the -ıе-вѣ of the verbs of the third conjugation, where the change -*jo*- > -*je*- is regular (§11.2).

(*j*) The ending -тд of the 2nd pers. du.—used also for the 3rd pers. in later OCS texts: Supr., Savv. Kn., and sporadically also in Zogr. and Ass.—is formed on the analogy of the dual forms of the nouns; for that reason it appears also as -тѣ when the noun-subject is feminine: посъластѣ (aor.) же сестрѣ (Savv. Kn., Ostr.) 'the two sisters sent'.

(*k*) The ending of the 3rd pers. du. is -те (Mar., Cloz., Ps. Sin.), which is often replaced by the -тд of the 2nd pers. (Zogr., Ass., Euch. Sin., Supr., Savv. Kn.) and may appear as -тѣ when the subject is feminine or neuter. The dual forms, which have survived in the Slavonic languages, have, in the 3rd pers., the ending -*ta*.

2. *The secondary endings* originally formed the aorist, the imperfect, and the optative-imperative forms. These endings were: 1st pers. sg. -*m*, 2nd pers. sg. -*s*, 3rd pers. sg. -*t*. In Slavonic, following the tendency towards open syllables (§ 5), the final consonants were dropped. In the 1st pers. the suffix -*o*-(+*m*) developed into -*ŭ* which is the ending of the aorist (§ 15.3). In the 2nd and 3rd pers. sg. there remained no suffix. The dual and plural forms (1st and 2nd persons) have identical endings with the present primary ones. The 3rd pers. pl. has the ending -ѧ, -ѫ which represents -*e*-+*nt*, -*o*-+*nt* (§ 14.3). The result in OCS was therefore as follows:

Sing.	1st -*o*-+*m* > ъ	Plur.	1st -мъ
	2nd -*s* (zero)		2nd -те
	3rd -*t* (zero)		3rd -*e-nt*, -*o-nt* > -ѧ, -ѫ

Dual 1st -вѣ

2nd -та

3rd -те

The bibliography for the history of the verbal endings is given by N. van Wijk, *Geschichte der altkirchenslavischen Sprache*, 1931, 215.

Personal Verbal Forms

PRESENT TENSE

§ 68. The present tense forms are obtained by adding the primary endings (§ 67.1) to the stem (§ 60): несе-ши, бере-тъ, двигне-мъ, знае-тъ, мол-ѧтъ. In the 1st pers. the ending is added to the root: нес-ѫ, бер-ѫ, знａ-іѫ, мол-іѫ. In the forms of the first and second conjugation one would expect the thematic suffixes *-o-*, *-no-* instead of *-e-*, *-ne-*; these last result from analogy with the third conjugation where *-jo-* > *-je-* (§ 11.2, § 65).

The verbs of the fifth (athematic) conjugation add the endings directly to the stem: іес-лѫ, да-лѫ, дас-тъ < **dad-tĭ* (§ 61.V). The form сѫтъ of the 3rd pers. pl. follows the thematic conjugation, representing a stem with the grade *o*: **so-nt-*.

AORIST

§ 69. There are three aorist forms:

1. Simple (asigmatic, strong) aorist formed from the verbs of the first conjugation, with an infinitive-aorist stem ending in a consonant, and from the verbs of the second conjugation with a consonantal stem obtained after dropping the *-nǫ-* infix, e.g.:

мошти 'to be able', могѫ, stem: *mog-*; двигнѫти 'to move', двигнѫ, stem: *dvig-*:

Singular	Plural	Dual
могъ < **mog-o-m*	могомъ < **mog-o-mŭ*	моговѣ < **mog-o-vě*
може < **mog-e-s*	можете < **mog-e-te*	можета < **mog-e-ta*
може < **mog-e-t*	могѫ < **mog-o-nt*	можете < **mog-e-te*
двигъ < **dvig-o-m*	двиголъ < **dvig-o-mŭ*	двиговѣ < **dvig-o-vě*
движе < **dvig-e-s*	движете < **dvig-e-te*	движета < **dvig-e-ta*
движе < **dvig-e-t*	двигѫ < **dvig-o-nt*	движете < **dvig-e-te*

(*a*) One single verb of the third conjugation forms the asigmatic aorist: сърѣсти, съ-ращѫ 'to meet', обрѣсти, об-ращѫ 'to find', aor. -рѣтъ, -рѣте, &c.

(*b*) The asigmatic aorist forms are not frequent in the texts. Verbs having the vowel *e* in the radical syllable form this aorist only in the 2nd and 3rd pers. sg.: нести, aor. несе (2nd, 3rd pers.) but not *nesǔ (1st pers.). In general, forms of the 2nd and 3rd pers. sg. and 3rd pl. are frequent and regular, whereas the other persons appear very seldom. Not every verb has a complete paradigm of the asigmatic aorist forms, and from the same verb a sigmatic aorist may also exist.

Here are the most frequent asigmatic aorist forms recorded in the texts:

(*c*) *Of the first conjugation*: ити 'to go', 1st sg. pr. идѫ, aor.: 1st sg. идъ, 1st pl. идомъ, 2nd pl. идете, 3rd pl. идѫ, 3rd du. идете; мошти 'to be able', 1st sg. pr. могѫ, aor.: 1st sg. могъ, 1st pl. моголъ, 3rd pl. могѫ, 3rd du. можете; врѣшти 'to throw', 1st sg. pr. врьгѫ, aor.: 3rd pl. врьгѫ; красти 'to steal', 1st sg. pr. крадѫ aor.: 3rd pl. оукрадѫ; пасти 'to fall', 1st sg. pr. падѫ, aor.: 3rd pl. падѫ; сѣсти 'to sit down', 1st sg. pr. сядѫ, aor.: 1st sg. сѣдъ, 1st pl. сѣдомъ, 3rd pl. сѣдѫ; трясти 'to shake', 1st sg. pr. трясѫ, aor.: 1st sg. трясъ, 3rd pl. трясѫ; ꙗхати 'to drive (in a vehicle)', 1st. sg. pr. ꙗдѫ, aor.: 3rd pl. въ-ꙗдѫ, прѣ-ꙗдѫ.

(*d*) *Of the second conjugation*: -бѣгнѫти (изъ-, отъ-, при-) 'to run away', 1st sg. pr. -бѣгнѫ, aor.: 3rd pl. -бѣгѫ; -выкнѫти 'to get accustomed', 1st sg. pr. -выкнѫ, aor.: 3rd pl. на-выкѫ; глъбнѫти 'to sink', 1st sg. pr. глъбнѫ, aor.: 1st sg. оу-глъбъ (оу-глебъ), 3rd pl. оуглъбѫ; гыбнѫти, 'to perish', 1st sg. pr. гыбнѫ aor.: 3rd pl. по-гыбѫ; двигнѫти 'to move', 1st sg. pr. двигнѫ, aor.: 1st sg. двигъ, 3rd pl. двигѫ; жаснѫти ся 'to be frightened', 1st sg. pr. жаснѫ ся, aor.: 3rd pl. оу-жасѫ ся, 3rd du. оу-жасете ся; забнѫти 'to bud', 1st sg. pr. забнѫ, aor.: 3rd pl. про-забѫ; въс-крьснѫти 'to rise, to resurrect', 1st sg. pr. въскрьснѫ, aor.: 3rd pl. въскрьсѫ; кыснѫти 'to become sour', 1st sg. pr. кыснѫ, aor.: 3rd pl. въс-кысѫ; млькнѫти 'to become silent', 1st sg. pr.

млькнѫ, aor.: 3rd pl. оу-млѣкѫ; -никнѫти 'to rise', 1st sg. pr.
никнѫ, aor.: 3rd pl. въз-никѫ; оу-нъзнѫти 'to put in', 1st sg. pr.
нъзнѫ, aor.: 3rd pl. оу-нѣзѫ; свлнѫти (сваднѫти) intrans.
'to be singed', 1st sg. pr. свадѫ, aor.: 3rd pl. при-свадѫ; съхнѫти
intrans. 'to dry', 1st sg. pr. съхнѫ, aor.: 1st sg. и-съхъ (и-сохъ),
3rd pl. и-съхѫ; тонѫти 'to sink', 1st sg. pr. -тонѫ, aor.: 3rd pl.
оу-топѫ < *-topnǫt; тъкнѫти 'to push', 1st sg. pr. тъкнѫ, aor.:
3rd pl. по-тъкѫ; хрълнѫти 'to limp', 1st sg. pr. хрълнѫ, aor.:
3rd pl. оу-хрълмѫ; чезнѫти 'to disappear', 1st sg. pr. чезнѫ, aor.:
3rd pl. иштезѫ, 3rd du. иштезете < изчезете (§ 30.1.a).

2. Sigmatic aorist, so called because its stem is enlarged by the
suffix -s-, to which the secondary endings are attached by a
connecting -o- (in the 1st pers. sg. and du.) or directly (in the
other persons). The suffix -s- was either kept or changed into -x-
(§ 22).

The endings are parallel to those of the asigmatic aorist:

Sing. 1st -съ, -хъ　　Plur. 1st -сомъ, -хомъ　　Dual 1st -совѣ, -ховѣ
　　　2nd — —　　　　　　2nd -сте　　　　　　　　　2nd -ста
　　　3rd — —　　　　　　3rd -сѧ, -шѧ　　　　　　3rd -сте

The features of these aorist forms are: changes in the stems,
alternative suffixes -s- or -x-, and lengthening of the radical vowel.

(a) Verbs with a vocalic monosyllabic or polysyllabic stem could
form this aorist: бьрд-ти 'to carry', aor. sg. бьрд-хъ, бьрд, бьрд;
pl. бьрдхомъ, бьрдсте, бьрдшѧ; du. бьрдховѣ, бьрдста, бьрдсте;
зна-ти 'to know', aor. знахъ; пи-ти 'to drink', aor. пихъ; видѣти 'to see', aor. видѣхъ; пѣ-ти 'to sing', aor. пѣхъ.

(b) The -s- changed into -x- after -i- and -u- (§ 22), i.e. in verbs
of the type pi-ti and kry-ti 'to cover' (where y < ū); from this
type the ending -xŭ spread to the other types: бьрд-хъ, &c.

(c) The -s- ending was preserved by the verbs whose stem
showed a nasal -ę-: ѩ-ти 'to take, to grasp', aor. ѩсъ; клѧ-ти 'to
curse', aor. клѧсъ; на-чѧ-ти 'to begin', aor. начѧсъ. However,
analogous forms appear as well: рас-пѧти, 'to crucify', aor. -пѧхъ,
-пѧхомъ, -пѧшѧ (Zogr., Mar. have both forms; Supr., Savv. Kn.
have only x- forms; Ps. Sin., Euch. Sin. have s- forms almost exclusively).

(*d*) Verbs of the second class with a vocalic stem form the aor. in -хъ only: ми-нѫ-ти 'to pass, to overtake', aor. минѫхъ; помѣ-нѫ-ти 'to remember', aor. помѣнѫхъ; those with a consonantal stem may form the aor. in -хъ: двиг-нѫ-ти, aor. двиг-нѫхъ, but they prefer the asigmatic aorist двигъ (§ 69.1), or in a later period the enlarged sigmatic aorist in -охъ (§ 69.3) двигохъ. The number of -хъ aorists from verbs of the second class is small in the texts, and they occur alongside the asigmatic forms: коснѫти 'to touch', aor. 3rd pl. коснѫшѧ and коснѧ; дръзнѫти 'to dare', aor. 3rd pl. дръзнѫшѧ and дръзнѧ; тръгнѫти 'to pull', aor. 3rd pl. тръгнѫшѧ and тръгнѧ.

(*e*) Verbs with a monosyllabic stem ending in a consonant could form the sigmatic aorist by adding the endings and lengthening the vowel of the infinitive-aorist stem (§ 62) *o* > *a*, *e* > *ĕ*, *i* > *i*: бос-ти 'to sting', 1st sg. pr. бодѫ, aor. sg. басъ, боде боде; pl. басомъ, басте, басѧ; du. басовѣ, баста, басте; вес-ти 'to lead', 1st sg. pr. ведѫ, aor. вѣсъ, веде, &c.; чисти 'to count, to read', 1st sg. чьтѫ, aor. чисъ, &c.; пѧти 'to stretch, to hang', 1st sg. pr. пьнѫ, aor. пѧсъ, пѧ, пѧ, пѧсомъ, &c.; ꙗсти 'to eat', 1st sg. pr. ꙗмь, aor. ꙗсъ, из-ѣ, (-ꙗ), из-ѣ, ꙗсомъ (ꙗхомъ), ꙗсте, ꙗсѧ (ꙗшѧ), but also ꙗхъ, probably on the analogy of дахъ from дасти 'to give'. In the 3rd pers. ꙗстъ is the regular form parallel to дастъ; the ending -стъ is analogous to the 3rd sg. pr. ѥстъ.

(*f*) When the final consonant of the stem was *k*, *r* (§ 22), *g*, *l* the suffix -*s*- is changed into -*x*: рещи 'to tell', 1st sg. pr. рекѫ, aor. sg.: рѣхъ < *rēk-sŭ, рече, рече; pl. рѣхомъ, рѣсте, рѣшѧ; du. рѣховѣ, рѣста, рѣсте; мрѣти < *merti 'to die', 1st sg. pr. мьрѫ, aor.: мрѣхъ, мрѣ, мрѣ, &c.; жешти 'to burn', 1st sg. pr. жегѫ, aor.: жахъ; клати < *kolti 'to stab, to slaughter', 1st sg. pr. колѭ, aor.: клахъ, кла, кла, клахомъ, &c. (§ 6.3).

(*g*) The verbs по-жрѣти < *žerti 'to devour' and жрѫти 'to sacrifice' have 1st sg. pr. жьрѫ, and трѣти < *terti 'to rub' (also an infinitive трѫти) 1st sg. pr. тьрѫ and form their aorists: -жрѣхъ, жрѫхъ, трѫхъ (§ 10.4).

(*h*) Also these aorist forms occur in the texts only from a small number of verbs. Apart from those mentioned above, the texts

record aorist forms from: блюсти 'to watch (over)', aor. блюсъ; врѣсти 'to throw', aor. врѣсъ; грети 'to dig, to row', aor. грѣсъ; мѧсти 'to trouble', aor. мѧсъ; трѧсти 'to shake', aor. трѧсъ; влѣшти 'to drag', aor. влѣхъ; лѧшти 'to bend', aor. лѧхъ. Double forms occur from мѧсти, 3rd pl. aor. мѧсѧ and съ-мѧшѧ.

(i) In the 2nd and 3rd persons sg. an ending -тъ is added, especially to the aorist forms of verbs with the stem ending in -r-, -ę-, -i-, -ĕ-: оумрѣтъ, прострѣтъ from прострѣти 'to spread', питъ from пити 'to drink', начатъ from начати 'to begin', бꙑстъ from бꙑти 'to be', поѧстъ from ѧсти 'to eat', дастъ from дати, 'to give', alongside оумрѣ, прострѣ, пи, начѧ, бꙑ, поѧ, дѧ.

3. The new, enlarged sigmatic aorist is formed by the suffix -охъ added to the stem which ends in a consonant. The conjugation is the same as that of the -хъ aorist, and in the 2nd and 3rd persons sg. it also takes the forms of the simple aorist. This aorist is formed from verbs of the first conjugation, with the exception of those which have an infinitive stem in -a- (бьрⷶ-ти) and of those with a stem ending in -n- or in -r- (пѧти-пьнѫ, мрѣти-мьрѫ); it is also formed from verbs of the second conjugation with a consonantal radical:

Sing.	1st	несохъ	двигохъ	Plur.	1st	несохомъ	двигохомъ
	2nd	несе	движе		2nd	несосте	двигосте
	3rd	несе	движе		3rd	несошѧ	двигошѧ

Dual	1st	несоховѣ	двигоховѣ
	2nd	несоста	двигоста
	3rd	несосте	двигосте

The texts vary in the use of these aorist forms. Some texts show no trace of them (Mar., Ps. Sin., Cloz.), others seldom use this aorist (Aṣṣ., Euch. Sin.), and in others again it is regular or frequent (Savv. Kn., Supr., Zogr.). This aorist is a later creation and replaced the asigmatic aorist and the sigmatic aorist in -хъ in the history of the Slavonic languages. The Western Slavonic languages form this aorist with the ending -ech.

IMPERFECT

§ 70. The IE imperfect (cf. Gr. ἔ-φευγ-ον) was lost in OCS, because in many verbs it became identical with the simple aorist; e.g. from вєсти 'to move in a vehicle', 1st sg. вєзѫ, the imperfect should have been *vezŭ; from мошти 'to be able', 1st sg. pr. могѫ, impf. *mogŭ. These forms are, however, identical with the simple aorist forms.

In Slavonic a new formation replaced the old IE imperfect. The derivative suffix of the new imperfect is -ахъ or -ѣахъ added usually to the infinitive stem. The ending -ахъ is used to form the imperfect of verbs which have a second stem ending in -а- or -ѣ-, i.e. conjugation Ib (§ 61.I) бьра-ти-, impf. бьра-ахъ; conjugation III (§ 61.III) зна-ти-, impf. зна-ахъ, грѣ-ти-, impf. грѣ-ахъ, коупова-ти, impf. коупова-ахъ; conjugation IVb (§ 61.IV) сѣдѣ-ти-, impf. сѣдѣ-ахъ.

All other verbs form the imperfect by means of the suffix -ѣахъ: нес-ти-, impf. нес-ѣахъ, двигнѫти, impf. двигн-ѣахъ, молити, impf. мол-ꙗахъ (мол-ѣахъ) < *molj-ěaxŭ.

(a) The velar stem consonants k, g were palatalized into č, ž by a following -ě-. After the palatal consonants (č, ž, j) -ě- changed into -a- and so an ending -аахъ was obtained: текѫ, тешти 'to run, to flow', impf. течаахъ < *tek-ěaxъ; могѫ, мошти 'to be able', impf. можаахъ < *mog-ěaxъ; враштѫ, вратити 'to turn', impf. враштаахъ < *vortj-ěaxŭ; чюѭ, чюти 'to feel', impf. чюꙗахъ.

(b) Most of the endings are parallel to those of the aorist:

Sing. 1st -ахъ, -ѣахъ, -аахъ Plur. -ахомъ, -ѣахомъ, -аахомъ
      2nd -ашє, -ѣашє, -аашє   -ашєтє, (-астє); -ѣашєтє,
                                (-ѣастє); -аашєтє, (-аастє)
      3rd -ашє, -ѣашє, -аашє   -ахѫ, -ѣахѫ, -аахѫ

Dual 1st -аховѣ, -ѣаховѣ, -ааховѣ
      2nd -ашєта, (-аста); -ѣашєта, (-ѣаста); -аашєта, (-ааста)
      3rd -ашєтє, (-астє); -ѣашєтє, (-ѣастє); -аашєтє, (-аастє)

The ending -ѣахъ, &c. is also spelt -ꙗахъ.

(c) These endings were sometimes contracted, in the further de-velopment of the language, into -ачъ, -ѣхъ, and thus arose the impf. forms бьрахъ, несѥхъ alongside бьрадахъ, несѥкахъ (§ 32.5). The texts differ in their use of contracted and non-contracted impf. forms. Savv. Kn. uses only contracted forms, in Zogr. and Mar. the contracted forms are exceptions.

(d) The endings -сте (2nd pl., 3rd du.), -ста (2nd du.) are the aorist endings introduced into the imperfect paradigm. They do not appear in Zogr. and Cloz.; Savv. Kn. and Ostr. use them exclusively.

(e) The origin of the imperfect endings is not clear. The nearest approach to a satisfactory explanation is to be seen in -jaxŭ (ведѥкахъ < *vedě-jaxŭ) an old impf. from *es- (radical of the verb 'to be') preceded by an augment: e+es > ēs > *jasŭ, *jase, &c. The x for s (-jaxŭ) could be explained by analogy with the aorist endings -xŭ (§ 69.2). (Cf. J. Kurylowicz, Réflexions sur l'imparfait et les aspects en vieux slave. Esquisses linguistiques, 1960, p. 120.)

MOODS

IMPERATIVE MOOD

§ 71. Of the IE moods OCS retained only the indicative. The optative assumed in OCS the function of the imperative. The characteristic derivative element for the formation of the optative from the thematic verbs is -i-: *ber-o-i-mi, *ber-o-i-s, *ber-o-i-t, *ber-o-i-mŭ, *ber-o-i-te (cf. Gr. φέροιτε), &c. Forms for the 1st sg. and 3rd pl. have not been preserved in OCS. The imperative for these persons is formed with the particle да + indicative, which tense has then the meaning of a permissive mood.

1. The IE diphthong -oi- was monophthongized into -ě- (§ 10.2.3) which changed into -i- at the end of a word or when preceded by -j- or by a palatal consonant. Thus the following endings arose:

Sing. 1st —	Plur. 1st -ѣмъ, -ѣамъ,	Dual 1st -ѣвѣ, -ѣавѣ,
	-имъ	-ивѣ
2nd -и	2nd -ѣте, -ѣте,	2nd -ѣта, -ѣта,
	-ите	-ита
3rd -и	3rd —	3rd —

Accordingly, from вести, ведѫ the imperative is: веди, ведⷨ; ведѣмъ, ведѣте; ведѣвѣ, ведѣта. Dual forms are very rare. If the present stem contained a -j- the result was: знаи [znaji], знаи; знаимъ, знаите; знаивѣ, знаита; however, this category of verbs also has the ending -ѣмъ, -ѣте: глаголѣмъ and глагол- имъ, глаголѣте and глаголите. Euch. Sin. and Cloz. know only -i- forms; Savv. Kn. shows only -a- forms. Verbs with the present stem in -i- have -i- endings in the imperative: моли, молимъ, молите, which are identical with the indicative forms (where, however, the -i- is not of diphthongic origin). These verbs are of athematic origin (§ 61.IV) and have the endings of that class of verbs.

2. The athematic verbs add the -i- direct to the consonantal stem which is palatalized and gives the following result: даmь, imp. даждь, дадите; ѣmь, imp. ѣждь (ѣждь), ѣдите; вѣmь, imp. вѣждь, вѣдите. This ending has been extended, and the imp. from видѣти is виждь, видите. In Euch. Sin. the regular forms are даждн, вѣждн, виждн which are built by analogy with the thematic forms.

The athematic verb ѥсмь forms the imperative from another stem: бѫдѫ 'I will be', imp. бѫди; this verb alone has all three persons in imperative: бѫдѣмь, бѫди, бѫди; бѫдѣмъ, бѫдѣте, бѫдѫ; бѫдѣвѣ, бѫдѣта, бѫдѣте. Originally this form was a subjunctive. The first person form (бѫдѣмь) may have the meaning of an optative (§ 98.o).

3. The imperative forms illustrate the double treatment of the diphthong oi (§ 10.2). The OCS imperative represents the IE optative of the type Gr. φέροις, φέροι, φέροιμεν, φέροιτε. In the 2nd and 3rd sg. the final -oi is represented by -i: beri; in the 1st and 2nd pl. the medial -oi- is represented by -ĕ-: berĕmŭ, berĕte; when preceded by j the -oi- changes into -i-: znajimŭ, znajite. Some texts have forms with ĕ: ubiĕmŭ, bijate (Supr.). A. Meillet (Le slave commun, 1934, 330) considers the forms with ĕ, ja as old IE subjunctive forms, in which the a, ĕ represent an original long ō, ē of the type Gr. φέρωμεν, φέρητε (§ 6.2, 4).

The OCS imperative forms with -ĕ- (pl.) have been replaced in

the modern Slavonic languages by forms with -*i*-, which originates in the athematic verbs of the type *dadite, jadite, vĕdite*. This -*i*- represents an original -*jē*- in the reduced grade -*ĭ*-, as seen in Lat. *sīmus* (also *siem, sies*, &c., in Plautus.), Gr. εἶμεν (§ 37).

CONDITIONAL MOOD

§ 72. The athematic verb бъіти has a modal form used as an auxiliary to form the compound conditional-optative tense (§ 88). This auxiliary has a flexion similar to the imperative forms:

Sing. 1st бимь	Plur. 1st бимъ	(Dual 1st бивѣ
2nd би	2nd бисте	2nd биста
3rd би	3rd бѫ	3rd бисте)

In the compound conditional, instead of the auxiliary бимь, the aorist of the verb бъіти 'to be' could be used: бъіхъ, бъі, бъі (never бъістъ); бъіхомъ, бъісте, бъішѧ; бъіховѣ, бъіста, бъісте (§ 88). On the pattern of these forms the auxiliary of the compound conditional built new forms: бихомъ, бисте, бишѧ. The replacement of бимь by бъіхъ is characteristic for the later texts. So in Savv. Kn. and Supr. бимь, &c., are exceptions and бъіхъ is used regularly; Mar., Ass. keep the old form бимъ, while Zogr. has бихомъ; in Zogr., Mar., Ass. бишѧ appears as a new form alongside the more regular бѫ. Ostr. does not show бимь.

The form бисте is analogous to the aorist бъісте. The expected form of the 2nd pl. would be *bi-te*.

In the development of the Slavonic languages, formations with бимь are characteristic for OCS (Macedonian) and for the Western Slavonic languages; formations with бъіхъ are characteristic for Russian Church Slavonic and for Middle Bulgarian.

NOMINAL FORMS OF VERBS

PRESENT PARTICIPLE ACTIVE

§ 73. The present participle active is formed by means of the ending -ъі from verbs of the first and second conjugation, and from the athematic verbs, and by means of the ending -ѧ from verbs of the third and fourth conjugations.

One category of part. (conj. I, II, and athematic) has a stem ending in -ѫшт-, on which the other cases are built; the verbs of conj. III have a parallel stem ending in -ιѫшт-; the second category (conj. IV) builds the other cases on a stem ending in -ѧшт- (§ 52.2, § 58). So we have:

I.	ид-ы 'going'	G.	ид-ѫшт-а
II.	двигн-ы 'moving'	G.	двигн-ѫшт-а
III.	зна-ιѧ 'knowing'	G.	зна-ιѫшт-а
IV.	мол-ѧ 'demanding'	G.	мол-ѧшт-а
V.	дад-ы 'giving'	G.	дад-ѫшт-а

(a) The verb горѣти 'to burn' (intran.) горιѫ, гориши, fourth conj., has the pr. part. act. горѧ, G. горѫшта (alongside горѧшта); this verb originally belonged to the athematic class.

(b) The ending of the stem goes back to an IE suffix -nt- which, attached to the thematic vowel, gave: -o-nt- > -ǫ-, -e-nt- > -ę-, -i-nt- > -ę-, so *id-o-nt-ja > idǫšta (§ 13, § 21.2). The -y of the nom. (иды) has been explained as going back either to -ont-s or to -ōn (cf. Kul'bakin, Le vieux slave, 1929, 312). In Latin the cognate suffix appears in lauda-nt-is, &c. The -ιѧ of the soft stems is a regular result of the development -jont- > -jent- > -ję- (§ 14.3). The -ѧ of the fourth conjugation is analogous to the oblique cases: *modlint-ja > molęšta, &c. because *modlint-s would have developed into *modli, *moli (§ 5). The feminine forms in -i: идѫшти, молѧшти represent the zero-grade of a fem. -ja- stem: *modlint-ja/ *modlint-jī > molęšti (§ 37, § 39c).

PRESENT PARTICIPLE PASSIVE

§ 74. The present participle passive is an adjective formed by means of the ending -мъ, -ма, -мо added to the present stem:

	Masculine	Feminine	Neuter	
I.	несо-мъ	-ма	-мо	'carried'
II.	двиго-мъ	-ма	-мо	'moved'
III.	знаιє-мъ	-ма	-мо	'known'
IV.	моли-мъ	-ма	-мо	'asked'
V.	дадо-мъ	-ма	-мо	'given'

The originally athematic verbs видѣти 'to see' and алъкати 'to

be hungry' have the pr. part. pass. видомъ, лакомъ. The participles have nominal and pronominal declensions like adjectives (§ 49, § 56). They are used with any form of the auxiliary быти 'to be' to form a compound passive verbal form: несомъ ѥсмь 'I am carried', несоми быхомъ 'we were carried' (§ 89).

PAST PARTICIPLE ACTIVE I

§ 75. The past participle active I is formed by means of the suffix -ъ masc., neut., -ъши fem. attached to the consonantal infinitive stem. When the infinitive stem ends in a vowel the suffix is -въ masc., neut., -въши fem. (§ 52.3, § 58.2):

Masc., Neut.	Feminine
нес-ъ	нес-ъши
двиг-ъ	двиг-ъши
бьрд-въ	бьрд-въши
зна-въ	зна-въши

Verbs of the fourth conjugation form both types, in -ь: мольь, мольши, and in -въ: моливъ, моливъши. The first type is the older one and appears in the more archaic texts: Mar., Ass., Ps. Sin., Cloz.; the Supr. has a majority of participles in -ивъ; in Zogr., Euch. Sin., Savv. Kn. the -ивъ type appears exceptionally.

The ending -ŭ continues the IE suffix -ụs, -ụos/-ụes which in nom. sg. developed into -ŭx (§ 22) and changed into -ŭ (§ 5). The feminine form is a zero-grade of the feminine ending -ja: *nes-ŭx-i > nesŭši (§ 39c).

PAST PARTICIPLE ACTIVE 2

§ 76. The past participle active 2 is derived from the infinitive stem by means of the suffix -лъ masc., -ла fem., -ло neut., and declines only in N. sg. and pl. like a hard adjective (§ 49), usually in the indefinite form. These participles are used in the formation of compound verbal forms (§ 84, § 85, § 87, § 88):

Masculine	Feminine	Neuter
нес-лъ	нес-ла	нес-ло
двиг-лъ	двиг-ла	двиг-ло
зна-лъ	зна-ла	зна-ло

	Masculine	Feminine	Neuter
	моли-лъ	моли-ла	моли-ло
	да-лъ	да-ла	да-ло

Verbs of the first conjugation with a stem ending in -k or -r have, in this participle, the reduced root-vowel: влѣшти 'to drag, to pull', влѣкѫ, part. влъклъ (*vlk-lŭ*); трѣти 'to rub', тьрѫ, part. трьлъ; мрѣти 'to die', мьрѫ, part. мрьлъ (§ 37.5).

PAST PARTICIPLE PASSIVE

§ 77. The past participle passive has the form and the declension of a hard stem adjective (§ 49), derived from the infinitive stem by means of the suffix -енъ, -нъ, or -тъ: нес-енъ 'carried', движ-енъ 'moved'; зна-нъ 'known', да-нъ 'given'; би-тъ 'beaten'. It is used to form the passive voice (§ 89); cf. Lat. *pl-enus, pl-etus* E *full* < **pl̥n, fill-ed*.

1. The suffix -енъ forms the participles:

(*a*) from all verbs with an infinitive stem ending in a consonant: вести, ведѫ, part. веденъ 'lead'; решти, рекѫ, part. реченъ 'said', двигнѫти, двигнѫ, part. движенъ 'moved';

(*b*) from verbs of the third conjugation with the radical ending in -i, -y: бити, биѭ, part. биенъ 'beaten'; крыти, крыѭ, part. кръв-енъ 'covered', забыти, забѫдѫ, part. забъв-енъ 'forgotten';

(*c*) from verbs of the fourth conjugation: молити, молѭ, part. молиенъ 'requested'; просити, прошѫ, part. прошенъ 'solicited'; троудити, троуждѫ, part. троужденъ 'tired'; вратити, вращѫ, part. вращенъ 'turned'; любити, люблѭ, part. люблиенъ 'loved'. For the changes in the final stem consonant see § 17*b*, § 21.2.

(*d*) Verbs of the second conjugation seldom have a participle in -овенъ: отъринѫти 'to push', part. отъриновенъ; дръзнѫти 'to dare', part. дръзновенъ.

2. The suffix -нъ is used to form the participle from verbs with an infinitive stem ending in -a-, -ě-: пьса-ти 'to write', part. пьсанъ; да-ти 'to give', part. данъ; видѣ-ти 'to see', part. видѣнъ. The verbs with the radical ending in -l have the part. in -нъ, or in -енъ: клати < **kol-ti* 'to stab, to kill', part. кланъ or коленъ.

3. The suffix -тъ is used to form the participle from verbs with the infinitive stem ending in -ҏ: ѩ-ти 'to grasp, to seize', part. ѩтъ; клати 'to curse', part. клѧтъ; пѧти 'to stretch, to hang', part. пѧтъ.

The -тъ participle has become an adjective in forms derived from verbs with the stem ending in -s, -z: оувѧстъ 'crowned' from оувѧзѫ; извѣстъ 'known' from извѣдѣти; отъврьстъ 'open' from отъврѣсти, отъврьзѫ.

4. Some verbs may form both types of participles. Verbs having a radical ending in -r form the part. in -тъ: стрѣти 'to extend' < *ster-ti, part. стрьтъ, but the same verb also has a participle простьренъ. The verb бити, биѭ 'to beat' has the participles битъ and бьѥнъ; сѣти, сѣѭ 'to sow', participles о-сѣтъ or -сѣнъ; повити 'to swaddle' has the participle повитъ.

FUTURE PARTICIPLE

§ 78. The future participle has left a trace in texts of later date (Russian Church Slavonic) in the form бышѧшт-: (быти) 'which will be': не бышѧщи водѣ (Isaiah l. 2) 'because there will not be water'. Otherwise the future participle is expressed by the present participle of the perfective verb (§ 90) бѫдѫ, pr. part. act. бѫды, бѫдѫшта &c. 'who will be' (§ 73).

VERBAL NOUN

§ 79. The verbal noun is derived by means of the suffix -ije (-ĭje) (§ 40.2c) from the past part. pass. of transitive and intransitive verbs (which in reality have no past participle passive):
знати 'to know', past part. pass. знанъ : знаниѥ 'knowledge'; съпасти 'to save', past part. pass. съпасенъ : съпасениѥ 'salvation'; исцѣлити 'to cure', past part. pass. исцѣленъ : исцѣлениѥ 'the healing'; мыслити 'to think', past part. pass. мышленъ : помышлениѥ 'the thought'; зачати 'to conceive (a child)', past part. pass. зачатъ : зачатиѥ 'conception'; пропѧти 'to crucify', past part. pass. пропѧтъ : пропѧтиѥ 'crucifixion'; оумрѣти 'to die': оумрътиѥ 'death'; въскрьснѫти 'to resurrect': въскрьсениѥ, въскрьсновениѥ 'resurrection'; ити 'to go': шьстиѥ, шьствиѥ 'march'.

The verbal noun has a very extensive syntactic use. It has not only a nominal but also a verbal function: по глаголании его къ нимъ (Mt. xvi. 19) 'after he spoke to them'.

INVARIABLE VERBAL FORMS

INFINITIVE

§ 80. The infinitive is in origin a noun with a -*t*- stem, in the dative or locative case. The ending of the infinitive is -ти, which is added directly to a vocalic stem: зна-ти, да-ти, кры-ти, бьра-ти, коупова-ти. Verbs whose stem ends in a dental change the dental into -*s*- (§ 29.10): пас-ти 'to fall' < *pad-ti*, обрѣсти 'to find' < *obrēt-ti*; a final velar is palatalized (§ 30.1): решти 'to tell' < *rek-ti*, мошти 'to be able' < *mog-ti*; a labial is regularly dropped: гребѫ, грети 'to dig, to row' < *greb-ti* (§ 29.11). The later form погрести is a back formation on the analogy of нести, пасти. The *n, m* of the stem nasalize the preceding vowel when they belong to the same syllable: па-ти, пьн-ѫ 'to stretch', дѫ-ти, дъм-ѫ 'to blow' (§ 13, § 14). Radicals containing the diphthongs -*er*-, -*or*-, -*el*-, -*ol*- change them in the infinitive according to § 6.3, § 10.4: мьрѫ, мрѣти < *mer-ti* 'to die'; мелѭ, млѣти 'to mill' < *mel-ti*; борѭ, брати 'to defend' < *bor-ti*; колѭ, клати 'to stab' < *kol-ti*. The vocalic liquids are preserved in the stem: тьрѧ, трѣти 'to rub' < *tr̥ti*; тлък-нѫ, тлък-нѫ-ти 'to knock' < *tl̥knǫti* (§ 17).

SUPINE

§ 81. The supine is formed by replacing the infinitive ending -ти by the ending -тъ. This represents an original accusative from a stem in -*tu*-, and corresponds to Lat. -*tum* in the supine: *da-tu-m*. The changes of the stem consonant are the same as those which take place in the formation of the infinitive. When the stem ends in -*k*, ъ is replaced by ь: пекѫ, пешти inf. 'to bake', sup. пешть. The supine has the meaning of a verbal noun with final sense: идѫ рыбъ ловитъ (J. xxi. 3) 'I go fishing (to catch fish)'; придъ пролитъ кръве своеѩ (Cloz. i. 233) 'I came to shed my blood'; приде видѣтъ гроба (Mt. xxxviii. 1) '(she) came to see the sepulchre'; приде жена отъ самариѩ почрѣтъ воды (Zogr., J.

iv. 7) 'a woman of Samaria came to draw water'; огнѣ придъ
възврѣштъ въ землиѭ (Mar., L. xii. 49) 'I am come to send fire
on the earth'. The supine demands a genitive-object: чесо видѣтъ
изидите (Mt. xi. 7) 'what went ye out to see'.

The supine is used after a verb expressing motion, and translates
the Greek infinitive: идѭ рыбъ ловитъ 'I go to catch fish' = ὑπάγω
ἁλιεύειν (J. xxi. 3). The supine was already disappearing in OCS
and it has been replaced in Modern Slavonic languages by other
constructions (it survived in Slovene, Czech, and Lower Lusatian).
The OCS texts illustrate this development: thus in Zogr. the
example quoted above has an infinitive instead of the supine:
възврѣшти. Zogr. has: ї идѣахѫ вси кожьдо нап'сати сѧ въ свои
градъ (L. ii. 3) 'and all went to be taxed, (everyone) into his own
city'; Ass., Savv. Kn., Ostr. have a supine in this sentence in the
place of the infinitive: написатъ сѧ, and напсатъ сѧ (Savv.
Kn.). Another way of replacing the supine was by means of the
conjunction да 'in order that': се изиде сѣѧи сѣатъ (Mar.,
Mk. iv. 3) 'behold, there went out a sower to sow', but: изиде
сѣѧи да сѣетъ (Mar., Mt. xiii. 3) = Gr. ἐξῆλθεν ὁ σπείρων τοῦ
σπείρειν 'the sower went forth to sow'.

GERUND FORMS

§ 82. Isolated gerund forms in OCS texts mark the beginning of
the tendency to reduce participial declensions to a single form and
to create the gerund forms of the modern Slavonic languages:
повели ми древле шедъше погрети отца моего (Mar., Zogr., L.
ix. 59) 'suffer me first to go and bury my father', but Ass. and Ostr.
re-establish the agreement and have: шедъшоу; подоба ми ѥстъ
сѣдѣти мльчѧште (Supr. 20.5, 14) 'I like to be seated in silence'.

The past participle in the function of a gerund is recorded in
the example: отъ Адама до Моуса, рек'ше до закона (Supr.
35.1, 26) 'from Adam till Moses, namely (= си рѣчь) to the
Law'.

THE VERBAL FORM sętŭ

§ 83. An invariable verbal form of obscure origin is сѧтъ, сѧти
which occurs in Supr. (477.19) Ps. Sin. (35.2), and in Cloz. (28

times) with the meaning 'say(s)': послоушаі чъто сѫтъ еванге-
листъ: слꙑшавъше, сѫтъ, гласъ їдѫ въспѧть ї падѫ на земли
ници (Cloz.) 'hear what the Evangelist says: after they heard the
voice, he says, they went back and fell with their faces to the earth'.
This form сѫтъ has the meaning of the aorist рече (Supr.) and
is explanatory. Some scholars see in this form a 3rd person of
the present tense, others of the aorist, others again see an association of the reflexive сѧ+pronoun тъ(ти). It translates the Greek
φησί(ν) 'he says'.

COMPOUND VERBAL FORMS
PERFECT

§ 84. The IE perfect has disappeared in CS leaving only one form:
OCS вѣдѣ 'I know' (вѣдѣти, вѣмь) < *ṷoiḍāị corresponds to
the Gr. perfect (ϝ)οῖδα 'I know', Lat. vīdī 'I saw'.

The function of the perfect has been taken over by a form com-
pounded from the past participle in -лъ (§ 76) and the present of
бꙑти: неслъ masc., несла fem., несло neut., ѥсмь 'I carried';
несли masc., неслꙑ fem., несла neut., ѥсмъ 'we carried'.

The perfect often translates the Greek aorist; this shows that
it expressed the past in general without relation to the speaker.
Its development in the modern Slavonic languages seems to sup-
port this interpretation. Byzantine Greek had analytical tenses
consisting of participles and auxiliaries, and the Slavonic forms
may be built up on the analogy of such Greek constructions: ἦν
ἀποστείλας (plupf.) 'he had sent'; συναθροίζων ἦν (impf.) 'he was
gathering together'.

To such Greek constructions correspond in OCS parallel analytical verbal forms: бѣ оучѧ въ цръкве (L. xix. 47) 'he was
teaching in the church = he taught (daily) in the temple'; бѣ бо
оумираѩ (J. iv. 47) 'he was dying'.

PLUPERFECT

§ 85. An action which took place earlier than a past action is
expressed by the pluperfect. The formation is parallel to that of the
perfect, replacing the present of the auxiliary by the imperfect (or

the aorist): неслъ бѣахъ, бѣаше, &c.; бѣхъ, бѣше, &c. The auxiliary may also be replaced by the perfect of its form: неслъ бꙑлъ ѥсмь 'I had carried', и видѣ дъва анћела въ бѣлахъ (ризахъ) сѣдѧшта . . . идеже бѣ лежало тѣло исоусово (J. xx. 12) 'and saw two angels in white sitting . . . where the body of Jesus had lain'.

FUTURE

§ 86. The future tense is expressed either by the present of a perfective verb (§ 90), or by the infinitive associated with a verb which has a connotation of future action, like въчѧти, начѧти 'to begin', имѣти 'to have', хотѣти 'to will', fulfilling the function of an auxiliary: глаголати иматъ (Zogr., Mar., J. xvi. 13) 'he shall speak'; намъ хоштеши сѧ ѣвити (Zogr., Mar., J. xiv. 22) 'thou wilt manifest thyself unto us'; и ненавидѣти сѧ начьнѧтъ (Mt. xxiv. 10) 'they shall hate one another'; небрѣшти въчьнетъ (Zogr., Savv. Kn., L. xvi. 13) 'he will neglect'. The present of an imperfective verb could also express the future in the context of a sentence: отъсели не видите ме (Supr. 16.29) 'from now you shall not see me'.

FUTURE PERFECT

§ 87. The future perfect is usually expressed by the future tense (§ 86), but there is also a compound form, consisting of the past part. in -лъ and the auxiliary бѫдѫ: читалъ бѫдѫ 'I shall have read'; аще нꙑ деситъ день съмрътьнꙑ въ грѣсѣхъ, то въ-скѫѭ сѧ и родили бѫдемъ 'if the day of the death finds us in sins, then what for shall we have been born ?' (Euch. Sin. 71a. 4–6). The auxiliary бѫдѫ associated with a noun, an adjective, or a participle forms a periphrastic future: бѫдеши мльча (Zogr., L. i. 20) 'thou shalt be dumb'; живъ бѫдеши (Zogr., L. x. 28) 'thou shalt live'; бѫдѫ does not appear in OCS texts associated with the infinitive.

CONDITIONAL–OPTATIVE

§ 88. There exists a compound verbal form for conditional–optative which is obtained by adding the auxiliary optative бимь (§ 72) to

the past participle in -лъ: бꙑлъ бимь (бꙑхъ) 'I would (like to) be'; могли бимъ (бихомъ, бꙑхомъ) 'we would be able'; аште не би ... бꙑлъ ... не моглъ би (J. ix. 33) 'If he was not ... he could not'; аште сѧ би не родилъ (Mt. xxiv. 24) 'If he had not been born'.

The past. part. could also be used without the auxiliary to express a wish: ѥша и. не събрали събора (Supr. 386.6) 'if they had not been able to bring together the council'.

The conditional–optative could express a wish: іароу да бꙑ (би) обрѣлъ лютѣишѧ (Supr. 213.2) 'Oh, if he had found more cruel people!' (such constructions usually contain a particle: іароу); an unfulfilled condition: аште бо бисте вѣрѫ имали Мосеови, вѣрѫ бисте іали и мьнѣ (J. v. 46) 'for had ye believed Moses, ye would have believed me'; a possibility in final clauses: и дръжаахѫ и, да не би отъшелъ отъ нихъ (L. iv. 42) 'and they kept him, that he should not depart from them'; an uncertainty: и глаголахѫ дроугъ къ дроугоу, чьто биша сътворили Ісоусови (L. vi. 11) 'and communed one with another what they might do to Jesus'; и не оумѣхѫ чьто бѫ отъвѣштали ѥмоу (Mk. xiv. 40) 'neither wist they what to answer him'.

PASSIVE VOICE

§ 89. The passive voice has no special forms. It is expressed either by a reflexive verb (§ 60)or by the passive participle (§ 74, § 77) and an auxiliary form of бꙑти: азъ трѣбоуѭ отъ тебе крьстити сѧ (Mt. iii. 14) 'I have need to be baptized of thee'; сꙑнове цѣсарьствиіа изгънани бѫдѫтъ (Mt. viii. 12) 'the children of the kingdom shall be cast out'; гонимъ (pr. p. pass.) бꙑвааше (Mar., Zogr., Savv. Kn., L. viii. 29) 'he was driven out'; да пропѧтъ бѫдетъ (Mt. xxvii. 22) 'let him be crucified'; прѣданъ иматъ бꙑти (Mt. xvii. 22) 'he shall be betrayed'; бѫдете ненавидими (Mt. xxiv. 9) 'ye shall be hated'; прѣданъ бѫдетъ (Zogr., Mk. ix. 31; Mk. x. 33) 'he shall be delivered'.

The iterative (impft.–indeterminate) бꙑвати 'to be usually' may also function as auxiliary for the passive voice.

VERBAL ASPECTS

PERFECTIVE, IMPERFECTIVE, ITERATIVE VERBS

§ 90. Verbal tenses define the time *when* an event takes place; they indicate a relation in time between the speaker and the event (present, past, or future). An event, however, may be conceived independently of any time relation, and considered from the point of view of the quality *how* it develops. Thus, a verbal action may be conceived in its duration (non-completed): *I am going*, Lat. *venio* 'I come', OCS ид̯ѫ 'I go'. The quality of this event is *imperfective* (durative).

The event may be conceived from the point of view of its starting-point (Lat. inchoative verbs: *incānesco* 'I turn grey') or of its ending-point (Lat. *advenio* 'I arrive', OCS придѫ 'I shall arrive'). Again one may conceive an event as having the beginning and the end concentrated in one point, i.e. without consideration of its development. Such events are called *perfective* (completed) from the point of view of their quality.

The process may consist of several repeated durative actions: Lat. *ambulat* 'he walks habitually': Lat. *it* 'he goes'; OCS ходитъ 'he walks': идетъ 'he goes (in a certain direction)'. These repetitive events are *indeterminate* (without a definite term) compared with the imperfective events which are *determinate*. The indeterminate водитъ means 'he leads (in general), he is a leader', the determinate ведетъ means 'he leads (in a certain direction)'. The special verbal forms used to express these qualities of events are called *aspects*.

Not each verb has perfective and imperfective forms, just as not each verb has forms for all tenses. The perfective verbs have, as a rule, aorist and perfect tenses but no imperfect tense, the imperfective verbs have imperfect but no aorist forms. The present forms of the perfective verbs express the future tense. It is the totality of verbal forms which defines the verbal aspect.

Whereas some IE languages have developed a system of verbal tenses, and have reduced the aspects to a secondary function, CS developed a system of verbal aspects, creating two main categories: *perfective* and *imperfective*. The *iterative* category (indeterminate)

was restricted to a small number of verbs expressing a motion; many iterative verbs lost the idea of repetition and became imperfective, while the imperfect tense took over the function of expressing a repetitive action: и не дадѣаше николоуже лилю нести съсѫдъ (Mar., Mk. xi. 16) 'and would not suffer that any man carry any vessel', i.e. every time anybody carried a vessel he used to forbid him to do this.

Within the whole system of verbal forms the verbal aspect is featured by certain derivative elements, e.g. пасти 'to fall down', i.e. to reach the end point of falling, ıати 'to seize, to take', i.e. to put your hand on . . ., (о-)коньчати 'to finish', i.e. to bring an action to its completeness, are *perfective verbs*; whereas падати 'to fall', i.e. to be falling, имати 'to hold, to have', коньчавати 'to end', as a rule are *imperfective verbs*.

. By such derivative features indeterminate verbal forms were created in opposition to the determinate ones: determinate плоути 'to swim': indeterminate плавати; determinate коупити 'to buy': indeterminate коуповати; determinate клонити 'to bow': indeterminate клаıати; determinate скочити 'to jump': indeterminate скакати, &c.

The opposition perfective ⌣ imperfective may be obtained by prefixation; the prefix changes the imperfective into a perfective aspect: impft. нести 'to carry': pft. принести 'to bring'; impft. ити 'to go': pft. прити 'to arrive'.

The *iterative aspect* (indeterminate) is characterized by the vowel of the radical: ходити 'to go (habitually)', водити 'to lead (habitually)', носити 'to carry (habitually)'. The opposition iterative ⌣ imperfective may be obtained by secondary derivations: impft. творити: it. творıати 'to do repeatedly'; impft. лѣсти 'to step': it. лазити 'to crawl about'. The iterative (indeterminate) aspect forms merged with the imperfective (determinate) forms. The prefixed iterative forms either preserve their imperfective (-iterative) aspect: сътворıати 'to do repeatedly', or they become perfective: приходити 'to arrive'.

There are, however, no decisive formal characteristics for the determination of perfective and imperfective aspect forms. The aspect of a verbal form is in practice determined by the correla-

tion with the aspect of another verb derived from the same root.
Thus, we find oppositions of the following types: Perfective: ѩти,
стати, сѣсти, тлъкнѫти, пасти ◡ Imperfective: имати, стоѩти,
сѣдѣти, тлѣшти, падати ◡ Perfective: възѩти, въстати,
въсѣсти, сътлѣшти, въпасти ◡ Imperfective: приимати, въст-
аѩти, присѣдѣти, прѣдъстаѩти, нападати; Imperfective determinate: нести, ити, вести ◡ Imperfective indeterminate (Iterative): носити, ходити, водити ◡ Imperfective: приносити,
приходити, изводити ◡ Perfective: принести, прити, извести.

(a) It is not always easy to determine the aspect of a verb outside
the context. The aspect of some verbs is uncertain: видѣти 'to
see', бѣжати 'to run', сѫдити 'to judge', and other verbs vacillate
between the two aspects. It is the correlation with another aspect
and the context that defines usage and meaning.

(b) The main functional difference between the perfective and
the imperfective verbs is the fact that the present tense of the perfective verbs has the value of a future: имѫ 'I shall seize', станѫ
'I shall stand', сѧдѫ 'I shall sit down', коуплѭ 'I shall buy' ◡
ѥмлѭ 'I take', стаѭ 'I stand', сѣждѫ 'I am seated', коупоуѭ 'I
buy, I am buying'.

(c) Thus in OCS the perfective verbs could express the future
but could not express the present concept, and the imperfective
verbs could express the present but could not express the future.

The perfective verbs have as a rule no imperfect tense because
they express a completed action; the imperfective verbs have no
aorist forms because they express a durative action which is opposed
to the meaning of the aorist; however, the imperfective-indeterminate verbs have regular aorist forms which narrate durative events
in the past (cf. A. Meillet, *Le Slave commun*, 1924, pp. 217–18,
240–58).

FUNCTION OF VERBAL PREFIXES

§ 91. Some verbs express the opposition perfective ◡ imperfective
by forms derived from the same root, others by different verbs: pft.
ѩти (ѧти) 'to seize': impft. имати 'to have'; pft. тлъкнѫти 'to
knock': impft. тлѣшти 'to push; pft. решти 'to say': impft.
глаголати 'to talk'; others again supply the necessary forms by

prefixes: impft. творити 'to make': pft. сътворити 'to make';
impft. дѣлати 'to work': pft. съдѣлати 'to complete a work';
impft. нести 'to carry': pft. принести 'to bring'.

The prefixes originally had an adverbial function and defined
the verb semantically. Already in an early period some prefixes
lost their adverbial function and became derivative elements for
indicating the aspect; so, for example, въз-, о-, оу-, по-, съ- indicate perfectivity: блюсти impft.: съблюсти pft. 'to guard, to
watch'; вѣдѣти impft. 'to know': съвѣдѣти pft. 'to be aware',
also 'to know jointly', translating Gr. συνειδέναι, оувѣдѣти pft.
'to begin to know, to recognize, to learn'. Some verbs have very
numerous prefixed forms: e.g. ити shows about a score of forms,
ιати, дати have more than ten forms each. Generally speaking, it
may be said that a prefix changes the aspect of the verb. When,
however, the prefix has a clear adverbial function the verbal aspect
remains unchanged and the meaning of the verb is changed.

Verbal Prefixes and Their Meaning (see § 102)

§ 92. въ-, вън- (before vowels) express entry: въбѣгнѫти pft. 'to
run in', вънити 'to enter', въвести 'to lead into'.

въз- (възъ-), въс-, въж-, въ- 'up, upwards': възити 'to
climb', възалкати pft. 'to become hungry': алкати impft.
'to be hungry', въсходити 'to go up, to climb', въждадати
pft. 'to get thirsty.': жадати impft. 'to be thirsty'.

вы- 'out' occurs mainly in the Ps. Sin., Euch. Sin., and Cloz.
and seems to be of Western Slavonic origin; it is a parallel
form to изъ-, из-: выгънати pft. 'to drive out', изгънати,
иждєнѫ pft. 'to drive out, away': гънати 'to chase'.

до- 'up to, till': донти 'to arrive', донести 'to bring up to';
досадити 'to scold, to offend'.

за- 'behind, after, for': занти 'to go down = behind' (of the
sun), затворити 'to close in', забыти 'to forget', завидѣти
'to envy', закрыти 'to cover', заходити 'to go down, behind'.

из-, ис- 'out, from': изгорѣти 'to burn to the end', изити 'to go
out', иштезнѫти 'to disappear (altogether)'; a double prefix
gives the verb an expressive meaning: испроврѣшти,
опроврѣшти 'to turn upside-down'.

мимо- 'by, along': мимоити, мимоходити 'to pass by', мимотешти, мимотѣкати 'to run along'.

на- 'on, against': назьрѣти pft. 'to look at', назирати impft. 'to see, to observe, to watch', наложити 'to put upon', наити 'to attack'.

надъ- 'on, above' appears in a few examples: надълежати 'to lie on', надъити 'to invade'.

низъ- 'down' expresses the opposite of възъ-: низъврѣшти pft. 'to throw down', низъходити 'to descend, to go down', низити 'to descend'.

объ-, об-, о- 'round, about, at': обити, обидѫ pft. 'to go round, to surround', обити, обиѫ 'to waddle', обличити pft. 'to show, to announce, to accuse', обловъизати impft. 'to kiss', объходити 'to go round, to avoid', осльпнѫти pft. 'to go blind', оградити 'to hedge'.

отъ-, от-, о- 'from, off, away': отъыати (отати) 'to take away', отьмати (отъимати) 'to take away', оходити, отъходити 'to go away', отъпоуштати 'to set free, to forgive'.

по- has no definite adverbial function: помошти 'to help', поносити 'to reproach, to scold', подати 'to offer, to accord', показати 'to show, to indicate'.

подъ- 'under, beneath': подъкопати 'to dig under, to undermine', подъстьлати 'to stretch, to spread under', подъыати 'to undertake'.

при- 'at, near, by, along': привести 'to bring', призъвати 'to call near', приобрѣсти 'to gain, to win'.

про- 'through': пробити 'to split, to break', прорешти 'to prophesy', продати 'to sell', пропати 'to stretch, to crucify'.

прѣ- 'over': прѣдати 'to hand over, to betray', прѣлигати 'to spill', прѣселити 'to transfer, to colonize'.

прѣдъ- 'before, in front of, earlier': прѣдъложити 'to put before', прѣдъставити 'to put in front of, to represent', прѣдъити 'to precede'.

раз-, рас- expresses the idea of separation (cf. Lat. *dis*-, Gr. δια-): разбѣгнѫти сѧ 'to disperse', раздѣлити 'to separate, to distribute', растворити 'to dissolve, to mix'.

съ-, сън- 'downwards, from': съпасти 'to fall down', сънити

'to come down'; 'with, together': съвирати 'to gather, to collect', сънити са 'to gather' (intrans.), съвазати 'to tie together'.

оу- expresses the idea of separation, of bringing an action to the end, but in many cases this prefix emphasizes the meaning of the verb: оувити 'to kill', оусѣкнѫти 'to cut off', оузьрѣти 'to observe, to have a glimpse', оувоіати са 'to fear'; in denominatives: оувѣлити 'to make white', оувѣжати 'to run away'. This particle is also a conjunction (§ 104) and an interjection (§ 105).

Conjugations and the Verbal Aspect

§ 93. A certain correspondence has been established between the aspect and the conjugation classes of the OCS verb:

I. Verbs of the first conjugation have, in their great majority, imperfective aspect. The perfective verbs of this class are: бѫдѫ 'I shall be'; врѣшти, врьгѫ 'to throw'; жлѣсти (жласти), жлѣдѫ 'to recompense; іати, имѫ 'to seize'; лешти, лагѫ 'to lie down'; пасти, падѫ 'to fall'; решти, рекѫ 'to tell'; сѣсти, садѫ 'to sit down'.

II. The majority of verbs of the second conjugation are perfective. Imperfective in this class are: влѣснѫти, влѣснѫ 'to charm'; въікнѫти, въікнѫ 'to be accustomed'; гъібнѫти, гъібнѫ 'to perish' (intrans.); заɓнѫти, заɓнѫ 'to bud'; къіснѫти, къіснѫ 'to go sour'; съхнѫти, съхнѫ 'to dry' (intrans.); тонѫти, тонѫ 'to sink' (intrans.).

Many verbs of this class occur only with prefixes: -вѣгнѫти pft.: вѣгати impft.; -дъіхнѫти pft. 'to breathe': дъіхати impft.; -кликнѫти pft. 'to shout': клицати impft.; -трьгнѫти pft. 'to pull': трьгати impft.; -тагнѫти pft. 'to pull': тазати impft.

Perfective are: двигнѫти 'to move'; дрьзнѫти 'to dare'; коснѫти 'to touch', &c. It is the opposition to an imperfective aspect which determines the perfective aspect: двизати, дрьзати, -касати, &c.

III. Verbs of the third conjugation are imperfective. The

number of perfective aspects is very small and dubious: кончати 'to finish'; лобъзати, лобъжж 'to kiss': лобъзати, лобъзаж impft.; погасати сѧ, -ашж сѧ 'to girdle': погасаж сѧ impft.; разоумѣти (pft. and impft.) 'to understand': разоумѣвати 'id'. Two verbs derived from Greek aorist stems are perfective: власвимисати 'to blaspheme': власвимлꙗти 'id.' impft.(?); сканъдалисати 'to irritate'.

IV. Verbs of the fourth conjugation with the inf. in -ѣти are imperfective; however видѣти has a perfective aspect as well. Those with the inf. in -ити are divided between the two aspects.

Perfective are: варити 'to precede, to overtake', вратити 'to turn', врѣдити 'to hurt', гонозити 'to cure', живити 'to live', крьстити 'to baptize', коупити 'to buy', лишити 'to deprive', льстити 'to revenge', мѣнити 'to change', образити 'to imagine', простити 'to forgive', противити сѧ 'to oppose', поустити 'to let go, to send', родити 'to give birth', роушити 'to destroy', свободити 'to free', сватити 'to consecrate', скочити 'to jump', срамити 'to shame', ставити 'to stop', троудити сѧ 'to work, to take pains', ꙗвити (ѣвити) 'to appear'.

Imperfective are: благодарити 'to thank', водити 'to lead', возити 'to carry', влачити 'to drag', гонити 'to chase, to drive', гоубити (trans.) 'to destroy', молити 'to pray', мѫчити 'to torture', носити 'to carry', нѫдити 'to constrain', поити 'to water', просити 'to ask', сѫдити 'to judge', хвалити 'to praise', оучити 'to teach'.

Some verbs of this category may function in both aspects: простити, противити сѧ, вратити, скочити, сватити, благослов-ити 'to bless'; others have an uncertain aspect: благовѣстити 'to announce', благодарьствити 'to thank', благословестити 'to bless', благоволити, благоизволити 'to consent to', десити 'to meet', гнѫсити сѧ 'to nauseate', ключити сѧ 'to fit, to happen', прѧжити сѧ 'to relax, to lessen', стрѣлити 'to shoot', стѫпити 'to step', хватити 'to catch', ꙗзвити (ѣзвити) 'to wound, to hurt'.

A few verbs of this class are iterative-indeterminate: водити, возити, носити (§ 90).

V. Of the athematic verbs, дамь is perfective. The present tense is expressed by the impft. даꙗти, даж.

PATTERNS OF CONJUGATION

§ 94. FIRST CONJUGATION (§ 61.I, § 62, § 63)

Present

Sing.

1 НЕСѪ	МОГѪ	МЬРѪ	ПЬНѪ	ПЛОВѪ	ЗОВѪ	БЕРѪ
2 НЕСЕШИ	МОЖЕШИ	МЬРЕШИ	ПЬНЕШИ	ПЛОВЕШИ	ЗОВЕШИ	БЕРЕШИ
3 НЕСЕТЪ	МОЖЕТЪ	МЬРЕТЪ	ПЬНЕТЪ	ПЛОВЕТЪ	ЗОВЕТЪ	БЕРЕТЪ

Plur.

1 НЕСЕМЪ	МОЖЕМЪ	МЬРЕМЪ	ПЬНЕМЪ	ПЛОВЕМЪ	ЗОВЕМЪ	БЕРЕМЪ
2 НЕСЕТЕ	МОЖЕТЕ	МЬРЕТЕ	ПЬНЕТЕ	ПЛОВЕТЕ	ЗОВЕТЕ	БЕРЕТЕ
3 НЕСѪТЪ	МОГѪТЪ	МЬРѪТЪ	ПЬНѪТЪ	ПЛОВѪТЪ	ЗОВѪТЪ	БЕРѪТЪ

Dual

1 НЕСЕВѣ	МОЖЕВѣ	МЬРЕВѣ	ПЬНЕВѣ	ПЛОВЕВѣ	ЗОВЕВѣ	БЕРЕВѣ
2 НЕСЕТА	МОЖЕТА	МЬРЕТА	ПЬНЕТА	ПЛОВЕТА	ЗОВЕТА	БЕРЕТА
3 НЕСЕТЕ	МОЖЕТЕ	МЬРЕТЕ	ПЬНЕТЕ	ПЛОВЕТЕ	ЗОВЕТЕ	БЕРЕТЕ

Imperative

Sing.

1 ——	——	——	——	——	——	——
2 НЕСИ	МОЗИ	МЬРИ	ПЬНИ	ПЛОВИ	ЗОВИ	БЕРИ
3 НЕСИ	МОЗИ	МЬРИ	ПЬНИ	ПЛОВИ	ЗОВИ	БЕРИ

Plur.

1 НЕСѣМЪ	МОЗѣМЪ	МЬРѣМЪ	ПЬНѣМЪ	ПЛОВѣМЪ	ЗОВѣМЪ	БЕРѣМЪ
2 НЕСѣТЕ	МОЗѣТЕ	МЬРѣТЕ	ПЬНѣТЕ	ПЛОВѣТЕ	ЗОВѣТЕ	БЕРѣ
3 ——	——	——	——	——	——	——

Dual

1 НЕСѣВѣ	МОЗѣВѣ	МЬРѣВѣ	ПЬНѣВѣ	ПЛОВѣВѣ	ЗОВѣВѣ	БЕРѣВѣ
2 НЕСѣТА	МОЗѣТА	МЬРѣТА	ПЬНѣТА	ПЛОВѣТА	ЗОВѣТА	БЕРѣ
3 ——	——	——	——	——	——	——

Present Participle Active

Masc., neut.

НЕСЫ	МОГЫ	МЬРЫ	ПЬНЫ	ПЛОВЫ	ЗОВЫ	БЕРЫ

Fem.

НЕС-	МОГ-	МЬР-	ПЬН-	ПЛОВ-	ЗОВ-	БЕР-
ѪШТИ	ѪШТИ	ѪШТИ	ѪШТИ	ѪШТИ	ѪШТИ	ѪШТИ

Present Participle Passive

несомъ	——	——	пьномъ	пловомъ	зовомъ	беромъ
несома	——	——	пьнома	пловома	зовома	берома
несомо	——	——	пьномо	пловомо	зовомо	беромо

Imperfect

Sing.

1 нес҆ѣахъ   лождаахъ   мьр҆ѣахъ   пьн҆ѣахъ   плов҆ѣахъ
2 нес҆ѣаше   можддаше   мьр҆ѣаше   пьн҆ѣаше   плов҆ѣаше
3 нес҆ѣаше   можддаше   мьр҆ѣаше   пьн҆ѣаше   плов҆ѣаше

Plur.

1 нес҆ѣахомъ   ложддахомъ   мьр҆ѣахомъ   пьн҆ѣахомъ   плов҆ѣахомъ
2 нес҆ѣашете   можддашете   мьр҆ѣашете   пьн҆ѣашете   плов҆ѣашете
3 нес҆ѣахѫ   можддахѫ   мьр҆ѣахѫ   пьн҆ѣахѫ   плов҆ѣахѫ

Dual

1 нес҆ѣаховѣ   можддаховѣ   мьр҆ѣаховѣ   пьн҆ѣаховѣ   плов҆ѣаховѣ
2 нес҆ѣашета   можддашета   мьр҆ѣашета   пьн҆ѣашета   плов҆ѣашета
3 нес҆ѣашете   можддашете   мьр҆ѣашете   пьн҆ѣашете   пчов҆ѣашете

Sing. 1 зов҆ѣахъ,   зъвдахъ   бьрдахъ
2 зов҆ѣаше,   зъвдаше   бьрдаше
3 зов҆ѣаше,   зъвдаше   бьрдаше

Plur. 1 зов҆ѣахомъ,   зъвдахомъ   бьрдахомъ
2 зов҆ѣашете,   зъвдашете   бьрдашете
3 зов҆ѣахѫ,   зъвдахѫ   бьрдахѫ

Dual 1 зов҆ѣаховѣ,   зъвдаховѣ   бьрдаховѣ
2 зов҆ѣашета,   зъвдашета   бьрдашета
3 зов҆ѣашете,   зъвдашете   бьрдашете

Simple (Asigmatic) Aorist

Sing. 1 логъ   Plur. 1 логомъ   Dual 1 логовѣ
2 може   2 можете   2 можета
3 може   3 логѫ   3 можете

Sigmatic Aorist

Sing. 1	нѣсъ	мрѣхъ	мрьхъ	пасъ	плоухъ
2	несе	мрѣ	мрь	па	плоу
3	несе	мрѣ(тъ)	мрь	па	плоу
Plur. 1	нѣсомъ	мрѣхомъ	мрьхомъ	пасомъ	плоухомъ
2	нѣсте	мрѣсте	мрьсте	пасте	плоусте
3	нѣса	мрѣша	мрьша	паса	плоуша
Dual 1	нѣсовѣ	мрѣховѣ	мрьховѣ	пасовѣ	плоуховѣ
2	нѣста	мрѣста	мрьста	паста	плоуста
3	нѣсте	мрѣсте	мрьсте	пасте	плоусте

Sing. 1	зъвахъ	бьрахъ	Plur. 1	зъвахомъ	бьрахомъ
2	зъва	бьра	2	зъвасте	бьрасте
3	зъва	бьра	3	зъваша	бьраша

Dual 1	зъваховѣ	бьраховѣ
2	зъваста	бьраста
3	зъвасте	бьрасте

New Aorist

Sing. 1	несохъ	могохъ	Plur. 1	несохомъ	могохомъ
2	несе	може	2	несосте	могосте
3	несе	може	3	несоша	могоша

Dual 1	несоховѣ	могоховѣ
2	несоста	могоста
3	несосте	могосте

Past Participle Active 1

Masc., neut.

несъ	могъ	пьнъ	плоувъ	зъвавъ	бьравъ

Fem.

несъши	могъши	пьнъши	плоувъши	зъвавъши	бьравъши

Past Participle Active 2

несл-ъ, -а, -о   могл-ъ, -а, -о   мрьл-ъ, -а, -о   пал-ъ, -а, -о
плоул-ъ, -а, -о   зъвал-ъ, -а, -о   бьрал-ъ, -а, -о

Past Participle Passive

НЕСЕН-Ъ, -а, -о,   ПАТ-Ъ -а, -о,   ПЛОВЕН-Ъ -а, -о,   ЗЪВАН-Ъ -а, -о,
ЕЬРАН-Ъ, -а, -о

Infinitive

НЕСТИ 'to carry'   МОШТИ 'to be able'   МРѢТИ 'to die'   -ПАТИ 'to stretch'
ПЛОУТИ 'to float'   ЗЪВАТИ 'to call'   ЕЬРАТИ 'to collect'

Supine

НЕСТЪ   ЛЮШТЪ   ЛРѢТЪ   ПАТЪ   ПЛОУТЪ   ЗЪВАТЪ   ЕЬРАТЪ

Verbal Noun

НЕСЕНИЮ   (РАС)ПАТНИЮ   (ПЛОУТНИЕ)   ОУМРЬТНИЕ, ОУЛРЪТВНЕ

(a) The infinitive stem may end in a labial (§ 62): ТѢТИ < *tep-ti, ТЕПѪ 'to beat'; in a dental: МАСТИ < *ment-ti, МАТѪ 'to stir, to trouble', ПАСТИ < *pad-ti, ПАДѪ 'to fall', ВЕСТИ < *ved-ti, ВЕДѪ 'to lead', ПРАСТИ < *prend-ti, ПРАДѪ 'to spin'; in a velar: ТЕШТИ < *tek-ti, ТЕКѪ 'to run, to flow', ПРАШТИ < *preng-ti, ПРАГѪ 'to span, to harness'; in a nasal: ПАТИ < *pen-ti, ПЬНѪ 'to stretch'; in a liquid: ЖРѢТИ < *žer-ti, ЖЬРѪ 'to devour', ЖРЪТИ, ЖЬРѪ 'to sacrifice'.

(b) The thematic vowel may be: e, ę, or—less frequently—o, ǫ, ě, a, i, ĭ, y; when the infinitive stem has the grade e the present stem may have zero grade: ЧРѢТИ < *čerp-ti 'to dip up, to draw (up) water': ЧРЬПѪ, ВРѢШТИ < *verg-ti 'to throw': ВРЪГѪ, НАЧАТИ < *načen-ti 'to start': НАЧЬНѪ (§ 37).

(c) Verbs with the thematic vowel e, ę: ГНЕСТИ, ГНЕТѪ 'to press', ЖЕШТИ, ЖЕГѪ 'to burn' (trans.), ВЛѢШТИ < *velk-ti, ВЛѢКѪ 'to pull', ЖЛѢСТИ, ЖЛАСТИ (cf. OHG geltan), ЖЛѢДѪ 'to reward', СТРѢШТИ < *sterg-, СТРѢГѪ 'to guard, to watch', НЕБРѢШТИ < *-berg-, НЕБРѢГѪ 'to neglect', БЛАСТИ, БЛАДѪ 'to err, to talk wildly', ОУВАСТИ, ОУВАЗѪ 'to crown', ГРАСТИ, ГРАДѪ 'to come', ЗВАШТИ, ЗВАГѪ 'to ring out', ПРАСТИ, ПРАДѪ 'to spin', ТРАСТИ, ТРАСѪ 'to shake'.

(d) Verbs with the thematic vowel o, ǫ: БОСТИ, БОДѪ 'to sting, to prick', ВЛАСТИ < *vold-ti, ВЛАДѪ 'to rule', ДѪТИ, ДЪМѪ 'to blow'.

(*e*) Verbs with the thematic vowel *ě, a*: лѣсти, лѣзѫ 'to climb, to walk', сѣщи, сѣкѫ 'to cut', ꙗхати, ꙗдѫ 'to be driven' (Lat. *vehor*), класти, кладѫ 'to put, to load', красти, крадѫ 'to steal', пасти, пасѫ 'to graze, to watch'.

(*f*) Verbs with the thematic vowel *i, ī*: ити, идѫ 'to go', стрищи, стригѫ 'to shear', цвисти, цвьтѫ 'to bloom', чисти, чьтѫ 'to count, to read'.

(*g*) One verb has the thematic vowel *y*: грꙑсти, грꙑзѫ 'to gnaw, to bite'.

(*h*) The imperative forms of the verbs рещи 'to say', тещи 'to run', пещи 'to cook', жещи 'to burn' (trans.) have the radical vowel in the zero grade: рьци, тьци пьци, жьзи. Forms of жещи also show the zero grade in present and aorist tenses, and in participles: въжъжеши (Supr. 457.11), зажьже (Mar., Mt. xxii. 7), жьгомъ (for жъгомъ) (Supr. 476.17).

(*i*) The verb грасти, градѫ 'to come' has a nasal vowel in both stems, whereas сѣсти, сѧдѫ 'to sit down', лешти, лѧгѫ 'to lie down' have infinitive stems without nasals: *sěd-, leg-*. The simple aorist and the past part. are derived from the infinitive stem: сѣдъ, легъ; сѣлъ, леглъ.

(*j*) The verb ꙗти has a nasal in the infinitive stem, which represents the *-e-* grade (**j-em-*), as against the zero grade in the present stem: имѫ, имеши, &c. < **j-ĭm-* > *jim-* (with a prosthetic *j-*) at the beginning of the word (§ 33.4), but without *j* in the middle: възьмѫ, вьньмѫ. The same explanation applies to the verb дѫти, дъмѫ, 'to blow', past part. pass. надъменъ; the infinitive stem has the *o*-grade.

(*k*) Whereas some verbs show a regular alternation of vowels in the present and the infinitive stems: врьгѫ ⌣ врѣщи 'to throw', врьзѫ ⌣ врѣсти 'to tie, to open', -вьрѫ ⌣ -врѣти 'to close', цвьтѫ ⌣ цвисти 'to bloom', чьтѫ ⌣ чисти 'to count'; others show an irregular alternation: -брѣгѫ ⌣ -брѣщи 'to neglect, to disregard', past part. act. -брѣгъ; влѣщи, влѣкѫ 'to pull', past part. act. влъкъ, влъклъ also влѣкъ, past part. pass. влъченъ and влѣченъ.

(*l*) The verb ити has a stem *i-* for infinitive and supine, a stem *id-*

< * jĭ-d- (-d- is a suffix) for present, imp., impf., aor., and a stem
šĭd- < *chĭd- for the past participles шьдъ, шьлъ. The same stem
with another gradation appears in ходити. A similar case is that of
the verb 'кхати (іахати), 'кдж 'to drive' with a stem ĕ- in past part.
act. I прѣ-'квъ, a stem ĕ-d- for present imp., impf., aor., and a
stem ĕx- in inf. and past part. act. I при-'кхавъ.

(*m*) Verbs with an infinitive stem ending in -*a*- show, as a rule,
in this form, the reduced or zero grade: бьрати, 'to collect' гънати
'to chase', дьрати 'to tear, to flay', жьдати 'to wait', зъвати
'to call', пьрати 'to fly' ⌣ беρж, деρж, женж, жидж, зовж, пеρж.
The imperfect is derived either from the zero grade stems of the
infinitive (in the older texts): жьдаахъ, зъваахъ, or from the
present stems with the *e/o* grade (in the later texts, e.g. Supr.):
жиджаахъ, зов'каахъ (§ 37).

(*n*) The verb бѫдж (an original subjunctive form) has only present, imp., and pr. part. act. forms: бѫдеши, &c.; бѫди, бѫдѣмъ,
бѫдете; бѫдꙑ, бѫджшти (fem.).

(*o*) Alongside the forms жрѣти, жьρж 'to devour', мρѣти, мьρж
'to die', жьρти, жьρж 'to sacrifice', exist the infinitive forms
-мьρти(ти), мьρ'кти 'to die', built on the analogy of the present
form мьρж. The aorist forms are жьρ'кхъ, мьρ'кхъ. The origin of
жρьти is not clear; its aor. is жρъхъ, жρъ, жρъ.

(*p*) The regular ending of the present part. act. is -ꙑ. However,
the texts also show isolated forms in -ѧ or -ѫ: грѧдѧ (Zogr., Mt.
xi. 3; Mk. xi. 9), несѧ (Zogr., Mk. xiv. 13; Mar., L. xxii. 10);
the pr. part. act. from іесмь is сꙑ, but сѫ, сѧ also occur as secondary
forms (Ass., J. iii. 31).

(*q*) There exists an aorist form отвѣ, отвѣшѧ 'he, they replied'
(Ass., Savv. Kn.) having same stem as отвѣтъ, and an aorist
изли'ктъ сѧ (Ps. Sin.) 'he changed', cf. the noun мѣна.

§ 95. SECOND CONJUGATION (§ 61.II, § 64)

Present

Sing.	1	двигнж	станж	ринж
	2	двигнеши	станеши	ринеши
	3	двигнетъ	станетъ	ринетъ

Plur. 1 двигнемъ   станемъ   ринемъ
    2 двигнете   станете   ринете
    3 двигнѫтъ   станѫтъ   ринѫтъ

Dual 1 двигневѣ   станевѣ   риневѣ
    2 двигнета   станета   ринета
    3 двигнете, -та   станете, -та   ринете, -та

Imperative

Sing. 1 ——   ——   ——
    2 двигни   стани   рини
    3 двигни   стани   рини

Plur. 1 двигнѣмъ   станѣмъ   ринѣмъ
    2 двигнѣте   станѣте   ринѣте
    3 ——

Dual 1 двигнѣвѣ   станѣвѣ   ринѣвѣ
    2 двигнѣта   станѣта   ринѣта
    3 ——

Present Participle Active

Masc., neut.

    двигны   станы   рины

Fem.

    двигнѫшти   станѫшти   ринѫшти

Present Participle Passive

двигномъ-ъ, -а, -о   ——   риномъ-ъ, -а, -о

Imperfect

Sing. 1 двигнѣахъ   о-станѣахъ   ринѣахъ
    2 двигнѣаше   о-станѣаше   ринѣаше
    3 двигнѣаше   о-станѣаше   ринѣаше

Plur. 1 двигнѣахомъ   о-станѣахомъ   ринѣахомъ
    2 двигнѣашете   о-станѣашете   ринѣашете
    3 двигнѣахѫ   о-станѣахѫ   ринѣахѫ

Dual 1   двигнѣаховѣ   о-станѣаховѣ   ринѣаховѣ
     2   двигнѣашета   о-станѣашета   ринѣашета
     3   двигнѣашете, -та   о-станѣашете, -та   ринѣашете, -та

Simple (Asigmatic) Aorist

Sing. 1   двигъ   *станъ
     2   движе   ста
     3   движе   ста

Plur. 1   двигомъ   *станомъ
     2   движете   *станете
     3   двигж   *станж , -станжшѧ

Dual 1   двиговѣ   *становѣ
     2   движета   *станета
     3   движете, -та   *станете

Sigmatic Aorist

Sing. 1   дрѣзнжхъ   двигохъ   ринжхъ
     2   дрѣзнж   движе   ринж
     3   дрѣзнж   движе   ринж

Plur. 1   дрѣзнжхомъ   двигохомъ   ринжхомъ
     2   дрѣзнжсте   двигосте   ринжсте
     3   дрʼѣзнжшѧ   двигошѧ   ринжшѧ

Dual 1   дрѣзнжховѣ   двигоховѣ   ринжховѣ
     2   дрѣзнжста   двигоста   ринжста
     3   дрѣзнжсте, -та   двигосте, -та   ринжсте, -та

Past Participle Active 1

Masc., neut.
     двигъ   дрѣзнжвъ   ринжвъ

Fem.
     двигъши   дрѣзнжвъши   ринжвъши

Past Participle Active 2

двигл-ъ, -а, -о   стал-ъ, -а, -о   ринжл-ъ, -а, -о

Past Participle Passive

движен-ъ, -а, -о   дръзновен-ъ, -а, -о   риновен-ъ, -а, -о

Infinitive

двигнѫти 'to move' стати 'to get up, to stand' ринѫти 'to push'

Supine

двигнѫтъ   статъ   ринѫтъ

Verbal noun

движение   въстание 'resurrection'   риновение

(*a*) The suffix -нѫ- of the infinitive and present stems was dropped in the aorist and past participle forms: aor. двигъ, past part. двигъ, двиглъ. By analogy, however, the -нѫ- suffix was also introduced into these forms: дръзнѫти 'to dare', past part. act. 1 дръзнѫвъ, past part. act. 2 дръзнѫлъ. The texts differ in the use of these analogical forms. They are more numerous in Supr.

(*b*) The past part. pass. sometimes also appears with the ending -новенъ which represents a suffix -*неи*-: дръзновенъ from дръзнѫти 'to dare', плиновенъ from плинѫти 'to spit', косновенъ from коснѫти 'to touch'. From these participles are then derived the verbal nouns: плиновение, косновение, въскрьсновение 'resurrection', from въскрьснѫти.

(*c*) Some forms of the paradigms do not occur in OCS texts.

§ 96. THIRD CONJUGATION (§ 61.III, § 65)

1. *Verbs with original infinitive stems ending in a vowel.*

Present

Sing. 1	знаѭ	грѣѭ	биѭ	мыѭ	чюѭ
2	знаеши	грѣеши	биеши	мыеши	чюеши
3	знаетъ	грѣетъ	биетъ	мыетъ	чюетъ
Plur. 1	знаемъ	грѣемъ	биемъ	мыемъ	чюемъ
2	знаете	грѣете	биете	мыете	чюете
3	знаѭтъ	грѣѭтъ	биѭтъ	мыѭтъ	чюѭтъ

Dual	1	знаіевѣ	грѣіевѣ	биіевѣ	мъіиевѣ	чюіевѣ
	2	знаіета	грѣіета	биіета	мъіиета	чюіета
	3	знаіете,	грѣіете,	биіете,	мъіиете,	чюіете,
		-та	-та	-та	-та	-та

Imperative

Sing.	1	——	——	——	——	——
	2	знаи	грѣи	бии (бьи)	мъіи	чюи
	3	знаи	грѣи	бии	мъіи	чюи
Plur.	1	знаимъ	грѣимъ	биимъ	мъіимъ	чюимъ
	2	знаите	грѣите	бните	мъіите	чюите
	3	——	——	——	——	——
Dual	1	знаивѣ	грѣивѣ	биивѣ	мъіивѣ	чюивѣ
	2	знаита	грѣита	биита	мъіита	чюита
	3	——	——	——	——	——

Present Participle Active

Masc., neut.

знаіа	грѣіа	биіа	мъіиіа	чюіа

Fem.

знаіжшти	грѣіжшти	биіжшти	мъіиіжшти	чюіжшти

Present Participle Passive

знаіеми-ъ,	грѣіеми-ъ,	биіеми-ъ,	мъіиеми-ъ,	чюіеми-ъ,
-а, -о	-а, -о	-а, -о	-а, -о	-а, -о

Imperfect

Sing.

1	знаахъ	грѣахъ	биіаахъ	мъіиаахъ	чюѣахъ
2	знааше	грѣаше	биіааше	мъіиааше	чюѣаше
3	знааше	грѣаше	биіааше	мъіиааше	чюѣаше

Plur.

1	знаахомъ	грѣахомъ	биіаахомъ	мъіиаахомъ	чюѣахомъ
2	знаашете	грѣашете	биіаашете	мъіиаашете	чюѣашете
3	знаахѫ	грѣахѫ	биіаахѫ	мъіиаахѫ	чюѣахѫ

Dual
1 знадховѣ   грѣаховѣ   бигаховѣ   мъігааховѣ   чюѣаховѣ
2 знаашета   грѣашета   бигаашета   мъігаашета   чюѣашета
3 знаашете,   грѣашете,   бигаашете,   мъігаашете,   чюѣашете,
   -та   -та   -та   -та   -та

Sigmatic Aorist

Sing.
1 знахъ   грѣхъ   бихъ   мъіхъ   чюхъ
2 зна   грѣ   би   лъі   чю
3 зна   грѣ   би   лъі   чю

Plur.
1 знахомъ   грѣхомъ   бихомъ   мъіхомъ   чюхомъ
2 знасте   грѣсте   бисте   мъісте   чюсте
3 знаша   грѣша   биша   мъіша   чюша

Dual
1 знаховѣ   грѣховѣ   биховѣ   мъіховѣ   чюховѣ
2 знаста   грѣста   биста   мъіста   чюста
3 знасте, -та   грѣсте, -та   бисте, -та   мъісте, -та   чюсте, -та

Past Participle Active 1

Masc., neut.
знавъ   грѣвъ   бивъ   мъівъ   чювъ

Fem.
знавъши   грѣвъши   бивъши   мъівъши   чювъши

Past Participle Active 2

знал-ъ,-а,-о   грѣл-ъ,-а,-о   бил-ъ,-а,-о   мъіл-ъ,-а,-о   чюл-ъ,-а,-о

Past Participle Passive

знан-ъ, -а, -о   грѣнъ, -а, -о   бигенъ, -а, -о   битъ, -а, -о
мъівен-ъ, -а, -о   чювен-ъ, -а, -о

Infinitive

знати 'to know'   грѣти 'to warm' (intr.)   бити 'to beat'
мъіти 'to wash'   чюти 'to feel'

Supine

зндт҄ъ грѣтъ битъ мытъ чютъ

Verbal Noun

(по)знание грѣние биение битие (оу)мываниѥ чювение

(a) *Verbs of this category*: дѣти, дѣик҄ (дежд҄к҄) 'to put, to set', спѣти, спѣик҄ 'to succeed', съмѣти, съмѣик҄ 'to dare', сѣти, сѣик҄ 'to sow; to sieve', пѣти, поик҄ 'to sing', вити, вик҄ (вык҄) 'to wind up, to swathe', гнити, гник҄ 'to putrify', лити, лик҄ (лык҄) 'to pour', пити, пик҄ (пык҄) 'to drink', почити, почик҄ 'to rest', крыти, крык҄ 'to cover', оунъыти, оунъик҄ 'to weary, to be despondent', рыти, рык҄ 'to dig', шити, шик҄ 'to sew', оснъывати, оснъывак҄ 'to found, to create', надоути, надоук҄ 'to blow up', обоути, обоук҄ 'to put on shoes', изоути 'to take off', сиѣти, сииати, сиѣик҄ (сь-) 'to glimmer, to shine'.

The form дежд҄к҄ is derived from a root with reduplication: *de-d-jǫ > dēždǫ, cf. Lith. *demi*, Lat. *facio*: Old Ind. *dadhāmi* 'I set'.

(b) In texts appear forms which have dropped the intervocalic *j* with resulting assimilation of the vowels: знддте < знаиете, зндатъ < знаиетъ, сѣиати 'to sow', сѣатъ < сѣиетъ, ддатъ < даиетъ (§ 32.5).

(c) In the imperfect verbs of the type вити, пити take the endings -иддхъ or -ѣдхъ, &c. The verb пѣти, поик҄ has also contracted imperfect forms: поиаше, поиахк҄ (Supr. 118. 11, 70. 26). The OCS texts show only contracted imperfect forms from крыти and чюти: крыиаше (крыѣкше), чюѣкше, чюиаста.

(d) In the 2nd and 3rd sg. aor. verbs with the stem in -и- or -ѣ- may attach the ending -тъ: витъ, питъ, пѣтъ.

(e) The past part. pass. has the ending -нъ or -тъ. There is no clear-cut rule as to the distribution of these endings. Verbs in -ѣ- have -нъ: сѣнъ 'sown', одѣнъ 'dressed', but осѣтъ 'sown'. Verbs in -и have -тъ: извитъ 'unwound', повитъ 'swaddled', пролитъ 'slipped', пѣтъ 'sung', but вьиенъ 'beaten', which is formed like кръвенъ from крыти, мъвенъ from мыти, шьвенъ from шити, обоувенъ from обоути.

(*f*) The verbs скѣти 'to sow, to sieve', грѣти сѧ 'to warm' (refl.), спѣти 'to thrive' have also enlarged infinitives: скꙗти, скати; грѣꙗти, грѣати; спѣꙗти, which put them in category 3 of this conjugation.

2. *Verbs with original infinitive stems ending in a consonant.*

Present

Sing.	1	колѭ	жьнѭ	мелѭ
	2	колѥши	жьнѥши	мелѥши
	3	колѥтъ	жьнѥтъ	мелѥтъ
Plur.	1	колѥмъ	жьнѥмъ	мелѥмъ
	2	колѥте	жьнѥте	мелѥте
	3	колѭтъ	жьнѭтъ	мелѭтъ
Dual	1	колѥвѣ	жьнѥвѣ	мелѥвѣ
	2	колѥта	жьнѥта	мелѥта
	3	колѥте	жьнѥте	мелѥте

Imperative

Sing.	1	——	——	——
	2	коли	жьни	мели
	3	коли	жьни	мели
Plur.	1	колимъ (колꙗмъ)	жьнимъ	мелимъ
	2	колите (колꙗте)	жьните	мелите
	3	——	——	——
Dual	1	коливѣ	жьнивѣ	меливѣ
	2	колита	жьнита	мелита
	3	——	——	——

Present participle active

Masc., neut.	колѧ	жьнѧ	мелѧ
Fem.	колѭшти	жьнѭшти	мелѭшти

Present participle passive

колѥм-ъ, -а, -о   жьнѥм-ъ, -а, -о   мелѥм-ъ, -а, -о

Imperfect

Sing.	1	колѣахъ	жьнѣахъ	мелꙗахъ
	2	колѣаше	жьнѣаше	мелꙗаше
	3	колѣаше	жьнѣаше	мелꙗаше
Plur.	1	колѣахомъ	жьнѣахомъ	мелꙗахомъ
	2	колѣашете	жьнѣашете	мелꙗашете
	3	колѣахѫ	· жьнѣахѫ	мелꙗахѫ
Dual	1	колѣаховѣ	жьнѣаховѣ	мелꙗаховѣ
	2	колѣашета	жьнѣашета	мелꙗашета
	3	колѣашете	жьнѣашете	мелꙗашете

Sigmatic aorist

Sing.	1	клахъ	жахъ	млѣхъ
	2	кла	жа	млѣ
	3	кла	жа	млѣ
Plur.	1	клахомъ	жахомъ	млѣхомъ
	2	класте	жасте	млѣсте
	3	клаша	жаша	млѣша
Dual	1	клаховѣ	жаховѣ	млѣховѣ
	2	класта	жаста	млѣста
	3	класте, -та	жасте, -та	млѣсте, -та

Past participle active 1

Masc., neut. клавъ   Fem. клавъши

Past participle active 2

клал-ъ, -а, -о   жал-ъ, -а, -о   млѣл-ъ, -а, -о

Past participle passive

-колен-ъ, -а, -о (-кланъ)

Infinitive

клати (кълати) 'to stab'   жати 'to harvest'   млѣти 'to grind'

Supine

клатъ   жатъ   млѣтъ (мьлѣть Supr. 565. 4)

Verbal noun

-колениѥ

(*a*) This group consists only of a few verbs, to which may be added a verb with the radical ending in -*t*-: -рѣсти, -рашѫ (об- 'to find', съ- 'to meet', приоб- 'to gain, to earn'), from which the verbal nouns are сърѣтениѥ 'meeting', обрѣтениѥ 'finding'.

(*b*) Forms of these verbs, other than the present tense forms, occur very rarely in the texts.

(*c*) From брати, борѭ 'to fight' occur a form борѣахѫ and a form в'рахомъ = върахомъ (Supr. 72. 27); aorist прѣбра, въраша, браша. The verbal noun appears in two forms: върание and борение, and these indicate two past parts. pass.: бранъ and борюнъ.

(*d*) The verb клати 'to stab' appears in aor. клахъ, закла (закъла), &c., in past part. pass. кланъ, коленъ, verbal noun коление. The imperfect колѣахъ, клаахъ does not occur in OCS texts.

(*e*) The verb млѣти 'to grind' appears in an imperfect form мелꙗаше and in an aorist form млѣша.

(*f*) From жати 'to reap' there is an aorist пожа.

(*g*) The verb обрѣсти 'to find' forms the imperfect from the present stem: обраштаахъ, обраштахомъ. More numerous are the forms derived from the infinitive stem: aor. обрѣтъ, обрѣте, обрѣтомъ, обрѣтѫ and обрѣтохъ, обрѣтохомъ; past part. act. 1 обрѣтъ, past part. act. 2 обрѣлъ; pres. part. pass. обрѣтенъ; sup. обрѣстъ.

(*h*) From the verbs клати, брати, and млѣти the infinitive stem appears also with a secondary reduced vowel: кълати, възати, мьлѣти. The reduced vowel results from analogy with verbs like: съ лати 'to send', зьрѣти 'to see'.

3. *Verbs with original infinitive stems (ending in a vowel or a conso- nant) enlarged by -a-.*

Present

Sing.

1 даѭ	важѫ	глаголіѭ	наричѭ	нарицаѭ
2 даѥши	важеши	глаголюши	наричеши	нарицаѥши
3 даѥтъ	важетъ	глаголютъ	наричетъ	нарицаѥтъ

Plur.

1 даіемъ	важемъ	глаголıемъ	наричемъ	нарицаıемъ
2 даіете	важете	глаголıете	наричете	нарицаıете
3 даıѫтъ	важѫтъ	глаголıѫтъ	наричѫтъ	нарицаıѫтъ

Dual

1 даıевѣ	важевѣ	глаголıевѣ	наричевѣ	нарицаıевѣ
2 даıета	важета	глаголıета	наричета	нарицаıета
3 даıете,	важете,	глаголıете,	наричете,	нарицаıете,
-та	-та	-та	-та	-та

Imperative

Sing.

1 ——	——	——	——	——
2 дан	важи	глаголи	нарьци	нарицан
3 дан	важи	глаголи	нарьци	нарицан

Plur.

1 димъ	важимъ	глаголимъ	нарьцѣмъ	нарицаимъ
2 даите	важите	глаголите	нарьцѣте	нарицаите
3 ——	——	——	——	——

Dual

1 данвѣ	важивѣ	глаголивѣ	нарьцѣвѣ	нарицаивѣ
2 данта	важита	глаголита	нарьцѣта	нарицаита
3 ——	——	——	——	——

Present participle active

Masc., neut.

даıѧ	важѧ	глаголıѧ	наричѧ	нарицаıѧ

Fem.

даıѫшти	важѫшти	глаголıѫшти	наричѫшти	нарицаıѫшти

Present participle passive

даıемъ-ъ, -а, -о   важемъ-ъ, -а, -о   глаголıемъ-ъ, -а, -о

наричемъ-ъ, -а, -о   нарицаıемъ-ъ, -а, -о

Imperfect

Sing.

1	дѣашхъ	вѧздаахъ	глаголаахъ	нарицаахъ
2	дѣаше	вѧздааше	глаголааше	нарицааше
3	дѣаше	вѧздааше	глаголааше	нарицааше

Plur.

1	дѣаахомъ	вѧздаахомъ	глаголаахомъ	нарицаахомъ
2	дѣаашете	вѧздаашете	глаголаашете	нарицаашете
3	дѣаахѫ	вѧздаахѫ	глаголаахѫ	нарицаахѫ

Dual

1	дѣааховѣ	вѧздааховѣ	глаголааховѣ	нарицааховѣ
2	дѣаашета	вѧздаашета	глаголаашета	нарицаашета
3	дѣаашете	вѧздаашете	глаголаашете	нарицаашете

Sigmatic aorist

Sing.

1	-дѣахъ	вѧзахъ	глаголахъ	нарицахъ
2	-дѣа	вѧза	глагола	нарица
3	-дѣа	вѧза	глагола	нарица

Plur.

1	-дѣахомъ	вѧзахомъ	глаголахомъ	нарицахомъ
2	-дѣасте,	вѧзасте,	глаголасте,	нарицасте,
	-та	-та	-та	-та
3	-дѣашѧ	вѧзашѧ	глаголашѧ	нарицашѧ

Dual

1	-дѣаховѣ	вѧзаховѣ	глаголаховѣ	нарицаховѣ
2	-дѣашета	вѧзаста	глаголаста	нарицаста
3	-дѣашете	вѧзасте	глаголасте	нарицасте

Past participle active 1

Masc., neut.

дѣавъ	вѧзавъ	глаголавъ	нарицавъ

Fem.

дѣавъши	вѧзавъши	глаголавъши	нарицавъши

Past participle active 2

даіалъ,	вѧзалъ,	глаголалъ,	нарицалъ,
-а, -о	-а, -о	-а, -о	-а, -о

Past participle passive

даіанъ,	вѧзанъ,	глаголанъ,	нарицанъ,
-а, -о	-а, -о	-а, -о	-а, -о

Infinitive

даіати 'to give'   вѧзати 'to tie'   глаголати 'to speak'

нарицати 'to name'

Supine

даіатъ   вѧзатъ   глаголатъ   нарицатъ

Verbal noun

даіаниѥ   вѧзаниѥ   глаголаниѥ   нарицаниѥ

(a) Verbs with stems ending in a vowel: ваіати, ваіѫ 'to sculpt', вѣіати, вѣіѫ 'to blow', дѣіати, дѣіѫ 'to do', каіати, каіѫ сѧ 'to repent', лаіати, лаіѫ 'to spy, to lay traps; to bark', -маіати, -маіѫ 'to make a sign, to call', стаіати, стаіѫ 'to stand, to be standing', сѣіати, сѣіѫ 'to sow', таіати, таіѫ 'to melt', зніати, зѣіѫ 'to yawn, to gape', ліати, лѣіѫ 'to pour', смиіати сѧ, смѣіѫ сѧ 'to laugh', грѣіати, грѣіѫ 'to warm', рѣіати, рѣіѫ 'to push', чаіати, чаіѫ 'to wait', блѣвати, блюіѫ 'to vomit', плѣвати, плюіѫ 'to spit'.

(b) Verbs with stems ending in a consonant: ал(ъ)кати, алчѫ 'to be hungry', навыцати, -вычѫ 'to learn', гасати, гашѫ 'to extinguish', гыбати, гыбліѫ 'to perish', жадати, жаждѫ 'to be thirsty', зьдати, зьждѫ 'to build', зобати, зобліѫ 'to devour', зыбати, зыбліѫ 'to shake', искати, иштѫ, искѫ 'to seek', клепати, клепліѫ 'to push against', лизати, лижѫ 'to lick, to lap', лъгати, лъжѫ 'to tell a lie', лѣгати, лѣжѫ 'to take to one's bed', лацати, лачѫ 'to stretch', мрьцати, мрьчѫ 'to grow dark', ницати, ничѫ 'to bud', пьсати, пишѫ 'to write', плакати, плачѫ 'to wash; to cry', плъзати, плѣжѫ 'to crawl', пласати, плашѫ 'to dance', ристати, риштѫ 'to run', ръзати, ръжѫ 'to neigh', рѣзати, рѣжѫ 'to cut', скрьжьтати, скрьжьштѫ 'to

gnash', сльпати, слѣплѭ 'to sputter', сълати, сълѭ 'to send', оувѧдати, оувѧждѫ 'to wither', стрѣкати, стрѣчѫ 'to sting', сыпати, сыплѭ 'to scatter, to shed', стрьгати (строугати), строужѫ 'to lacerate', тесати, тешѫ 'to hew, to cut', трьзати, трѣжѫ (трьзаѭ) 'to tear to pieces, to rend', тазати, тажѫ 'to pull', чесати, чешѫ 'to comb, to strip', чрьпати, чрѣплѭ 'to draw water', стьлати, стелѭ 'to spread', мрьмьрати, мрьмрѭ 'to gnaw', орати, орѭ 'to plough', стенати, стенѭ 'to sigh, to complain', имати, иемлѭ 'to take', страдати, страждѫ 'to suffer', лобъзати, лобъжѫ 'to kiss', оугльбѣти, оугльблѭ 'to sink in', тратати, трашѫ 'to pursue', исъхати, исъшѫ 'to dry'.

(c) The present and the infinitive stems of some verbs of this category are differentiated by vowel alternation: зѣѭ — зьѧти, зиѧти; лѣѭ — льѧти, лиѧти; слѣѭ сѧ — сльѧти, смиѧти сѧ; блюѭ — бльвати; плюѭ — пльвати; стелѭ — стьлати, стьлати; иемлѭ — имати; пишѫ — пьсати, писати.

(d) The imperfect is, with few exceptions, formed from the infinitive stem: казаахъ : казати; писаахъ : писати; метаахъ: метати, but also мешта́ахѫ (Supr. 216. 25) from the present stem; приимаахъ : приимати, but also приюмлꙗаше (Supr. 383. 26) from the present stem. The endings -ашета, -ашете in the 2nd pl. and in the 2nd and 3rd pl. are exceptionally replaced by -аста, -асте.

(e) The intervocalic j in the endings of these verbs tends to disappear; the vowels are then in some cases assimilated and contracted (§ 32.5): даѥтъ > даатъ, дѣѥтъ > дѣатъ, даѥте > даате; разбиваѥтъ > разбиваатъ; послоушаѥте > послоушате; повѣдаѥши > повѣдаши. Isolated forms of this kind occur in various OCS texts.

(f) Verbs of this category, as well as those of 1, have plural and dual forms in the imperative also enlarged by -ꙗ-, -ѣ-, which recall the imperative forms of the first and second conjugation: бинꙗмъ, бинꙗте for бинмъ, бините; глаголꙗамъ, глаголꙗте for глаголимъ, глаголите; накажѣте; възништѣте; пиꙗте; покажате, &c. The derived verbs of category 4 have no imperative forms in -ꙗ-, -ѣ-.

(g) There is no precise difference between verbs of category 3

and category 4. The primary and the derived verbs form a single category from the point of view of descriptive grammar.

4. Derived verbs.

Present

Sing.	1	дѣлаѭ	разоумѣѭ	вѣроуѭ
	2	дѣлаеши	разоумѣеши	вѣроуеши
	3	дѣлаетъ	разоумѣетъ	вѣроуетъ
Plur.	1	дѣлаемъ	разоумѣемъ	вѣроуемъ
	2	дѣлаете	разоумѣете	вѣроуете
	3	дѣлаѭтъ	разоумѣѭтъ	вѣроуѭтъ
Dual	1	дѣлаевѣ	разоумѣевѣ	вѣроуевѣ
	2	дѣлаета	разоумѣета	вѣроуета
	3	дѣлаете, -та	разоумѣете, -та	вѣроуете, -та

Imperative

Sing.	1	——	——	——
	2	дѣлаи	разоумѣи	вѣроуи
	3	дѣлаи	разоумѣи	вѣроуи
Plur.	1	дѣлаимъ	разоумѣимъ	вѣроуимъ
	2	дѣлаите	разоумѣите	вѣроуите
	3	——	——	——
Dual	1	дѣлаивѣ	разоумѣивѣ	вѣроуивѣ
	2	дѣлаита	разоумѣита	вѣроуита
	3	——	——	——

Present participle active

Masc., neut.

     дѣлаѩ   разоумѣѩ   вѣроуѩ

Fem.

     дѣлаѭшти   разоумѣѭшти   вѣроуѭшти

Present participle passive

дѣлаюм-ъ, -а, -о   разоумѣюм-ъ, -а, -о   вѣроуюм-ъ, -а, -о

Imperfect

Sing.	1	дѣлаахъ	разоумѣахъ	вѣроваахъ
	2	дѣлааше	разоумѣаше	вѣровааше
	3	дѣлааше	разоумѣаше	вѣровааше
Plur.	1	дѣлаахомъ	разоумѣахомъ	вѣроваахомъ
	2	дѣлаашете	разоумѣашете	вѣроваашете
	3	дѣлаахѫ	разоумѣахѫ	вѣровадхѫ
Dual	1	дѣлааховѣ	разоумѣаховѣ	вѣровааховѣ
	2	дѣлаашета	разоумѣашета	вѣроваашета
	3	дѣлаашете, -та	разоумѣашете, -та	вѣроваашете,-та

Sigmatic aorist

Sing.	1	дѣлахъ	разоумѣхъ	вѣровахъ
	2	дѣла	разоумѣ	вѣрова
	3	дѣла	разоумѣ	вѣрова
Plur.	1	дѣлахомъ	разоумѣхомъ	вѣровахомъ
	2	дѣласте	разоумѣсте	вѣровасте
	3	дѣлашѧ	разоумѣшѧ	вѣровашѧ
Dual	1	дѣлаховѣ	разоумѣховѣ	вѣроваховѣ
	2	дѣласта	разоумѣста	вѣроваста
	3	дѣласте, -та	разоумѣсте, -та	вѣровасте, -та

Past participle active 1

Masc., neut.

дѣлавъ	разоумѣвъ	вѣровавъ

Fem.

дѣлавъши	разоумѣвъши	вѣровавъши

Past participle active 2

дѣлал-ъ, -а, -о	разоумѣл-ъ, -а, -о	вѣровал-ъ, -а, -о

Past participle passive

дѣлан-ъ, -а, -о	разоумѣн-ъ, -а, -о	вѣрован-ъ, -а, -о

Infinitive

дѣлати 'to work'   разоумѣти 'to understand'
вѣровати 'to believe'

Supine

дѣлатъ   разоумѣтъ   вѣроватъ

Verbal noun

дѣланиѥ   разоумлѣниѥ   вѣрованиѥ

(*a*) It is not possible to draw a line between the derived verbs of this category and the radical verbs of category 3 of this conjugation. A verb like глаголати may be considered as being derived from the noun глаголъ 'word'; нарицати may be considered as derived from нарешти, нарекѫ 'to name'.

(*b*) To this category of derived verbs belong: знаменати, знаменаѭ 'to mark, to point out': знамѧ n. 'mark', отъвѣштати, отъвѣштаѭ 'to answer': отъвѣтъ 'answer', бꙑвати, бꙑваѭ 'to be (habitually)': бꙑти 'to be', нарицати, нарицаѭ 'to name' which is, however, also considered as a radical verb and has the present наричѫ, желѣти, желѣѭ 'to wish': желіа 'wish, longing', имѣти, имѣѭ 'to have', питѣти (питати), питѣѭ 'to feed', ослабѣти, ослабѣѭ 'to become weak', ветъшати, ветъшаѭ 'to become old': ветъхъ adj., обништати, обништаѭ 'to become poor': ништь adj., коуповати, коупоуѭ 'to buy', съвѣдѣтельствовати, -воуѭ 'to witness': съвѣдѣтель, скандалисати, -саѭ 'to scandalize', коньчати, коньчаѭ 'to finish, to come to an end', цѣсарьствовати, -воуѭ 'to reign': цѣсарь 'emperor'.

(*c*) Some onomatopoeic verbs may be considered as derived from the corresponding nouns: клеветати, клевештѫ 'to slander': клюти, рꙑпътати, рꙑпьштѫ 'to grumble': рꙑпътъ, скрьжътати, скрьжьштѫ 'to gnash': скрьжьтъ, шьпътати, шьпъштѫ 'to whisper': шьпътъ.

(*d*) The majority of verbs with infinitive stem ending in -*a*- of the type дѣлати are derived from nouns, and from a purely formal point of view they should be assigned to category 3 of this conjugation. They have, however, been considered as secondary, derived verbs with stems enlarged by -*a*- and as forming à separate category—4.

(*e*) In the present tense endings, the intervocalic *j* again shows the tendency to disappear, and the vowels are assimilated:

разоумѣ́ютъ>разоумⷠ́катъ, вѣроⷢютъ>вѣроⷢ́оѵтъ, разбива-
ютъ > разбиваатъ > разбиватъ (§ 32.5, § 96.3. e).

(f) The imperfect is formed from the infinitive stem: дѣлаахъ,
разоумⷠ́каше. Verbs in -овати also have exceptional imperfect
forms derived from the present stem: бесⷠ́ковати, бесⷠ́доуⷤ
'to speak' — бесⷠ́доуꙗше (Supr. 304.18. d) and бесⷠ́коваꙗше,
даровати, дароуⷤ 'to present' — дароуꙗше and дароваꙗше, &c.
The endings -аꙗшета (2nd du.) and -ашете (3rd du. and 2nd pl.)
are sometimes replaced by -аста, -асте.

(g) The suffix -ova- appears as -eva- after palatal consonants:
польбевати 'to profit', непьштевати 'to suppose' (§ 11.2, § 65.3).

(h) Some verbs in -овати show present forms derived from a
stem in -аю-: готовати 'to prepare', готоваютъ 'he prepares',
растрьбовати 'to tear to pieces', растрьбоваютъ (Supr. 350. 28)
'he tears to pieces'. The first verb is derived from готовъ and
belongs only formally to this verbal category.

§ 97. FOURTH CONJUGATION (§ 61.IV, § 66)

Present

Sing.

1 молⷤ	любл҄ⷤ	вращⷤ	виждⷤ	слꙑшⷤ	кричⷤ
2 молиши	любиши	вратиши	видиши	слꙑшиши	кричиши
3 молитъ	любитъ	вратитъ	видитъ	слꙑшитъ	кричитъ

Plur.

1 молимъ	любимъ	вратимъ	видимъ	слꙑшимъ	кричимъ
2 молите	любите	вратите	видите	слꙑшите	кричите
3 молатъ	любатъ	врататъ	видатъ	слꙑшатъ	кричатъ

Dual

1 моливѣ	любивѣ	вративѣ	видивѣ	слꙑшивѣ	кричивѣ
2 молита	любита	вратита	видита	слꙑшита	кричита
3 молите,	любите,	вратите,	видите,	слꙑшите,	кричите,
-та	-та	-та	-та	-та	-та

Imperative

Sing.
1 —— —— —— —— —— ——
2 моли ла́юби врати виждь слꙑши кричи
3 моли ла́юби врати виждь слꙑши кричи

Plur.
1 молимъ ла́юбимъ вратимъ видимъ слꙑшимъ кричимъ
2 молите ла́юбите вратите видите слꙑшите кричите
3 —— —— —— —— —— ——

Dual
1 молив҆ѣ ла́юбив҆ѣ вратив҆ѣ видив҆ѣ слꙑшив҆ѣ кричив҆ѣ
2 молита ла́юбита вратита видита слꙑшита кричита
3 —— —— —— —— —— ——

Present participle active

Masc., neut.
мола ла́юба врата вида слꙑша крича

Fem.
молашти ла́юбашти врат аꙗшти видашти слꙑшашти
кричашти

Present participle passive

молимъ-ъ, -а, -о   ла́юбимъ-ъ, -а, -о   вратимъ-ъ, -а, -о
видимъ-ъ, -а, -о   слꙑшимъ-ъ, -а, -о   кричимъ-ъ, -а, -о
(видомъ-ъ, -а, -о)   невидимъ-ъ, -а, -о

Imperfect

Sing. 1 моліꙗахъ   люблꙗахъ   враштаахъ
2 моліꙗаше   люблꙗааше   враштааше
3 моліꙗаше   люблꙗааше   враштааше

Plur. 1 моліꙗахомъ   люблꙗаахомъ   враштаахомъ
2 моліꙗашете   люблꙗаашете   враштаашете
3 моліꙗахѫ   люблꙗаахѫ   враштаахѫ

Dual 1 моліꙗаховѣ   люблꙗааховѣ   враштааховѣ
2 моліꙗашета   люблꙗаашета   враштаашета
3 моліꙗашете,   люблꙗаашете,   враштаашете,
       -та   -та   -та

Sing. 1 виждаахъ   слышаахъ   кричаахъ
2 виждааше   слышааше   кричааше
3 виждааше   слышааше   кричааше

Plur. 1 виждаахомъ   слышаахомъ   кричаахомъ
2 виждаашете   слышаашете   кричаашете
3 виждаахѫ   слышаахѫ   кричаахѫ

Dual 1 виждааховѣ   слышааховѣ   кричааховѣ
2 виждаашета   слышаашета   кричаашета
3 виждаашете,   слышаашете,   кричаашете,
     -та   -та   -та

Sigmatic aorist

Sing. 1 молихъ   любихъ   вратихъ
2 моли   люби   врати
3 моли   люби   врати

Plur. 1 молихомъ   любихомъ   вратихомъ
2 молисте   любисте   вратисте
3 молишѧ   любишѧ   вратишѧ

Dual 1 молиховѣ   любиховѣ   вратиховѣ
2 молиста   любиста   вратиста
3 молисте, -та   любисте, -та   вратисте, -та

Sing. 1 видѣхъ   слышахъ   кричахъ
2 видѣ   слыша   крича
3 видѣ   слыша   крича

Plur. 1 видѣхомъ   слышахомъ   кричахомъ
2 видѣсте   слышасте   кричасте
3 видѣшѧ   слышашѧ   кричашѧ

Dual 1 видѣховѣ   слышаховѣ   кричаховѣ
2 видѣста   слышаста   кричаста
3 видѣсте, та   слышасте, -та   кричасте, -та

Past participle active 1

Masc., neut.

моль   любль, любивъ   вративъ   видѣвъ   слышавъ   кричавъ

Fem.

  мольши любльши, любивъши вративъши видѣвъши
        слышавъши кричавъши

Past participle active 2

молилъ-ъ, -а, -о любилъ-ъ, -а, -о вратилъ-ъ, -а, -о видѣлъ-ъ, -а, -о
слышалъ-ъ, -а, -о кричалъ-ъ, -а, -о

Past participle passive

моленъ-ъ, -а, -о любленъ-ъ, -а, -о враштенъ-ъ, -а, -о
видѣнъ-ъ, -а, -о слышанъ-ъ, -а, -о

Infinitive

молити 'to ask' любити 'to love' вратити 'to turn' видѣти 'to see'
слышати 'to listen' кричати 'to call, to shout'

Supine

молитъ любитъ вратитъ видѣтъ слышатъ кричатъ

Verbal noun

моление любление враштение видѣние слышание
кричание

(a) To this conjugation belong verbs in -ити (inf.) which are derived from nouns: авити 'to show', хвалити 'to praise', сѫдити
'to jᵘ Ige', мыслити 'to think', съмотрити 'to observe', гвоздити
'to nail', хранити 'to protect', блазнити 'to lead astray', мѫчити
'to torture', постити сѧ 'to fast', славити 'to praise', &c.

(b) Some iterative (indeterminate-imperfective) verbs belong to
this class: водити 'to lead', носити 'to carry', гонити 'to chase',
лазити 'to crawl', ходити 'to walk', влачити 'to drag', возити
'to drive in a vehicle', мѫтити 'to trouble'; these verbs have
corresponding determinate-imperfectives: вести, нести, гънати,
лѣсти, ити, влѣшти, вести – везѫ, ма(сти.

(c) This conjugation comprises a good number of causative
verbs: поити 'to water' : пити 'to drink', боудити 'to awake':
бъдѣти 'to wake, to watch', оучити 'to teach' : въкнѫти 'to get
accustomed', оуморити 'to kill' : мрѣти 'to die', посадити 'to set

down': сѣсти 'to sit down', въскрѣсити (trans.) 'to raise': въскрьснѫти (intrans.) 'to rise from the dead', гоубити 'to destroy': гъіенѫти 'to perish', исѫчити, исѫцати 'to make dry': исакнѫти 'to get dry', &c.

(d) Verbs in -ѣти (inf.) of this class are primary verbs which indicate a state and are therefore intransitive: вльштати 'to shine, to glitter', волѣти 'to be ill', воіати сѧ 'to fear', въдѣти 'to watch', вѣжати 'to run', велѣти 'to order, to command', висѣти 'to hang', вьртѣти 'to turn', вьрѣти 'to boil', горѣти 'to burn', грьлиѣти 'to thunder', движати 'to move', дрьжати 'to hold, to rule', жадѣти, жадати 'to be thirsty', зьрѣти 'to look', клачати to kneel', късиѣти 'to abide', къпѣти 'to boil', лежати 'to lie', летѣти 'to fly', прильпѣти 'to stick', льштати сѧ 'to shine, to sparkle', мльчати 'to be silent', мрьзѣти 'to be detested', мъчати 'to shake, to carry away', мьнѣти 'to think, to mean', пльзѣти 'to crawl', полѣти 'to flame, to blaze', пьрѣти сѧ 'to dispute', свьтѣти сѧ 'to be light, to shine', скрьвѣти 'to sorrow, to grieve', смрьдѣти 'to stink', стоѣти (стоіати) 'to be standing', стъідѣти сѧ 'to be ashamed', сѣдѣти 'to sit', трьпѣти 'to suffer', тьштати сѧ 'to hurry', сътѧжати 'to acquire', штадѣти 'to spare, to forbear'.

(e) The verb хотѣти (хътѣти) 'to wish' belongs to this conjugation only in the 3rd pl. and in pres. part. act. It forms the present from a stem in -ю-, and the imperfect and aorist from a stem хот-:

Present

Sing.	1 хоштѫ	Imperative:	хошти
	2 хоштеши, хоште	Pres. part. act.:	masc., neut.
	(Supr. 169. 21)		хотѧ
	3 хоштетъ		fem. хотѧшти
Plur.	1 хоштемъ	Imperfect:	хотѣахъ
	2 хоштете	Aorist:	хотѣхъ
	3 хотѧтъ	Past. part. act. 1, masc., neut.: хотѣвъ
Dual	1 хоштевѣ		fem. хотѣвъши
	2 хоштета	Past part. act. 2: хотѣлъ-ъ, -а, -о
	3 хоштете, -та	Verbal noun: хотѣниіе

(*f*) The verb довьлѣти (довълѣти) 'to suffice' has the same conjugation in the present as хотѣти, according to the third conjugation. However, only a few forms of the paradigms are recorded in the texts. The imperfect and aorist are formed from a stem довьлѣ-:

Present

Sing.	1	довьлѭ, довьлѣѭ	Plur.	1	довьлѭемъ, довьлѣѭемъ
	2	довьлѭеши, довьлѣѭеши		2	довьлѭете, довьлѣѭете
	3	довьлѭетъ, довьлѣѭетъ		3	довьлѭтъ, -лѭтъ, -лѣѭтъ

Dual	1	довьлѭевѣ, -лѣѭевѣ
	2	довьлѭета, -лѣѭета
	3	довьлѭете, -лѣѭете

Pres. part. act.:   довьлѩ, довьлѣѩ
Imperfect: довьлѣахъ
Aorist: довьлѣхъ
Past part. act. 2:   довьлѣлъ

(*g*) The verb съпати 'to sleep' (оусъпити, -съплѭ, -съпиши 'to fall asleep') forms the imperfect and aorist from a stem съпа-; the present is regular: съплѭ, съпиши, &c., 3rd plur. съплѭтъ. Imperfect: съпаахъ, aorist съпахъ. Imperative: съпи, pres. part. act. съпѩ (§ 66).

(*h*) The verb видѣти has irregular forms in imperative (виждь, видимъ, cf. § 98) and in pres. part. pass. However, завидѣти 'to envy' обидѣти 'to hurt' have in imperative завиди, обиди, and in pres. part. pass. the form видимъ occurs beside видомъ. Parallel to видомъ the verb питѣти, питѣѭ forms a pres. part. pass. питомъ.

(*i*) The verbs горѣти 'to burn', летѣти 'to fly', вьрѣти 'to boil' have in pres. part. act. forms with -ѭ- instead of -ѩ-: N. горѩ, N.-pl. горѭште, I. pl. горѭштиими (Ps. Sin. cxix. 4), but Savv. Kn. has горѩште. The Russian Church Slavonic forms летоуцꙗ and вроуцꙖ- presuppose forms with ρ in CS.

(*j*) The stems of this verbal category end in -*i*-. When the derivative element began with a vowel, this *i* changed into *j* and the

foregoing consonant was palatalized (§ 17. *b*, § 21). The verbal forms
in which this palatalization took place are: 1st sg., impf., past part.
act. 1, and past part. pass.:

возити	вожѫ	возиши	вождаахъ	вожь	воженъ
водити	вождѫ	водиши	вождаахъ	вождь	вожденъ
мѫтити	мѫштѫ	мѫтиши	мѫштаахъ	мѫшть	мѫштенъ
поустити	поуштѫ	поустиши	поуштаахъ	поушть	поуштенъ
любити	любліѫ	любиши	любліаахъ	любль	любліенъ

Forms without palatalization occur exceptionally: съмотрити
'to look', съмоштрѫ and съмотріѫ alongside съмоштріѫ.

§ 98. FIFTH CONJUGATION (ATHEMATIC VERBS) (§ 61.V)

Present

Sing. 1	ѥсмь	дамь	вѣмь, вѣдѣ	іамь (ѣмь)
2	ѥси	даси	вѣси	іаси
3	ѥстъ	дастъ	вѣстъ	іастъ
Plur. 1	ѥсмъ	дамъ	вѣмъ	іамъ
2	ѥсте	дасте	вѣсте	іасте
3	сѫтъ	дадѧтъ	вѣдѧтъ	іадѧтъ
Dual 1	ѥсвѣ	давѣ	вѣвѣ	іавѣ
2	ѥста	даста	вѣста	іаста
3	ѥсте, -та	дасте, -та	вѣсте, -та	іасте, -та

Future   *Imperative*

Sing. 1	бѫдѫ	бѫдѣмь	——	——	——
2	бѫдеши	бѫди	даждь	вѣждь	іаждь
3	бѫдетъ	бѫди	даждь	вѣждь	іаждь
Plur. 1	бѫдемъ	бѫдѣмъ	дадимъ	вѣдимъ	іадимъ
2	бѫдете	бѫдѣте	дадите	вѣдите	іадите
3	бѫдѫтъ	бѫдѫ	——		
Dual 1	бѫдевѣ	бѫдѣвѣ	дадивѣ	вѣдивѣ	іадивѣ
2	бѫдета	бѫдѣта	дадита	вѣдита	іадита
3	бѫдете, -та	бѫдѣте, -та	——		

Present participle active

Masc., neut.

съı   бѫдъı 'future'   дадъı   вѣдъı   ѩдъı

Fem.

сѫшти   бѫдѫшти   дадѫшти   вѣдѫшти   ѩдѫшти

Present participle passive

—   —   вѣдомъ, вѣдим-ъ, -а, -о   ѩдом-ъ, -а, -о

Imperfect

Sing.

1 *бѣахъ	бѣхъ	дадѣахъ	вѣдѣахъ	ѩдѣахъ
2 бѣаше	бѣ	дадѣаше	вѣдѣаше	ѩдѣаше
3 бѣаше	бѣ	дадѣаше	вѣдѣаше	ѩдѣаше

Plur.

1 *бѣахомъ	бѣхомъ	дадѣахомъ	вѣдѣахомъ	ѩдѣахомъ
2 бѣашете	бѣсте	дадѣашете	вѣдѣашете	ѩдѣашете
3 бѣахѫ	бѣшѧ	дадѣахѫ	вѣдѣахѫ	ѩдѣахѫ

Dual

1 *бѣаховѣ	бѣховѣ	дадѣаховѣ	вѣдѣаховѣ	ѩдѣаховѣ
2 бѣашета	бѣста	дадѣашета	вѣдѣашета	ѩдѣашета
3 бѣашете, -та	бѣсте, -та	дадѣашете, -та	вѣдѣашете, -та	ѩдѣашете, -та

Aorist

Sing.

1 бъıхъ	дахъ	вѣдѣхъ	ѩсъ (ѣсъ), ѩхъ
2 бъıстъ, бъı	дастъ, да	вѣдѣ	ѩстъ, из-ѩ (из-ѣ)
3 бъıстъ, бъı	дастъ, да	вѣдѣ	ѩстъ, из-ѩ (из-ѣ)

Plur.

1 бъıхомъ	дахомъ	вѣдѣхомъ	ѩсомъ, ѩхомъ
2 бъıсте	дасте	вѣдѣсте	ѩсте
3 бъıшѧ	дашѧ	вѣдѣшѧ	ѩсѧ, ѩшѧ

Dual

1 бъıховѣ	даховѣ	вѣдѣховѣ	ѩсовѣ
2 бъıста	даста	вѣдѣста	ѩста
3 бъıсте, -та	дасте, -та	вѣдѣсте, -та	ѩсте, -та

Past participle active 1

| Masc., neut. | БЪІВ'Ъ | ДАВ'Ъ | В'ѢД'ѢВЪ | ІАДЪ |
| Fem. | БЪІВЪШИ | ДАВЪШИ | В'ѢД'ѢВЪШИ | ІАДЪШИ |

Past participle active 2

| БЪІЛ-Ъ, -А, -о | ДАЛ-Ъ, -А, -о | В'ѢД'ѢЛ-Ъ, -А, -о | ІАЛ-Ъ, -А, -о |

Past participle passive

ЗА-БЪВЕН-Ъ, -А, -о 'forgotten'   ДАН-Ъ, -А, -о   -В'ѢД'ѢН-Ъ, -А, -о

ІАДЕН-Ъ, -А, -о

Infinitive

БЪІТИ 'to be'   ДАТИ 'to give'   В'ѢД'ѢТИ 'to know'   ІАСТИ 'to eat'

Supine

БЪІТЪ   ДАТЪ   В'ѢД'ѢТЪ   ІАСТЪ

Verbal noun

БЪІТИЮ, (ЗА)БЪВЕНИЮ   ДАНИЮ   В'ѢД'ѢНИЮ   ІАДЕНИЮ

(a) For the conditional of БЪІТИ see § 72.

(b) The form Б'ѢХЪ, &c., has the conjugation of an aorist, but it fulfils the function of the imperfect tense, though once it translates thè Greek aorist ἐγένοντο = Б'ѢША (Zogr., Mar., L. xiii. 2, 4). It seems that Б'ѢХЪ is the older imperfect form, and was replaced, starting with the 3rd pl., by Б'ѢАХЪ, a newer creation, on the analogy of the other imperfect forms. Forms of the first person imperfect Б'ѢАХЪ do not occur in the texts.

(c) In the 3rd sg. pres. there also appears the short form Е, ІЕ (Zogr., Mar., Ass., Cloz., Savv. Kn., Supr.). In the 2nd sg. pres. we find СИ for ІЕСИ (Zogr., L. xi. 27). In the 3rd pl. pres. a short form СѪ appears (Supr. 38. 12, etc.).

(d) The negative present is: sg. Н'ѢСМЬ, Н'ѢСИ, Н'ѢСТ'Ъ (Н'Ѣ); pl. Н'ѢСМЪ, Н'ѢСТЕ, НЕ СѪТЪ; du. Н'ѢСВ'Ѣ, Н'ѢСТА, Н'ѢСТЕ, -ТА.

(e) Forms of a future participle are preserved in Euch. Sin., Supr., Mar. (once): БѪДѪШТ-, and a future part. БЪІШАЦІЕЮ, БЪІШАЦІЕЮ appears in Izbornik 1073, and in later texts.

(*f*) The iterative (impft.-indeterminate) бꙑвати, бꙑваѭ (: бꙑти, бѫ ꙗ) appears in compound formations: забꙑвати, -ваѭ: забꙑти (impft.), -бѫдѫ (pft.) 'to forget' (§ 89).

(*g*) The verb бꙑти is built on an infinitive stem бꙑ- < IE *bhū- (cf. Lat. *fūit*) and a present stem with vowel alternation: *e ~ zero*, *(i̯)es- ~ *s-ontŭ (§ 37); бѫдѫ seems to be a perfective form built on the same stem.

(*h*) The present stems of the other athematic verbs end in a dental: *dad-, věd-, ěd-*; *dad-* keeps the dental in the originally re-duplicated forms; the dental disappears when followed by *m* or *s*, and changes into *s* when followed by *t*: *dad-mĭ* > дамь, *dad-si* > даси, *dad-tŭ* > дастъ (§ 29. 4. 10); on the analogy of these verbs one finds бꙑстъ in the 2nd and 3rd sg. aor.

(*i*) The aspect of дати is perfective, except in the negative не дати; the imperfective form is даꙗти, даѭ, &c.

(*j*) In the imperative a form даждꙑ also appears.

(*k*) The athematic verb вѣдѣти also has in the 1st sg. pres. the form вѣдѣ (cf. Gr. perfect οἶδα; § 84), which also occurs in Old Slovene (Freis.), Old Czech, and Old Russian. This form appears twice in Zogr., twice in Ass., six times in Savv. Kn.; in Supr. вѣдѣ is more frequently used than вѣмь. The two forms may have belonged to two different dialects. The stem вѣдѣ- is replaced, mainly in imperfective forms, by вѣда-: повѣдати, повѣдовати.

(*l*) In the 3rd sg. pres. a short form вѣ is recorded in Supr. (382. 17) and проповѣ сѧ '(it) shall be proclaimed' in Ass. (L. xii. 3).

(*m*) In the past part. pass. there appear the isolated forms извѣстъ (Supr. 363. 3) 'well informed' and in later texts вѣстъ 'known'; these are adjectival forms.

(*n*) The verb ꙗсти has a single stem *jad- = *ēd- (cf. Lat. *ēdo*) from which all the forms are built: *jad-ti* > ꙗсти, *jad-sŭ* > ꙗсъ, ꙗхъ (ѣхъ).

(*o*) The form бѫдѫ is used as the imperative for the 3rd pers. pl.: бѫдѫ чрѣсла ваша прѣпоѣсана (Mar., L. xii. 35) 'Let your loins be girded about'; бѫдѫ днье его мали (Ps. Sin. cix. 8) 'Let his days be few'; бѫдѫ чѧда его въ пагоубѫ (Ps. Sin. cix. 13)

'Let his posterity be cut off', &c. But this imperative is expressed, in the same text, by да and the present-future form: да бѫдѫтъ прѣдъ господьмъ вꙑнѫ (Ps. Sin. cix. 15) 'Let them be before the Lord continually' (§ 71.2).

(*p*) The forms -бѫдѫ are always perfective: избꙑти, избѫдѫ 'to abound in, to escape', добꙑти, добѫдѫ 'to attain', събꙑти, събѫдѫ сѧ 'to happen', забꙑти, забѫдѫ 'to forget'; the forms -бꙑти, -бꙑвати are imperfective избꙑти 'to escape', забꙑти 'to forget', избꙑвати 'to be abundance of, to be liberated', прѣбꙑвати 'to remain'.

(*q*) The perfective бѫдѫ replacing the imperfective бꙑти in the perfect forms (§ 84) creates a future perfect form: далъ бѫдѫ 'I shall have given' (§ 87).

(*r*) The verb имѣти 'to have' forms the present according to the third conjugation (§ 96): имѣѭ, имѣѥши, &c., or according to the athematic verbs from a stem има-. Its conjugation is built on two stems:

	Present	*Imperative*	*Aorist*	*Imperfect*
Sing.				
1	имамь	——	имѣхъ	имѣахъ
2	имаши	имѣи	имѣ	имѣаше
3	иматъ	имѣи	имѣ	имѣаше
Plur.				
1	имамъ	имѣимъ	имѣхомъ	имѣахомъ
2	имате	имѣите	имѣсте	имѣашете
3	имѫтъ, имѣѭтъ	——	имѣшѧ	имѣахѫ
Dual				
1	имавѣ	имѣивѣ	имѣховѣ	имѣаховѣ
2	имата	имѣита	имѣста	имѣашета
3	имате, -та	——	имѣсте, -та	имѣашете, -та

Pres. part. act. masc., neut.   имꙑ, имѣѩ, fem. имѫшти, имѣѭшти

Past part. act. 1 masc., neut.   имѣвъ, fem. имѣвъши

Past part. act. 2   имѣлъ, -ло, -ла

Verbal noun   имѣнию

INVARIABLE WORD-CATEGORIES
§ 99. ADVERBS

Nouns, adjectives, pronouns, numerals, in various cases, with or without prepositions, sometimes derived by means of suffixes, acquire the function of adverbs (§ 54), which may also function as conjunctions (§ 104) or prepositions (§ 103).

1. Locative sg. (masc., neut.): добрѣ 'well', долѣ 'down', вънѣ 'outside', горѣ 'up', кромѣ 'beside', митѣ 'alternating', поздѣ 'late', оутрѣ 'next day', нꙑнѣ 'now', лани 'last year', зади 'behind', сквозѣ 'through', междоу (loc. du.) 'between', долоу 'down', въноу 'out', врьхоу 'on (top of)', низоу 'down', тоу 'there, here', оноудѣ 'there', посрѣдоу (loc. du.) 'between', оу, ю (оуже, юже) 'already', оу-то 'of course'.

2. Accusative sg. (masc., fem., neut.) sѣло 'very', любо 'also'ꞈ любо ли 'or', мало 'a little', тако 'such', тоуне 'for nothing, in vain', сице 'so'; comparatives: боле 'more', вꙑше 'higher up', паче 'again', далече 'far', единаче 'yet, more', таче 'then', обаче 'however', еште 'more', противѫ 'opposite', вънъ 'outside', низъ 'down', близъ 'near', противъ 'against'.

3. Instrumental sg. (fem.) (§ 59.6.a): въшыѭ 'only', единоѭ 'once', въторицеѭ 'the second time', мъножицеѭ 'often', тъчиѭ 'just, only', ноштиѭ 'at daybreak'.

4. Genitive sg.: вьчера 'yesterday'.

5. Dative sg.: домови 'at home'.

6. Instrumental pl.: въпрѣкꙑ 'however, again', правꙑ 'straight', трикратꙑ 'three times', and the adverbs in -ьскꙑ (§ 100); больми, большьмь 'more', вельми 'great, much', кольми 'how much', мьньшьми 'less', нѫдьми 'forcibly'.

7. Instrumental du.: дѣльма 'because of', ноудьма 'necessarily', полъма 'in two halves, through the middle', тольма 'so much', ельма (елѣ) 'in how far, how much'.

§ 100. ADVERBIAL SUFFIXES

The adverbial forms are very numerous. Some are clear nominal cases (§ 99), others continue prehistoric formations. The syntactic

use of adverbs has been studied by Al. Doritsch, 'Gebrauch der altbulgarischen Adverbia' (*Jahresbericht des Instituts für rumänische Sprache*, xvi, Leipzig, 1910). Here are the most frequent suffixes of historic and prehistoric origin:

-ъı: пакъı 'again', малъı 'a little', акъı 'as', окъı 'as, about'; adjectives in -ьскъ regularly form adverbs in -ъı: латиньскъı 'in Latin', роумьскъı 'in Roman', вьсѣчьскъı 'by all means' (§ 99.6).

-и: коли 'when', послѣди 'afterwards', прѣди 'in front', отаи, таи 'secretly' (§ 99.1).

-а: дома 'at home', едъва 'hardly, scarcely', нꙑнꙗ 'now', дѣлꙗ 'for the sake of'.

-амо derives local adverbs from pronouns: вьсѣмо 'in all directions', камо 'whither', тамо 'thither', сѣмо 'hither', овамо 'hither', онамо 'thither' (§ 54).

-ждоу, -ждѣ derive local (direction) adverbs from pronouns: (отъ) вьсѫдоу '(from) everywhere', (из) вънѫдоу '(from) outside' (из) вьнѣѭждоу '(from) outside', (отъ) кѫдоу, кѫдѫ, кѫдѣ 'whence', (отъ) тѫдоу, тѫдѫ, тѫдѣ 'thence', (отъ) сѫдоу 'hither', (отъ) обоѭдоу '(from) both sides', (из) ѫтрьѭдоу '(from) inside' (§ 99.1).

-де (-жде) derives local adverbs from pronouns: къде 'where', овъде 'here', онъде 'there', вьсьде 'everywhere', сьде ... овьде 'here ... there', инъде 'elsewhere', иде, идеже, ижде, иждеже 'where' (relative), дондеже, доньжде, доньдеже 'to, up to', послѣжде 'afterwards' (§ 99.4).

-гда derives temporal adverbs from pronouns: вьсегда 'always', егда(-же) 'when' (relative), къгда (когда) 'when', тъгда (тогда) 'then', иньгда 'once', овогда 'at that time', никъгдаже 'never', нѣкъгдаже 'sometimes'.

-ли, -ма derive modal adverbs: вельми 'very', ельми 'how far' (relative), кольми ... тольми 'so much ... as', бъхъма (бъхъмь бъхъмъ) 'throughout, absolutely', нодъма, ноудьма 'by force', радьма (радма, ради) 'for, because of', тъкъма (тъкъмо) 'only' (§ 99.6.7).

-ль, -ли, -лѣ derive qualitative adverbs (of degree) from pronouns: коль, коли, колѣ ... толь, толи, толѣ 'to what degree

(*quantum*) ... to such degree (*tantum*)', иже колижьдо 'whosoever', отъ сели, селѣ, 'from now on', доколѣ 'till', донелѣже
'as long as, till'. These adverbs also have temporal meaning.

-шьди, -шди, -жди derive multiplicative adverbs (§ 59. 4):
дъвашьди 'twice', трижди 'three times', многашьди,
многашти 'many times'.

-ь of unknown origin derives adverbs mainly from adjectives:
ашоуть 'in vain', бездобь 'untimely', въспать 'backwards',
въиспрь 'upwards', издрадь 'extraordinarily', изѫтрь 'from
inside', иностань 'continuously', искрь 'near by', окрьсть
'round', опать 'again', ѫтрь 'inside', изѫтрь 'from inside',
особь 'especially', отънѫдь, отьнѫдь 'altogether', правь
'indeed', прѣмь 'straight', прѣпрость 'simply', различь
'differently', сѫпротивь 'towards', стрьмоглавь 'straight
ahead', соугоубь 'twofold' (§ 54).

§ 101. PARTICLES

ли is the interrogative particle and follows the emphasized word;
ли ... ли 'either ... or', аште ли 'if however'.

не, ни are negative particles, the first being the simple negation,
the second expressing emphatic, absolute negation; неже after
comparatives means 'than', некъли, негли 'perhaps', ни
'no, neither', никъто 'nobody', ничьто 'nothing', ни ... ни
'neither ... nor' (§ 104).

The direct object of a negative sentence or verb takes the genitive:
никтоже бо не приставлѣатъ приставлениѣ плата не бѣлена
(Mar., Mt. ix. 16) 'No man putteth a piece of new cloth'; ни
въливаѭтъ вина нова въ мѣхы ветъхы (Mar., Mt. ix. 17)
'neither do men put new wine into old bottles'; бежнего
ничесоже не бысть еже бысть (Ass., J. i. 3) (Zogr. has
ничьтоже не бысть) 'without him was not any thing'; ѣко
не имамь къде събирати плодъ моихъ (L. xii. 17) 'because
I have no room where to bestow my fruits'.

нѣ- prefixed to a pronoun or adverb gives it an indefinite
meaning: нѣкъто 'somebody', нѣкъгда 'sometime', нѣ оу
кого 'with somebody', ни оу кого 'with nobody' (§ 55. 3. b).

си is a particle which strengthens an interrogative sentence: что (ли) си юн бѫдетъ, въпраша юиѧ (Mar.) 'what then will happen to her, he asked her'.

-жде suffixed to a pronoun emphasizes the identity: тъжде 'the same', такожде 'also', пр‘кжде 'before' (§ 55. 2. *b. c.*, § 100).

-жьдо, -ждо suffixed to a pronoun generalizes the meaning: къжьдо 'every one' (§ 55. 2. *b*).

-же suffixed to a demonstrative pronoun gives a relative meaning: иже 'who', югдаже 'when', &c., or emphasizes the negation: никътоже 'nobody', никъгдаже 'never' (§ 55. 2. 6).

§ 102. PREFIXES AND PREPOSITIONS

1. Certain particles are used only as prefixes and modify the meaning of verbs (§ 91, § 92) and nouns: про- 'through', пр‘к- 'over, through', раз- (разъ-), рас- 'asunder', па-, пра-, сѫ-: проказа 'leprosy', пр‘кдрагъ 'very dear', разоумъ 'mind, intellect', пагоуба 'loss', памѧть 'memory', прадѣдъ 'ancestor', сѫпьрь 'adversary', сѫс‘кдъ 'neighbour'.

2. Other particles are used as prefixes (§ 92) and prepositions with nominal cases:

въ 'in' with A. (direction), with L. (place): въ тъ дьнь 'that day', въ коупѣ 'together'.

въз (възъ), въс 'for, in exchange for' with A. въс кѫиѫ 'why ?'; въс краи 'near by' (prep. with G.).

за 'for, after, behind' with A. (direction), with I. (place), with G. it means 'because': ѧти за власы 'to seize by the hair'.

из (изъ), ис 'from, out' with G.: издрѫкъı (= из рѫкъı) 'from the hand', ис корабліа 'from the boat'. This particle is seldom used as a preposition.

на 'on, to, upon' with A. (direction), with L. (place): излиіаша огнь на землѭ (Supr. 6. 18) 'they poured fire on earth'.

надъ (надо) 'on, upon, over' with A. (direction), with I. (place): надъ главѫ 'over the head', надъ сіономъ горѫѫ (Ps. Sin. ii. 6) 'upon (my holy) hill of Zion'.

о, об (объ) 'over, round, about', with A. (direction), with L.

(place): ѡБ ношть вьсѫ 'the whole night through', ѡбъ онъ
полъ 'on the other side', о деснѫіѫ 'on the right'.

отъ 'from, away' with G.: отъ небесе 'from heaven'.

по, the original meaning of this preposition was 'under, below',
with D. it expresses extension in space: по морю ходѧ 'walking
over the sea'; with A. it indicates direction in space or time:
по вьсѧ градъі 'through all towns', по вьсѧ часъі 'through
all times'; with numerals it gives a distributive meaning:
по двѣма (dat.)' two each'; with L. (temporal and local): по
томь же 'after that'.

подъ 'under, beneath' with A. (direction), with I. (situation):
подъ ногъі 'under the feet', подъ ногама 'under the feet.'

при 'at, at the time' with L.: възвратилъ нъі еси въспиѧтъ
при вразѣхъ нашихъ (Ps. Sin. xliv. 11) 'and hast scattered
us among the (our) heathen'.

прѣдъ 'in front of, before' with A. (direction), with I. (situation):
прѣдъ цѣсарⷶ 'before the king', прѣдъ градомь 'in the
vicinity of the city'.

съ (со, сь) 'with' with I. (expressing association, not the instrument), with G. 'from, off, away' (separation), with A. indicates measure (in later texts): съ нимь 'with him', съ
небесе 'down from heaven', съ лакъть 'a cubit long'.

оу 'at' with G.: оу двьрьць 'at the doors'.

(a) The particles без, въз, из, ѡб, раз, used as prepositions or
as prefixes, have, as a rule, no final vowel (-ъ). Forms with
final -ъ are exceptional in Mar., Euch. Sin., more frequent in
Ass., Supr. Also отъ appears in the texts without the final
vowel -ъ.

(b) Forms with vocalized reduced vowels in strong position in a
sentence (§33. 1) occur in the texts: воз, во, ото, надо,
подо, прѣдо.

(c) An isolated preposition въі occurs in front of words beginning with и-: въі истинѫ (въістинѫ = въ истинѫ) 'in
truth', въі инѫ весь (Mar., L. ix. 56) 'in another village'. The
change vŭ- > vy- could be explained according to § 33. 3.

§ 103. ADVERBS IN PREPOSITIONAL FUNCTION

Certain adverbs and nominal case-forms with adverbial signi-
ficance are used as prepositions (§ 99):

With G.: близъ 'near' (also takes D.), вънѣ 'outside', дѣлꙗ,
дѣльма 'because of', искрь 'nearly', кромѣ 'besides, except',
прѣжде 'before', ради, радьма 'because, for', развѣ 'outside,
except'.

With D.: противѫ 'against, opposed to', прѣмⷻ 'against, in front
of, opposite'.

With A.: подлъгъ 'along', сквозѣ 'through'.

With I.: междоу 'between'.

§ 104. CONJUNCTIONS

а, али 'but' translates Gr. δέ, co-ordinates the parts of the
sentence by opposing them: небо и землѣ милю идетъ, а
словеса моѣ не милю идѫтъ (Mar., L. xxi. 33) 'heaven and
earth will pass, but my words will not pass away'; with the
conditional it means 'if': а би былъ сьде не бы ли оумрьлъ
братъ (Supr. 307. 21) 'if he had been here my brother would
not have died'; а бы былъ пророкъ (L. vii. 39) 'if he were a
prophet'; followed by the interrogative ли, it developed into
an emphatic conjunction: инꙑ съпасе, али себе не можетъ
съпасти (Mar., Mk. xv. 31) 'He saved others, himself he cannot save'.

акꙑ, ꙗкꙑ, ако, ѣко, ꙗко, ꙗкоже, окꙑ 'how, so that, when',
introducing a complemental clause after the verbs 'to say, to
think', &c. It translates Gr. ὡς, ὅτε. It may also introduce
oratio recta, imitating Gr. ὅτι: вꙑ глаголете ѣко власвими-
ѣеши (Mar., J. x. 36) 'you say (say ye): Thou blasphemest'
Gr. ὑμεῖς λέγετε, ὅτι βλασφημεῖς; 'when, as': и ѣко приближи
сѧ, видѣвъ градъ плака сѧ о немь (Mar., L. xix. 41) 'when
he was come near, he beheld the city, and wept over it', сотона
проситъ васъ да би сѣлъ ѣко пшеницѫ (Mar., L. xxii. 31)
'Satan hath desired (to have) you, that he may sift (you) as
wheat'; и отъпоусти намъ длъгꙑ нашѧ, ꙗко и мꙑ

отъпоуштаıемъ длъжъникомъ нашимъ (Mar., Mt. vi. 12) 'and forgive us our debts, as we forgive our debtors'; meaning 'because, for': мене же ненавидитъ, ѣко азъ съвѣдѣтельствоуѭ о немь, ѣко дѣла его зъла сѫтъ (Mar., J. vii. 7) 'but me it hateth, because I testify of it, that the works thereof are evil'.

ацѣ, цѣ 'although, however' translates Gr. καίτοι: не бо рече· Июда прѣдавникъ, ацѣ лѣпо бѣ ... и сего отъ зълобы прозъвати (Supr. 410. 20) 'for he did not say: Judas the traitor, although (however) it was right to call also this one by the name of his crime', и не видѣаше тоу сѫшта ıегоже хотѣаше прѣдати, цѣ свѣштамъ сѫштамъ и свѣтоу толикоу (Supr. 412. 15) 'he did not see that he whom he wanted to sell was there, though there were torches and so much light'.

аште (ıаште), аште ли 'if, whether' (conditional): аште хоштеши, можеши 'if thou wilt, thou canst', аште би вѣдѣлъ ... бъдѣлъ оубо би 'if he had known ... he would have watched'; аште и 'even if': аште и съмрътъно что испиѭтъ ничътоже ихъ не врѣдитъ (Mar., Mk. xvi. 18) 'and if they drink any deadly thing, it shall in no wise hurt them'; аште 'whether' introduces an indirect interrogative clause translating Gr. εἰ: остани да видимъ, аште придетъ илиѣ (Mar., Mt. xxvii. 49) 'let be, let us see whether Elijah will come'; after a relative pronoun аште generalizes the relative meaning by imitating the Greek construction ὃς ἄν (ἐάν): иже аште съблазнитъ (Mar., Mk. ix. 42) 'whosoever shall offend', и идеже аште вънидетъ рьцѣта господиноу домоу (Mar., Mk. xiv. 14) 'and wheresoever he shall go in, say to the goodman of the house'; аште ли 'else, otherwise': отъженѣмъ и отъ прѣдѣлъ сихъ, аште ли вьса люди привлѣчетъ къ севѣ (Supr. 215. 30) 'let us drive him away from these lands, otherwise he will attract to him all people', аште ли же ни, просѧдѫтъ сѧ мѣси (Mar., Mt. ix. 17) 'else the skins burst'; иже аште 'whoever', аште ли да 'if however, lest', аште ли же ни, аште да не 'if not, lest'.

ЕО used enclitically 'for, because'; НЕО 'and really, for even' corresponds to Gr. καὶ γάρ, Lat. *etenim*: НЕО И ПСИ 'ѢДѦТЪ (Mar., Mt. xv. 27) 'for even the dogs eat'; НЕО may be separated into И and ЕО: И ТИ ЕО ПРИДѪ ВЪ ПРАЗДЬНИКЪ (Mar., J. iv. 45) 'for they also went unto the feast'; ОҮЕО 'but' translates Gr. (οὐκ)οῦν: ОҮЕО Ц'ѢСѦРЬ ЛИ ЕСИ ТЪІ (Mar., J. xviii. 37) 'art thou a king then?'; ОҮЕО . . . ЖЕ translates Gr. μὲν . . . δέ: 'ѢКО ТИ ОҮЕО ИЗЕИШѦ ІѦ, ВЪІ ЖЕ ЗИЖДЕТЕ ИХЪ ГРОЕЪІ (Mar., L. xi. 48) 'for they (indeed) killed them, and ye build their sepulchres'; ОҮЕО also renders the conditional expressed by Gr. ἄν: ѦШТЕ ЕИСТЕ ЛЮЕИЛИ ЛІѦ, ВЪЗДРѦДОВѦЛИ СѦ ЕИСТЕ ОҮЕО (Mar., J. xiv. 28) 'if ye loved me, ye would rejoice'; НЕЕОНЪ 'and really, however', when divided into its component parts НЕ ЕО НЪ, means 'because that is not, namely, but': НЕЕОНЪ И ѦЗЪ ИздрѦилиТ'ѢНИНЪ ІЄСЛЬ (Romans xi. 1) 'for I also am an Israelite'.

ВЪНЕГДѦ, see ІЄГДѦ.

ДѦ (ДО) 'in order that' (final); in negative sentences ДѦ НЕ or ІЄДѦ: ПОСЪЛѦШѦ ЗѦС'ѢДЬНИКЪІ, ТВОРѦШТѦ СѦ ПРѦВЕДЬНИЦИ СѪШТЕ ДѦ ИМѪТЪ И ВЪ СЛОВЕСИ, ДѦ ЕѪ И ПР'ѢДѦЛИ ВЛѦДЪІЧЪ-СТВОҮ (Mar., L. xx. 20) 'they sent forth spies, which feigned themselves to be righteous, that they might take hold of his speech, that so they might deliver him unto the power', 'ѢКО СЪНИДЪ С НЕЕЕСЕ, ДѦ НЕ ТВОРѪ ВОЛѦ МОІЄІѦ, НЪ ВОЛІѪ ПОСЪ-ЛѦВЪШѦѦГО МѦ (Mar., J. vi. 38) 'for I came down from heaven, not to do mine own will, but the will of him that sent me'; preceding the 3rd person forms it expresses the imperative: ДѦ ЕѪДЕТЪ 'let it be', also with the 2nd pers.: ДѦ В'ѢСИ 'thou shalt know; ДѦ introduces a complemental clause: ЧТО ХОШТЕШИ ДѦ ТИ СЪТВОРІѪ (Mar., L. xviii. 41) 'what wilt thou that I shall do unto thee?', И ВРѦТНИКОҮ ПОВЕЛ'Ѣ ДѦ В'ѢДИТЪ (Mar., Mk. xiii. 34) 'he commanded also the porter to watch', НЕ ВЪЗМОЖЪНО ЕСТЪ ДѦ НЕ ПРИДѪТЪ СКѦНЪДѦЛИ (Mar., L. xvii. 1) 'it is impossible but that offences will come'.

In a few cases ДѦ introduces a consecutive sentence: ТОЛИКѦ

бо сила бѣаше оучителга, да и блѫдница привлѣкши на своіе послоушаніе (Supr. 408. 20) 'for the power of the Master was such that he also attracted the fornicatresses to obey him'; as a rule the consecutive да is followed by the aorist and not by the present: чъто ти естъ море да побѣже (Ps. Sin. cxiii. 5) 'what aileth thee, o thou sea, that thou fleddest?', къто съгрѣши, сь ли или родителѣ его, да слѣпъ роди са (Mar., J. ix. 2) 'who did sin, this man or his parents, that he was born blind?'; аште да 'if . . . that': аште ли его п'си да въскоусатъ, р̅ денъ да поститъ са (Euch. Sin. 103a. 15) 'or if (it happens) that the dogs taste it, 100 days he should fast'; даже не, прѣжде даже не 'till', неже да 'rather than', гако да 'so that' (ut consecutive), да ако, да гако 'when however, when then': идѣмъ оубо братига мога въкоупѣ даже не придетъ (Supr. 16. 20) 'let us go, brethren, together before he comes', не видѣти съмрьти прѣжде даже видитъ Хрьста Господинѣ (Mar., L. ii. 26) 'that he should not see death, before he had seen the Lord's Christ', оунѣе емоу би било, аште би камень жрьновънъ възложенъ на выѭ его, и въвьрженъ въ море, неже да сканъдалисаатъ . . . (Mar., L. xvii. 2) 'it were better for him if a millstone were hanged about his neck, and he were thrown into the sea, than that he should offend . . .', искаахѫ лъжа съвѣдѣтелѣ на Icoyca, ѣко да оубиѭтъ i (Mar., Mt. xxvi. 59) '(they) sought false witness against Jesus, that they might put him to death', прѣжде даже въторицеѭ кокотъ не възгласитъ (Mar., Mk. xiv. 30) 'before the cock crow twice'.

дажи до, дожи и до, и до 'till, until, as far as'.

The conjunction да may mean 'and (then)', indicating an emphatic contrast between two clauses. This use developed into an affirmation: глагола имъ Icoycъ: азъ есмъ . . ., да ѣко рече имъ азъ есмъ, идѫ въспать (Mar., J. xviii. 6) 'Jesus said unto them: I am . . ., as soon then as he (had) said unto them: I am, they went backward', не десать ли ищистиша са; да девать како не обрѣтѫ са (Mar., L. xvii. 17) 'were there not the ten cleansed? but (then, yes) why were the nine not found?'

доⷩнелиⷤже, доⷩнелѣⷤже 'till, until': доⷩнелѣⷤже ꙗмь (Savv. Kn., L. xvii. 8) 'till I have eaten'.

доⷩньдеⷤже, доⷩндеⷤже 'as long as, until': ходите доⷩньдеⷤже свѣтъ имате (Mar., J. xii. 35) 'walk while ye have the light', доⷩньдеⷤже ѣмь и пиѭ (Mar., L. xvii. 8) 'till I have eaten and drunken'.

же, used enclitically, renders Gr. δέ, emphasizes contrast between clauses, and as a rule is not to be translated. Its meaning is 'on the other hand, or'; further, it is attached to pronouns and adverbs: бꙑстъ же належаштю емь народоу (absolute dative) (Zogr., L. v. 1) 'and it came to pass, that, as the people pressed upon him', и за ꙗⷩегоже съмрьтъ изволисте, тъ же то чоудо сътвори (Supr. 67. 4) 'and for whom you chose to die, he made this miracle', и обрѣтѫ Мариѭ же и Иосифа (Mar., L. ii. 16) 'and they found Mary and (as well as) Joseph'.

заⷩе 'because, for' emphasizes the cause: и се бѫдеши мльча . . . заⷩе не вѣрова словесемъ моимъ (Mar., L. i. 20) 'thou shalt be silent . . . because thou believedst not my words', и прѣстѫпьникомъ зъвати и, заⷩе заповѣди божиꙗ прѣстѫпивъшоу юмоу коумиромъ жрьти (Supr. 214. 5) 'and to call him a sinner, because he sacrificed to the idols, by disregarding God's commandment given to him'.

и 'and' is used proclitically; и . . . и 'as well . . . as'; и is also used as an adverb meaning 'too, also': посъла и того къ нимъ (Mar., Mk. xii. 6) 'he sent him also unto them', и избравъ отъ нихъ дъва на десѧте, ꙗже и апостолꙑ нарече (Mar., L. vi. 13) 'and he chose from them twelve, whom also he named apostles'.

ибо, see бо.

иде, идеⷤже 'for' (also an adverb): како бѫдетъ се иде мѫжа не знаѭ (Mar., L. i. 34) 'how shall this be, seeing I know not a man?', оуслꙑши мѧ, иде ичезѫ ѣко дꙑмъ дьни мои (Ps. Sin. ci. 3–4) 'hear me, for my days are consumed like smoke'.

или 'or', see ли.

иликже 'because' is I. sg. of the relative pronoun: не въдаше себе въ вѣрѫ ихъ, илигъже самъ вѣдѣаше вьсѧ (Mar., J. ii. 24) '(Jesus) did not commit himself unto them, because he knew all men'.

кѫде 'where, when': кѫде же свѣтъ быстъ въставъ молгаше стрѣгѫштаѧ воины (Supr. 16. 11) 'when daylight came, getting up, he asked the watching soldiers'.

ли, или 'or', ли ... ли, или ... или 'either ... or'; used enclitically, ли introduces direct (seldom also indirect) interrogative sentences: ни ли сего есте чъли еже сътвори давидъ (Mar., L. vi. 3) 'Have ye not read even this, what David did?', онъже рече кръстигангыии ли геси (Supr. 132. 19) 'he said: art thou a Christian woman?', чимъ вѣси, прости ли гего или не прости (Supr. 361. 1) 'how do you know whether he forgave him or not?', въпрошѫ вы что достоитъ въ сѫботы добро ли творити или зѣло творити, доушѫ съпасти ли погоубити (Mar., L. vi. 9) 'I will ask you one thing, is it lawful on the sabbath days to do good, or to do evil? to save a soul, or to destroy it?', хоштеши ли исплънити, иди продаждъ имѣнше твое (Savv. Kn., Mt. xix. 21) 'If thou wilt be perfect, go, sell that thou hast'.

ли may be used enclitically to аште: аште ли трѣвѫ дьнесь на селѣ сѫштѫ (Mar., L. xii. 28) 'If the grass which is to-day in the field'; for али see а.

When used proclitically ли means 'or': ли како речеши братроу твоемоу (Mar., Mt. vii. 4) 'or how wilt thou say to thy brother?'

ли is replaced by или in later texts, especially after the interrogative particle: Бараева ли или Исоусъ (Mar., Mt. xxvii. 17) 'Barabbas, or Jesus?', вечеръ ли въ полоу ношти, ли въ кокотоглашеные, ли ютро (Mar., Mk. xiii. 35) 'in the evening, or at midnight, or at cockcrow, or in the morning'; with comparatives: паче или 'more than': не вы ли паче ихъ лоучъши есте (Mar., Mt. vi. 26) 'are ye not much better than they?'.

любо, любо ли 'or'; любо ... любо 'either ... or': любо во

въторꙗ, любо въ третиѭ стражѫ придетъ (Mar., L. xii. 38) 'if he shall come in the second watch, or come in the third watch'.

небонъ 'namely, really', see бо.

неже, нежели means 'and not, than' and has a variant негъли, некъли 'perhaps': оуне бо іестъ ... чистъ имѣти оумъ негли ... (Supr. 403. 30) 'for it is better ... to have a pure mind than ...', посълѭ сынъ мои възлюбленъи, негъли сего видѣвъше оусрамлꙗѭтъ сѧ (Mar., L. xx. 13) 'I will send my beloved son: it may be they will reverence him, when they see him'.

не ... ни, ниже 'neither ... nor'; не оставитъ ли въсего, ниже сънидетъ съ нимъ слава домоу его (Ps. Sin. xlviii. 19) 'will he (not) leave everything, (neither) shall his glory descend after him'.

нъ 'but': татъ не приходитъ, нъ да оукрадетъ (Mar., J. x. 10) 'the thief cometh not, but for to steal'.

отъиели, отъиелиже 'since': си же отъиели въпидъ, не прѣста облобызаѭшти ногоу моіею (Mar., L. vii. 45) 'but since the time I came in (this woman) hath not ceased to kiss my feet'.

поие, поиеже 'because' (see заие): почьто поие не бѣ врѣмꙗ (Supr. 351. 19) '(why) because it was not the time', не достоино естъ въложити его въ карꙋванѫ, понеже цѣна кръве естъ (Mar., Mt. xxvii. 6) 'it is not lawful for to put them into the treasury, because it is the price of blood'.

та, таже 'and, then' is later confused with таче 'then, after'.

ти 'and, also, then'.

то 'then, so', correlative to the conjunction аште 'if' in the subordinate clause. A variant of то is тѣ, used very seldom: аште ли хоштеши въ животъ вънити, то съхрани заповѣди (Savv. Kn., Mt. xix. 17) 'but if thou wilt enter into life, keep the commandments', аште оубо свѣтъ иже въ тебѣ тъма естъ, тѣ тъма кольми (Mar., Mt. vi. 23) 'If therefore the light that is in thee be darkness, how great is that darkness!'

т‑кмь 'then' is correlative to имьже.

оу, ю 'yet': не оу ли разоумѣсте, ни помьните д̃ хлѣбъ (Mar., Mt. xvi. 9), 'do ye not yet understand, neither remember the five loaves?'

оүбо, see бо.

цѣ, ацѣ 'however, though, also' corresponds to Gr. καίτοι, καίτοιγε, Lat. *et quidem*; see ацѣ.

ꙗко, see ако.

иегда, иегдаже, въиегда 'when, if': придѫтъ же дьние, егдаже отъиимѥтъ сѧ отъ иихъ женихъ (Mar., Mt. ix. 15) 'but the days will come, when the bridegroom shall be taken from them', въиегда възвратити сѧ врагоу моемоу вьспѧтъ (Ps. Sin. ix. 4) 'when mine enemies (enemy) are turned back'.

иеда 'surely not' is a conjunction and interrogative particle corresponding to Gr. μή, Lat. *num, ne*: еда и мꙑ слѣпи есмъ (Mar., J. ix. 40) 'are we blind also?', на рѫкахъ возмѫтъ тѧ, еда когда прѣтъкнеши о камень ногѫ твоѭ (Ps. Sin. xc. 12) 'they shall bear thee up in their hands, lest thou dash thy foot against a stone'.

иели, иель (иелѣ), иельма 'while, as if': ꙗли бо овъ противѫ женъскꙋ прѣштению не сътрьпѣ . . ., како можаахѫ противѫ цѣсаремъ и кнѧземъ и народомъ стати (Supr. 442. 25) 'if he has not resisted the threats of the women, how could he have resisted the kings, the princes, and the peoples?', иельма не послоуша мене . . . 'as you did not listen to me . . .', иель далече отъстоѧтъ вьстоци отъ западъ (Ps. Sin. cii. 12) 'as far as the east is from the west'. See also дойелиже.

INTERJECTIONS

§ 105. These words are imitative formations or, in some cases, flexional forms of other parts of speech:

горе 'woe!'

ѡ, ѡле, ѡвеле 'oh!'

оу 'oh!'

оүва 'boohoo!'

оүвъі, оүвъі мьнѣ 'alas!, woe is me!'

іароү 'ah!, oh!, woe!' (іаръ adj. 'bitter, vehement')

ієн, єн 'yes!, indeed!'

ієсє, сє 'see!, lo!'

ієша, ієша да 'may it please God!'

SUBJECT INDEX

WORD INDEX

THIS index of OCS words occurring in the *Grammar* is comple-
mentary to the Glossary to Part II, *Texts and Glossary*. Words
explained in the *Grammar*, which appear also in the Glossary, are
not registered in this index. Only the basic forms (nominative,
infinitive) are recorded; other morphological forms and variants
will normally be found under the paragraph reference of the
basic form.

Ⰰ

абл҄ько § 32.2.
авел҄ь § 45.
авраамиовъ § 50*a*.
агнѧ § 44.4, § 46.1, § 48.2.
агода § 32.2, 6*a*.
агрипа § 45.
ако § 104.
алнии § 36.
алъдии § 36, § 39*c*.
алъинии § 36, § 39*c*.
алъчьба § 48.7.
анина § 45.
ацѣ § 104.
аште ли § 104.
ашоуть § 32.6*a*, § 100.

Ⰱ

блати § 48.1.
безлобь § 100.
безлилъвиие § 47, § 48.1.
безрѫ-къ, -чьнъ § 50*d*.
безоумиль § 48.5.
бичь § 48.2.
благодар-ити,-ьствити § 93.IV.
благодѣтель § 41.
благоизволити § 93.IV.
благословлюениие § 47.

благость § 48.3.
блазнити § 97*a*.
ближика § 39*h*, § 48.2.
блискати § 30.3.
блисцати § 29.5, § 30.3.
бльвати § 96.3*a*, *c*.
бльснѫти § 29.5.
бльштати § 17*e*, § 97*d*.
блѣскъ § 29.5, § 30.3.
блюсти § 8.2, § 37.5*c*, § 62.2, § 69.2*h*, § 91.
власти § 37.5*g*, § 94*c*.
блѫдити § 37.5*g*.
богатъ § 48.3, § 50*h*.
богатьство § 48.3.
богꙑнꙗ § 38.1.I, § 39*b*, § 46.1, § 52.3.
божьство § 40.2*b*.
боль § 43.
боль-ми, -шьмь § 99.6.
болѣзнь § 43.
болгаринъ § 41.
болие § 99.2.
бости § 37.5, § 69.2*e*, § 94*d*.
боꙗти сѧ § 66.
брадꙑ § 44.1.
брань § 43.
брати § 61.III*b*, § 80, § 96.2*c*, *h*.

Λ

Ш

шаръчии § 39*c*.
шити § 12.3, § 65.1, § 96.1*a*, *c*.
штьлѧгъ § 30.1*a*, 3*f*.
штѧдѣти § 97*d*.
шоулгъ § 3, § 31*a*.
-шьди, шьдъ § 59.4.
шьпътати § 65.1, § 96.4*c*.
шьст-ние, -вие § 79.

Ꙗ (Ѣ)

ꙗблъко § 32.2.
ꙗгньць § 32.2.
ꙗгода § 32.2.
ꙗдро § 32.6*b*.
ꙗдъ § 42.
ꙗдь § 47.
ꙗдьца § 48.2.
ꙗзвити § 93.IV, § 97.
ꙗкъ,-же § 30.3, § 55.2.I.
ꙗможе § 32.6*b*.
ꙗрость § 32.6*b*.
ꙗроу, ꙗръ § 88, § 105.
ꙗхати § 32.6*b*, § 59.1*c*, § 94*e*, *l*.
ꙗште § 104.
ꙗьце § 48.2.

Ѥ (Є)*

ѥ- § 11.2, § 55.4.
евдокиꙗ § 45.
ѥдва § 100.
ѥдинакъ § 50*i*.
ѥдиначе § 99.2.
ѥдиноѭ § 99.3.
ѥже § 32.2.
ѥзеро § 32.2.
ѥђѵпьтъ, еѓюптъ § 2.II Note 1.
ѥлень § 44.2.
ѥли, ѥль § 104.
ѥлинѓꙑн҃и § 39*b*.
ѥльми § 100.
ѥремиꙗ § 45.
ѥсе § 105.
ѥша § 105.

Ю

ю § 104.
юность § 43.
юнота § 39*h*.
ютро § 32.2.

Ѫ

ѫгль § 43.
ѫдолие § 47.
ѫдоль § 32.4.
ѫза § 19.2, § 32.3, 4, § 48.5.
ѫзълъ § 48.5.
ѫтрь § 48.7, § 100.
ѫтрьждоу § 100.
ѫхати § 32.3.

Ѩ

ѩзь § 16.5.
ѩти, имѫ § 91.
ѩчьмень § 44.2.

* Initial є, in words and in syllables, is usually preiotized, except in loanwords: евдокиꙗ, елинъ, ефесъ; but also ѥлисаветь (§ 3*b*).